# RESTORING THE KINGDOM

# RESTORING THE KINGDOM

## The Radical Christianity of The House Church Movement

## Dr. Andrew Walker

## HODDER AND STOUGHTON
### LONDON SYDNEY AUCKLAND TORONTO

**British Library Cataloguing in Publication Data**

Walker, Andrew, *1926–*
    Restoring the Kingdom : the radical Christianity
of the House Church Movement.
    1. House churches
    I. Title
    270.8'2        BV601.85

ISBN 0 340 37280 X

*Printed in Great Britain for Hodder and Stoughton Limited, Mill Road, Dunton Green, Sevenoaks, Kent by Richard Clay (The Chaucer Press) Ltd, Bungay, Suffolk. Typeset by Hewer Text Composition Services, Edinburgh.*

*Hodder and Stoughton Editorial Office: 47 Bedford Square, London WC1B 3DP.*

To my mother and the memory of my father,
Rev. Victor John Lacey-Walker.

# Contents

Prologue:   Finding the Kingdom      11

**Part One**   The Establishment of the Kingdom      15

  1  'House Churches? Never Heard of Them!'   17
  2  The Origins of Restoration   35
  3  The Restored Kingdom Emerges   50
  4  The Kingdom Established in Division   72
  5  Extending the Kingdom   95

**Part Two**   The Radical Kingdom      115

  6  The Radical Principles of Restoration (Part One)   117
  7  The Radical Principles of Restoration (Part Two)   139
  8  The Structure and Shape of Kingdom Life   160
  9  A Kingdom Tour   185
 10  Is the Restoration Movement a Denomination?   201
 11  Catholic Apostolics and Christian Brethren as the Forerunners of Restorationism   218
 12  Classical Pentecostalism and Restorationism   239
 13  The Kingdom Under Attack   258

Epilogue:   Does the Kingdom Have a Future?   289

Author's Postscript   298

**Appendix**   The Sealing of George Tarleton   299

# Tables

Graph of Church History                                133
The Sectarian Origins of Restorationism                255

# Acknowledgements

During the early work and preparation for the book in 1982 and 1983, I was particularly helped, when working for the BBC, by interviews with Joyce Thurman, Arthur Wallis, Keri Jones, Terry Virgo, Dick Simms, Martyn Dunsford and David Matthew. I am particularly indebted to Richard White, the press officer for the Dales Bible Week in 1982, for his helpfulness.

Special gratitude to David Matthew in 1984 for his in-depth interview, phone calls and material sent. I enjoyed my frank interview with Bryn Jones and Goos Vedder (and subsequent phone calls to Bryn Jones). David Tomlinson offered me hospitality as well as information, and was extremely helpful as a sounding board for my ideas. My weekend at Middlesbrough with his family, elders, and friends showed me a new dimension of Restorationist life. Gerald Coates and John Noble gave me an invaluable in-depth interview together, and I was able to see them both subsequently. Gerald became used to my many phone calls. Special mention must be made of Maurice Smith, who not only saw me for a day, but kept sending me letters, books, and further information; he was almost a research assistant. George Tarleton and I spent literally hours on the phone, and his insights and honest reflections taught me a great deal. I am grateful for the help given me by David Mansell and John MacLauchlan in my brief contact with them. A special thanks to Ted Rotherham who came to see me for a day and told me his story. John Race not only shared his story, but passed on information and ideas about kingdom life. Perhaps most importantly of all, I owe a great debt to all those hundreds of Restorationists that I met at

Festival 84, the Dales Bible Week, Community Churches and fellowships.

I would like to thank Tom Smail, Michael Harper, Tom Walker and Douglas McBain for their help in relating the Renewal to house churches. Thanks also to Roger Forster of Ichthus, and charismatics at the 'Third Wave' conference in October 1984.

My historical chapters were greatly helped by the expertise of John Baigent and John Boyes of the Christian Brethren, Desmond Cartwright of Elim, trustees and members of the Catholic Apostolic Church, and Gordon Strachan on Irving. John Lancaster of Elim, and Brian Long of the United Apostolic Church of Faith gave me invaluable help also.

Dr. David Russell, the Rev. Bernard Green and the Rev. Stephen Quicke helped me to see things from the perspective of the Baptist Union, and I was grateful for the talks with people from the Baptist fellowship at Lytham St. Annes. Thanks also to the Youth Unit and members of the Ecumenical Board of the BCC for their views.

Postgraduate students of All Souls, Oxford, and the London School of Economics helped me to sharpen up my sociology. My colleague, Sebastian Garman supported me throughout the highs and the lows.

A great many Evangelicals, Pentecostals, and Restorationists did not want to be named. I thank them all for their help. None of the many people who made this book possible can be held responsible for any of the views expressed here. Any distortion of the truth, or unfair bias will have to remain my responsibility.

I would like to thank the BBC for permission to use material from the programme *Front Room Gospel* and for the support of the producer, David Coomes and the presenter Rosemary Hartill.

Lastly, I would like to thank my wife who did all she could to keep our three young children quiet and amused whilst I ate up the long hours typing in the front room. Without her selfless support, I could not have finished the book.

# FINDING THE KINGDOM

It was the 6th of August 1982. I was at the Dales Bible Week in Yorkshire preparing a report for the BBC's Radio 4 programme, *Sunday*.[1] As I walked round the hundreds of tents and caravans housing some eight thousand people, it was impossible not to feel the excitement and enjoyment that people were experiencing. Everywhere I went, people were only too eager to tell me how they had been healed, delivered from demons, or simply blessed.

Going into a large tent that morning, I found hundreds of children laughing and clapping at the antics of a clown who was combining slapstick humour with stories from the Bible. Entering another tent, I saw a hundred or so teenagers— with hands lifted and eyes far away—singing in tongues, and praising God.

Later in the day, while some were playing a version of *It's A Knockout*, I came across a group of people being baptised by immersion in an outside pool. Quite a few of them appeared to be Anglicans! Little knots of people praying, singing with guitar, or locked in passionate discussion were commonplace. There seemed to be a great deal of talk about 'the kingdom': 'rule', 'reign', 'majesty', 'glory' were words I kept hearing everywhere.

In the evening, a huge wave of some five thousand (maybe seven thousand) people surged into the giant hall of the Great Yorkshire Showground. The rousing songs and choruses reflected the language of majesty and kingship that I had been hearing throughout the day. 'All hail King Jesus' was

11

one song I remember. Another was 'Jesus we enthrone you, We proclaim you are king'.

This language of sovereignty and glory was matched by a corresponding sense of being kingdom people: soldiers of the king.

> Gird up your armour ye sons of Zion
> Gird up your armour let's go to war.
> We'll win the battle with great rejoicing
> And so we'll praise him more and more.

> I hear the sound of the army of the Lord
> I hear the sound of the army of the Lord
> It's the sound of praise, it's the sound of war.
> The army of the Lord.
> The army of the Lord.
> The army of the Lord is marching on.[2]

The praise in the Showground was joyful and loud.

Much of it was accompanied by leaping, dancing, clapping (and even some high kicks). These, mainly young, people were geared up for war; rattling their spiritual shields, they were defying the Devil himself. The whole scene, though in a Christianised form, resembled some massive tribal war dance in preparation for an imminent battle.

And, of course, that is exactly what it was. When the preacher for the evening, Bryn Jones, strode to the microphone, he described the reality of the demonic powers that controlled our cities. His sermon contrasted the kingdom of God with the principality of Satan. He left us in no doubt that we were in a state of war.

After the service, as I made my way out by the back of the rostrum, there was a sudden commotion. 'Don't, don't,' someone screamed. A number of men gathered round a young man on the ground. They were commanding evil spirits to leave him in the name of Jesus. 'I won't go,' boomed an angry voice. The leaders ignored me as I stood there. These leaders turned exorcists were too busy holding down the young man whose limbs were twitching and jerking involuntarily. The exorcism became wilder and more intense; I decided to move on.

Outside in the growing dark, the crowds weaving their way through the caravans were singing and humming songs of the kingdom. (I noticed that I was singing too.) The sound was harmonious, and with the torchlights bobbing and twinkling it made a dramatic contrast to the discordant cry of the demons.

> The church of God is moving,
> The church of God is moving,

sing the crowd. Everybody is relaxed yet triumphant. More music strikes up a little further off:

> We're singing and dancing and shouting and marching
> As we execute the justice and rule of our God.
> We'll take the nations for Jesus as Satan's kingdom falls.
> Righteousness and truth will prevail through our God.[3]

That night, looking back, was the night I abandoned my investigation into House Church Movements, and decided to concentrate on the kingdom people.

## Notes

1   I was also there the previous year with the BBC's *Everyman* team. Most of my brief stay was spent talking to leaders.

2   Songs 72 and 27 respectively, *All Hail King Jesus* (Harvestime Press, 1982).

3   Song 63, ibid. (These songs were heard by me on both Thursday and Friday night, but I have recorded my impressions of them not a literal description of when exactly each song occurred.)

*Part One*

# THE ESTABLISHMENT
# OF THE KINGDOM

# 1

# 'HOUSE CHURCHES?
# NEVER HEARD OF THEM!'[1]

In the event, my decision to concentrate on what I call the 'kingdom people' was the right decision both practically and tactically. When I first became interested in the so-called 'house churches' in 1979,[2] I had no idea that there were so many different brands. By 1982, it was clear to me that the term 'House Church Movement' did not index a specific phenomenon. It is an inappropriate label—a misnomer— that I think we should drop.

## 'House Church Movement' as an Inappropriate Label

The phrase 'House Church Movement' has become one of those convenient labels that we stick onto a variety of churches because they seem to be outside typical Christian experience. Certainly, as we shall see, these House Churches do typically belong outside the mainline denominations. Unfortunately, convenient labels are difficult to remove once they become attached to anything; they become sanctioned by usage even if they are misleading in fact. There are four reasons, it seems to me, why we should make the effort to abandon the House Church label.

First, the label 'House Church Movement' masks the fact that there are quite different fellowships and organisations that come under this rubric. There is, for example, the Ichthus Christian Fellowship. There are also the fellowships founded by Pastor G. W. North. The groups linked to Chard in Somerset have been around for a long time. More recently we have seen the establishment of the so-called base line churches. In addition to these movements, there are the 'apostolic' churches under the direction of Bryn Jones and his colleagues, and the less structured churches affiliated to John Noble, Gerald Coates, David Tomlinson and their associates. There are the thriving Basingstoke communities, The Invisible Church, Union Life, and a host of independent groups who are not attached to anybody.

Second, the members of the various groups who make up this extra-denominational phenomena do not like to be identified by the blanket term 'House Church Movement'. (Unfortunately, for those of us who are outsiders, neither do many of them like to be called by any name that clearly identifies them.)

The third reason why the label is not very helpful is because although it is true that many of these groups started in homes, most of them have now grown into full-blown churches with house groups attached. The church at Bradford, under Bryn Jones's leadership, for example, has over six hundred members, and in Hove Terry Virgo's church can boast five hundred members. Many other churches now have membership exceeding a hundred and even three hundred members.

All these churches do have some things in common: they exist outside the mainline denominations of Great Britain; many are Evangelicals, and most of them are Pentecostals. However, they are different in style and organisation. Furthermore, and perhaps most importantly, these different movements have virtually nothing to do with each other.[3]

The fourth and final reason why the notion of a House Church Movement is not very useful is because it confuses extra-denominational churches with house churches inside the denominations. There are scores, if not hundreds of these churches within the Protestant and Catholic ambits. Many of these churches are neither charismatic nor evangelistic. Some of these house churches do claim to be radical. It is certainly difficult to think of a more non-conformist church in a house than Canon Ivor Smith-Cameron's at The Chase, South London.

He once described his church to me as a sort of spiritual cafeteria: people—regardless of religious affiliation—can come in and help themselves to whatever they fancy. (On offer might be Eastern style prayer, Church of England Eucharist, discussions on politics and racism, or experiments in inter-faith worship.) If this sounds like a recipe for anarchic or syncretic religion, it is based on Canon Smith-Cameron's conviction that you should not force inquiring people to have to eat the traditional three-course meal of Anglicanism; they may only want a quick snack, or to share in human fellowship.

What the Canon's house church shares with most of the denominational versions of house churches, is not only that they are primarily extensions of the denominations (or, at least, recognised by them), but that they are 'one offs': in no sense do they belong to a movement of any kind. Indeed, in Canon Smith-Cameron's case, he sees his work at The Chase as essentially parochial in the sense of reaching out to those who live in his locality regardless of their religion or church ties.

In no sense am I suggesting that denominational house churches are insignificant. But they are a separate phenomenon from the house churches outside the denominations, and are not a subject that I shall be discussing in this book.

I have used the phrase 'House Church Movement' in the sub-title of this book, because it is a term already in usage. But I wish to orient readers to a religious movement outside the recognised denominations. This creates an immediate problem: what shall we call them? In order to help facilitate the identification of the phenomenon under study, I have invented a terminology that I think fits the facts and is not offensive to the members of the churches with which we shall be dealing.

That I have decided to concentrate on what I have called the kingdom people allows us to go right to the heart of the new movements. To try and deal with all the movements' designated house churches would be virtually an impossible study. Not only are there simply too many to make this practically possible, but also there would be no conceptual warrant for such a study: what we would end up with would be a collection of disparate phenomena, not something that hangs together.

## Enter the Kingdom

My major justification for concentrating on kingdom people is not because they cohere together as a movement (which they do), but because they are the largest and most significant religious formation to emerge in Great Britain for over a half a century. Not since the Pentecostal movements of Elim and the Assemblies of God were established in the late 1920s has such a distinctive and indigenous Christian grouping arrived on the religious scene.[4]

Furthermore, like all new groups, they have arrived in clouds of controversy. Nearly all the mythologies, criticisms and accusations levelled at so-called house churches, turn out on investigation to be aimed at people of the kingdom: 'House Churches steal Christians from the established churches'; 'all the money goes into the leaders' pockets'; 'they operate a system of authoritarian control'; 'they are a new brain-washing cult'; 'it's a pyramid structure'; 'house churches are part of the international "shepherding" movement with its headquarters in North America.' All these statements, and many similar ones, are the sorts of things that I hear people say in Evangelical circles.

In other religious groups, very little is known about kingdom people. Many Anglicans and Roman Catholics, for example, have never come across any. Until recently, the national press has taken little notice of the emerging phenomenon. However, things are changing. During the writing of this book, I know of one major Sunday newspaper that was threatening an exposé of the Bradford Community Church, and Bryn Jones's apostolic team. Many rumours were circulating: 'did you know that Bryn Jones has a forty-thousand-pound Mercedes car?' 'His house in Yorkshire cost well over a hundred and fifty thousand pounds!' I mention these two because I happen to know that they have no foundation in fact.

Increasingly too, the religious trade press are carrying

major articles on the new groups. Both radio and television have now completed several programmes.[5] In short, kingdom people are becoming newsworthy. Because interest in them is growing, and as their churches are larger, doctrinally distinct, and more radical than their rivals, it is obviously timely as well as logical that we should look at them rather than the many other house church structures.

I have decided, on careful consideration, to reject a number of names which people have kindly suggested to me as possible titles for the new churches. Some names are simply too parochial. Bryn Jones and his churches are sometimes called 'Harvestime' after the name of the commercial organisation which handles many of their products. Such a name excludes the two apostolic teams of Tony Morton and Terry Virgo, who are closely linked with Bryn Jones. At the other extreme, a number of people suggested the term 'shepherding movement'. This is much better because it is the case that a great many loosely knit churches, which differ in other respects, hold to similar doctrines of radical discipleship or 'shepherding'. However, I decided to resist this title for three reasons.

First, the term 'shepherding movement' is usually seen as something with its origins in America. I do not think that the movement that I have been investigating has its origins in America (although there are undoubtedly direct influences). Second, kingdom people would object to the term, because they understand what they are doing as far more than incorporating discipleship doctrines into their churches. Third, kingdom people are essentially involved in trying to fulfil an eschatological vision: that vision is to replace denominations with the kingdom of God that will fill the whole earth before the Second Coming of Christ. To talk of shepherding principles is totally to miss this eschatological dimension.

Perhaps, with the great deal of talk about kingship and kingdom, it would have been possible to talk about Kingdom as a proper noun and title? There are also three problems with this terminology. First, the movement of the kingdom people is in fact two movements that were once one; so we would have to have two Kingdoms. Second,

Gerald Coates once tried calling his fellowships at Cobham, 'Kingdom Life'. He found that people tended to confuse this with the Jehovah's Witnesses. I feel that we would have the same trouble if we used the term on a less parochial basis. Third, whilst I am happy to use the notion of kingdom as a metaphor (which I shall do constantly throughout this book), I do not wish to confuse 'kingdom' as a spiritual and theological concept with 'kingdom' as an organisational construct.

It is not my intention to deny that the kingdom of God is to be found in this new religious movement, but I do insist that we should not see the two as synonymous or interchangeable. Leaders of the new movements such as Bryn Jones and David Tomlinson, for example, would agree with me that the kingdom of God is too big to be exclusively identified with a particular segment of the Christian Church.

## Restorationism

I have decided to adopt the term 'Restorationism' to index the two interrelated movements that I see as incorporating the people of the kingdom. This rubric I have broken down into the somewhat algebraic Restoration One and Restoration Two (R1 and R2 for short). In no sense should these terms be seen as the correct or proper names of the movements under investigation: they are a device—a rubric—to help our understanding; nothing more. A number of house church leaders have found the rubric helpful, and none of them violently objected to the schema. All of them understood that I was trying to create a framework for understanding them, not condemning them to be for ever called by my invented terminology.

The term 'Restorationism' denotes a qualitative understanding of (so members believe) the work of the Holy Spirit. Leaders of the new movements insist that denominations are not in the plan of God. Restorationists wish to restore or return to the New Testament pattern (as they see it) of the Early Church. The restoring of the Church as it was in its pristine form is to restore a charismatically ordained church, and one in which Christians are seen as living in a kingdom run according to God's order and rules. The nature of kingdom life is itself one of the distinguishing features of Restorationism. To see God's kingdom established (or re-established) is understood eschatologically. The 'end-time', which Restorationists believe is now, will be characterised by not so much world chaos and 'wars and rumours of wars', but an outpouring of God's Spirit culminating in the establishment of the kingdom that is ready and fit for the return of the King. (This is analogous to the Church as the Bride of Christ 'without blemish', who alone is worthy of full intimacy with the Bridegroom.)

Restorationists see themselves as Evangelicals and Pentecostals, but in a new radical mould. The crucible for this new shape is the doctrines of church order stemming from the ecclesiology of the Epistle to the Ephesians, Chapter 4, verses 8–12. The key verses are 11 and 12:

> And these were his gifts: some to be apostles, some prophets, some evangelists, some pastors and teachers, to equip God's people for work in his service, to the building up of the body of Christ. (New English Bible)

From this Restorationists believe that the Church should be run by divinely appointed apostles, prophets and elders. Furthermore, they hold to a doctrine of 'discipleship', or 'shepherding', whereby church members submit themselves to those deemed to be their overseers and spiritual counsellors. Restorationists eschew notions that they are a new denomination or sect, preferring to see themselves as part of a potential worldwide church where brethren will meet to 'break bread' and follow the Apostles' teaching.[6]

Restorationism, on one level then, refers to a recognisable cluster of doctrines and practices adhered to by a considerable number of churches who nevertheless prefer to see themselves as non-denominational. This self-perception does not preclude, however, the recognition that there are distinctive strands, or streams, within the movement. I think that there are basically two forms of Restorationism. One is clearly identifiable, with increasingly adhered-to 'house rules' on behaviour, beliefs, worship, and a pattern of recognised leadership. This group consists of inter-related apostolic teams each with its own spheres of influence, churches and personnel. However, the apostolic leaders share platforms together (at the Dales Bible Week, for example) and are editorial associates of the magazine *Restoration*. Like the *Elim Evangel* of the Elim Pentecostal Movement, *Restoration* magazine has an official ring about it.

Many of the people in this group refer to themselves as 'in the Restoration', and both apostles and elders prefer the term 'Restoration' to any other attempt to classify or pigeonhole them. Terry Virgo, the apostolic leader of a team based in Hove, West Sussex, is as adamant as the other apostles that he dislikes labels being attached to their work, but he does admit[7] that if they have to be called something in order to help facilitate identification, then 'Restoration' would be the best term to use. I suggest that we stick with the designation 'Restoration One', or R1 for short. Certainly, the other Restorationist formation have no difficulty in seeing R1 as an organised movement in denominational form; they usually refer to it by my generic term, 'Restoration'.

If we can apply that designation, with some confidence, to R1 as a proper noun, it is more difficult to do so to the second group. This is not due to any major doctrinal differences; it is more a question of style and history. Many of the people who make up this second group, are either refugees from R1, or belonged in an earlier stage to a nascent Restorationism that had not yet hardened into different factions. I believe, in that sense, that there was a generic movement that can be said to have split into two factions by 1976. If R1 is a clearly identified faction, let me call for convenience's sake the other faction 'Restoration Two'', or R2 for short. There is a problem with this terminology. Members of R2 are not keen to be called Restorationists, not because they dislike the qualitative associations with that word, but because they do not wish to be seen as identical to R1.

Nevertheless, I have decided on the use of Restoration Two, though for mainly pragmatic reasons. Gerald Coates, one of the leaders of R2 explained to me[8] that he and John

Noble's churches were briefly referred to as 'Fulness' after their magazine. Since its demise, a new name has not been forthcoming. Acutely aware, as he is, of the need of a name to help instant recognition, I am sure that it will not be too long before a more official designation becomes available. In the meantime, I intend to continue with R2. To say that R2 is a 'rag-bag' is to point not only to its amorphous nature, but also to the large number of independent yet affiliated churches which make up its constituency. This sense of affiliation is evidence that R2 is not purely a random collection of Restored churches. They come together at such organised events as the annual 'Banquet' and 'Festival' conferences where several thousands attend. Their common ideological beliefs and similar liturgical practices are further evidence that R2 is more than a bundle of disconnected pieces that just happen to bear close resemblance to each other.

And yet, my usage of R2 has one further function in this book: as a lowest common denominator, I shall use it to refer to all those groups who are not in R1, but share similar doctrines and life styles. This usage enables me to enlarge the 'rag-bag' to include not only the John Noble, Gerald Coates, David Tomlinson axis (which is at the core of R2) but also other independent groups such as the Basingstoke fellowships, and John MacLauchlan's groups in Somerset. I shall make it quite clear in the text when I shall invoke this extended usage. My reason for wishing to extend the stricter use of R2 is simply to avoid the infinite regress of R3 to Rn.[9]

## The South Chard and Pastor North Groups

Having decided (a) not to concentrate on house churches within the mainstream denominations, and (b) to concentrate on R1 and R2 as our central phenomenon, I cannot dismiss all other house church movements without comment. The Chard and North fellowships, for example, both precede Restorationism, and are important in its historical development. Indeed, most Restorationists pay tribute to South Chard and the North fellowships as the forerunner of the house system within their own movement. It would not be inaccurate to say that in the 1960s the House Church Movement was Chard and North.

The origins of South Chard prefigure much that will happen in the House Church Movement over the next fifteen years. It was founded by 'Uncle' Sid Purse as early as the 1940s. Sidney Purse was a member of the Open Brethren, and when he began to speak in tongues this caused friction with the rest of the Brethren in the local church. Sidney Purse and his wife, who too claimed the Pentecostal experience, began to hold meetings in their aptly named Manor House. By 1956, a church was opened which was built adjacent to the Manor House. Influenced by a very small Pentecostal sect with the unlikely name of 'Henry's Revival', South Chard built up what is known in house church jargon as a 'praise and preaching ministry'. By the 1960s, South Chard began to reach out to many areas both nationally and abroad with this ministry. Chard associates would train and encourage others to set up house churches, but with little evidence of empire building. This became clear during the 'heyday' of the Charismatic Renewal Movement from the late 1960s to the mid-1970s. Chard teachings and methods (and personnel) could be found both inside Pentecostal denominations, the historic churches, and the extra-denominational house churches. Many people now in Restoration, and some in Charismatic Renewal circles first encountered both Pentecostalism and house churches through the Chard work.

However, Chard charismatics became provocateurs in a controversy that has existed since the inception of Pentecostalism at the beginning of this century. They adopted a baptismal formula whereby they baptised in the name of Jesus only. Bryn and Keri Jones—soon to become apostles in R1—were to find themselves involved in this controversy during a 'mini-revival' in Cornwall at the end of the 1960s. South Chard leaders were declaring that those baptised in the name of the Holy Trinity were receiving an invalid baptism. Ill feeling was caused in the area, and rather than become embroiled—or take sides—the Jones brothers left the West Country. Shortly afterwards in 1969, Bryn Jones moved to Bradford, which was to see the commencement of the Restoration movement in Yorkshire.

This doctrinal controversy highlights (I do not say it was a cause) the beginning of Chard's decline. In a way the Charismatic Movement stole much of their fire in the mid-1970s. It could be argued, of course, that Chard helped the Renewal on its way. Without doubt it became inter-related with it in many areas of Great Britain. After the 'discipleship' issue raised its head from 1975 onwards, the Chard Movement with its emphasis on praise rather than discipline and kingdom authority began to lose out against the new rising Restoration groups.[10] Today, South Chard is a shadow of its former self. Its historical moment may have passed, but there is little doubt that it was the pace-setter in the House Church Movement(s).[11]

Pastor G. W. (Wally) North's fellowships also have their roots outside the classical Pentecostal denominations and before the Charismatic Renewal Movement. Pastor North is a truly charismatic figure in the way in which his character and doctrines are treated as out of the ordinary by his followers. The North fellowships are throwbacks to the Holiness movements of the nineteenth century and the perfectionist teaching of John Wesley. Wally North established his reputation at an independent Holiness church in Bradford where he was pastor from 1952 to 1965.

In 1965, he moved to Liverpool, where he became chaplain to the Longcroft (a sort of spiritual rehabilitation centre in the Wirral) and founder of a number of fellowships in the city. The trustees of the Longcroft released North from his position as chaplain in 1968 in order that he could pursue a full-time itinerant ministry. This he did with considerable success, and to this day he travels to all parts of the world.

Pastor North has always insisted that he is not the founder of a denomination, but it would not be unfair to say that all the fellowships that he has encouraged or overseen bear the imprint of his personality and teachings. It is these teachings, rather than his personality, that have ensured that the North approach would never become a recipe for large organisations. His doctrines, by Evangelical and Pentecostal standards, contain elements of heresy. For instance, to be 'born again' for North is not the 'being saved' of Evangelicism or the initial forgiveness of sins. 'New Birth' is to enter the fullness of the Holy Spirit. This not only means the collapse of the 'second blessing' of Pentecostalism to one experience of spiritual initiation, it also implies a 'walking in the Spirit' that is synonymous with sinlessness.

From a sociological viewpoint, the North fellowships failed to appeal to the full range of social class membership that Restoration has done so successfully. Furthermore, its emphasis on personal holiness rather than 'kingdom living' meant that it failed to develop a communitarian and organisational ethos. Consequently, the North house churches tend to be inward-looking, small in numbers, and appear to have no influence outside their own circles. Since the 1970s when Pastor North moved to Scotland, his work seems to have dwindled in the southern part of Great Britain. New churches are still being formed (some in Northern Ireland, I heard recently) but not in great numbers. It would be honest to admit that nobody seems to know how large Pastor North's operation really is. Joyce Thurman is of the opinion that Pastor North's own view is rather optimistic.[12] Most leaders in R1 and R2, that I talked to, believe that the North fellowships have diminished as a result of their own appeal.

Wally North certainly provided a number of personnel for the new Restoration movement. David Tomlinson, formerly an apostle with R1 (and now in R2) was in the North movement, and, like most ex-members, holds the pastor in great regard. Furthermore, and with some irony, it was Bryn Jones, fresh from the squabbles of Cornwall, who appeared in Bradford in 1969 to become the temporary pastor of the New Covenant Church, which was the same church which Pastor North had built up until he left Bradford in 1965. According to Joyce Thurman, Pastor North sent a permanent pastor to Bradford, but in a short while Bryn Jones's influence held sway, and the North connection was broken.[13]

Neither the Chard movement, nor the North fellowships

had the aggressive discipline of the new Restoration churches. South Chard could really not offer anything that the Pentecostal churches and the Renewal Movement between them were not offering by the mid-1970s. And clearly, by that time they were not matching the radicality of Restorationism. It is only speculation, but it is difficult to envisage the perfectionist teaching of Pastor North having much success without his personal charisma. He has expressed the view himself that the vision dies with the man.[14] It would seem that by the 1980s even if the vision is still alive, fewer and fewer people are sharing it.

## Other Movements

However much I may extend my rubric of R1 and R2, it is not possible, without excessive Procrusteanism, to force everybody to fit it. To try and do so would be no better than the original misnomer of 'House Church Movement' with which we started. This being so, it is worth recapitulating that my schema is intended to inform us of a particular brand of extra-denominationalism. There are many other independent Pentecostal fellowships that look very similar on the surface, but they would not recognise themselves as belonging to my rubric. I am not sure whether the Ewell fellowship in Surrey fits, for example. There is also the recent importation from North America, 'Union Life' which certainly holds to no discipleship doctrines.[15]

Perhaps the most significant house church organisation that fits outside my categories is the Icthus movement. Headed by Roger Forster (who has one of the finest minds in the Evangelical constituency that I have ever encountered), this small group with their headquarters in Forest Hill is essentially a mission group. Its ethos is Open Brethren (as are its origins) and Renewalist Pentecostalism. Strongly attached to the work of the Evangelical Alliance, the movement also supports evangelism wherever it may be found. Whilst remaining a committed Evangelical, Forster is open to Catholic and Orthodox insights. His work is welcome in Restoration Two, and admired in Restoration One. Ichthus, however, do not subscribe to the discipleship teachings of R1 and R2. Neither do they have so narrow a definition of 'women's ministry' to be found in nearly all Restorationist churches (not to mention many Brethren Assemblies).

Having introduced enough caveats to avoid over-simplification, I would like to end this introductory chapter with a note on methodology and moral problems.

## Methods and Morals

I have not used any form of covert investigation believing it to be immoral and sometimes distressing to religious groups. My model here is Dr. Bryan Wilson of All Souls, Oxford. His reputation for fairness and gentlemanly conduct is as great amongst the religious groups he has investigated as it is amongst sociologists of religion.

My methodology has simply been to read journals, letters and propaganda sheets, attend meetings, talk to members and conduct in-depth interviews with some of the leaders. Many of the interviews were in the context of discussion and dialogue; friendships have emerged that I trust will survive a critical look at kingdom life.

In no sense have I attempted a definitive study. Such an approach would involve a standard of scholarship and a commitment of time beyond that which I have attempted here. Furthermore, I do not believe that such an approach could be attempted right now: the new movements are still in a period of flux, and they may grow rapidly or fade away just as quickly.

Although I am a committed Christian, I have primarily taken the role of an outsider using the tools of sociological, historical, and theological analysis rather than providing a series of spiritual comments and moral asides throughout the text. However, I am also a human being; not merely a cypher of knowledge, or impassive recorder of events; someone who has no opinions or prejudices at all, it seems to me, is an odd kind of investigator into human affairs. Part One of this book is really an interpretive narrative. I have often had to rely on my own judgement in the absence of firm or convincing data. Often evidence has been conflicting and nobody I met seemed to have an overall or clear picture of all the historical events.

Part One is also more personal and revealing (in an eaves-dropping sense) than I originally intended. The major reason for this is the nature of the material given me in conversation. But there is also another reason. Bryn Jones said to me, during interview, that he hoped that I would not make it all analysis. He hoped that the people I presented would have some life and character to them. I think basically that his instincts were right. Consequently, I have tried to balance analysis with personal pen-sketches; objective accounting is interspersed with subjective impressions.

The research was conducted under some strain and pressure. I discovered that Restorationism was extremely factional: there was ill-feeling and bitterness as well as health and life in the kingdom. There was also considerable anger and anxiety amongst many denominational groups. More than a few Christian opponents of Restorationism hoped that I would write a damning report of the movement. 'Make sure you show them up for what they are,' was one comment. One father remarked: 'If you don't get Bryn Jones, I will.' This sort of atmosphere was not helped by the imminent threat of a Sunday newspaper exposure, nor the discovery on my part that some scandals did exist.

However, this was compensated for in many ways by an openness to investigation that I found everywhere. When I did stumble upon some unpleasant facts (or, more typically, alleged unpleasantries), nobody made any attempt to stop me or curtail my activities. I am by nature a nosey person, and I saw no attempts at a cover-up.

As I am a member of the Russian Orthodox church, I was obviously not the kind of observer that Restorationists are used to meeting. On the whole this was an advantage. The closer you are to division, the closer you view it with dismay. Roman Catholics and Orthodox do not even know of Restorationism. It is the Baptists, Open Brethren, classical and neo-Pentecostals, who view the new dissenters with concern. Restorationist liturgy is not to my taste, but I do not find kingdom people in any way alien. In the first place I have been a professional investigator of charismatic groups for fifteen years. Secondly, my experience is by no means purely academic. I was brought up in a Pentecostal denomination (though I left it twenty-five years ago). In recent years I have represented the British Council of Churches at the World Council's consultation on Charismatic Renewal in 1980, and I regularly speak in Pentecostal churches.

Quoting Herbert Spencer's dictum not to have contempt for the people prior to investigation, Arthur Wallis in an editorial of *Restoration* magazine makes the following comment:

> We do not ask our critics to take our word that we are not authoritarian or dictatorial, but that we seek to 'rule in the fear of God', as those who must give account. We invite them, if they are motivated with a genuine desire to know the truth, to come and see for themselves . . .[16]

I do not see myself as a critic, but I have tried openly to discover what Restoration really stands for. My approach is primarily (though not exclusively) rationalistic and investigative. It does not pretend, therefore, to tell the whole truth. I do not believe that the reality of the Holy Spirit can be encapsulated by these methods, and I concede that a more theological and spiritual approach would not only proceed in a different way, but come up with a different level of findings.

## Notes

1    This is the heading of an article I remember seeing from an old newsletter of David Tomlinson's house churches.

2    This was in October 1979, when I was a consultant observer at the British Council of Churches consultation on the Charismatic Renewal. (It was organised jointly with the Fountain Trust.) Tom Smail, former director of the Fountain Trust, and Dr. David Russell—then General Secretary of the Baptist Union—introduced the church leaders to the HCM.

3 Roger Forster of Ichthus, and Ian Andrews of Chard are exceptions.

4 The Charismatic Renewal is within the mainline churches, and the many West Indian Pentecostal churches were primarily started outside Britain. Those started here are very significant, in my opinion, but they are still small and fragmented on the whole.

5 'The Dales Bible Week' report, 8 August 1982 (Radio 4's *Sunday*); 'Front Room Gospel', a 45-minute documentary on house churches, 23 March 1984—repeated in slightly changed form in 1985 (Radio 4).

In 1981 'Charismania' on *Credo* (LWT), 'Unearthly Powers' on *Everyman*, and *Brass Tacks* (both BBC television), covered aspects of the HCM.

6 'Apostles' here denotes a deliberate ambiguity, i.e. following apostolic teaching is to follow the Apostles of the New Testament, and the modern apostles of Restorationism.

7 In interview with me on Wednesday 23 November 1983.

8 In interview with me on Friday 14 October 1983.

9 In fact as the Basingstoke fellowships are growing stronger, and as both R1 and R2 are in a state of flux, R3/4/5 is already on the cards.

10 See Michael Harper's important little booklet, *Charismatic Crisis, The Charismatic Renewal—past, present and future* (Hounslow Printing Company, 1980).

11 Its strong emphasis on the supernatural and miracles is still influential.

12 Joyce V. Thurman, *New Wineskins, A Study of the House Church Movement* (Verlag Peter Lang, 1982), p. 34. (Mrs. Thurman's work is the pioneering study of the HCM, and I will make considerable use of it throughout this study. However, all pioneering work soon becomes out of date and some of the material is no longer relevant. On a more problematic note: much of my historical material is ordered differently from Mrs.

Thurman's. I feel that she fails to recognise the historical linkage of 'Harvestime' with the London Brothers.)

13   Ibid., p. 26. Joyce Thurman refers here to Peter Paris who was the first major leader to defect from R1. Bryn Jones does not accept Joyce Thurman's version of this story.

14   Ibid., p. 33.

15   Founded by the well-known Evangelical, Norman Grubb, this movement sounds like an insurance company. 'Union' refers to the union of Christ with believer. Some charge it with antinomianism; a charge often levelled at John Noble and Gerald Coates from people in R1.

16   Arthur Wallis, 'Focus', *Restoration* magazine (July/August 1980), p. 5.

# 2

# THE ORIGINS OF RESTORATION

Restoration has twin roots, I believe, in two nineteenth-century religious movements: the Irvingites (or Catholic Apostolic church) and the Brethren Movement. In the twentieth century, immediate precursors of Restorationism were the classical Pentecostal movements of the Apostolic church, and Elim and Assemblies of God. A look at these movements throws a great deal of light on the doctrines and developments of Restoration. However, before attempting to show these linkages in later chapters, I think it important that we first identify the immediate sources of this Kingdom Christianity; and then trace its rise and early development.

This is vitally important because a major misunderstanding concerning not only R1 and R2, but most house church movements, is that they are an outgrowth of the Charismatic Renewal within the mainstream churches. Seeing them this way is to see them as neo-Pentecostalism, whereas both theologically and sociologically they are far more akin to classical Pentecostalism. To be more accurate, Restorationism does not spring from the old Pentecostal denominationalism (though it could end up there); neither is it a 'spiritual deviation that sprang from the authentic charismatic movement'.[1] It is a separate strand of Pentecostalism that begins to emerge in the 1950s.

## The Early Years
Whilst Restoration was not planned or orchestrated by any one person in particular, there is no doubt that Arthur

35

Wallis can claim not only the early vision but also considerable influence in the way that vision unfolded. (Restorationists, of course, see God, not Arthur Wallis, as the architect of His restored kingdom.)

Arthur Wallis is the son of a famous preacher, Captain Reginald Wallis. Starting off with the Open Brethren, Captain Wallis later became an itinerant evangelist. Finding the Brethren too sectarian for his tastes, he left the movement whilst maintaining contacts with Brethren Assemblies. Arthur Wallis was greatly influenced by his father, and as a young man he was very much brought up with an Open Brethren dislike of denominationalism. Despite his high-profile charismatic history, Arthur Wallis still reminds one today of a Christian 'Brother'.

It was in 1951 that Arthur Wallis was 'baptised in the Holy Spirit'. Having, like his father before him, already abandoned the Brethren, Arthur Wallis made two significant decisions which mark him off from many who receive the 'baptism of fire'. Firstly, he never aligned himself with the existing Pentecostal denominations. Secondly, although he became passionately committed to world revival, he had no time for denominational empire-building. He saw, in the 1950s, that praying for revival usually meant praying for Methodist, Baptist, or Pentecostal revival.

In 1956, he published a book that was to give him an international reputation. This book, *In The Day Of Thy Power—the Scriptural Principles of Revival*,[2] contained a similar vision to the earlier hopes of Principal George Jeffries (Elim) and Smith-Wigglesworth (Assemblies of God) in the late 1920s. They had dreamed of a worldwide 'latter rain' that would herald the return of Christ to the world. This revival would see the demise of denominations and the rise of the universal and Spirit-endowed Church.

Whilst Arthur Wallis had this 'burden' for world revival, he had come across other men, who like himself were looking towards a 'mighty outpouring of the Holy Spirit'. Chief amongst these was David Lillie, who was also a former member of a Brethren Assembly. David Lillie had (and still has) a major interest in church structures based on New

Testament principles. Both Arthur Wallis and David Lillie were Pentecostal by experience, but dissatisfied with the purely Pentecostal emphasis given by other groups that they were beginning to meet. Wallis has always been wary of extreme emotionalism, and the 'glory meetings' of early Chard and other small independent Pentecostal fellowships were not really to his taste. Nevertheless, he had become convinced of the authenticity of tongues and prophecy. He was influenced here by two former members of the Apostolic church, Cecil Cousen and Edgar Parkyns. Wallis himself admits[3] that by 1958, it was David Lillie who was the main protagonist of restoring a New Testament pattern of church life.

It was 1958 that could be seen as the first conference organised specifically to discuss the ordering of God's church and kingdom. The conference, which lasted three days, was entitled 'The Church of Jesus Christ—Its Purity, Power, Pattern and Programme in the Context of Today'. A young student was there named Graham Perrins, who became one of the earliest apostles in the Restoration movement in the 1970s, and also edited R2's magazine, *Fulness*. (Graham Perrins was also a former member of the Brethren.)

Two more early conferences were held developing this theme. There were some forty leaders at Okehampton in 1961, and eighty leaders at Mamhead Park near Exeter in 1962. Many were 'baptised in the Holy Spirit', and prophecies and interpretations of tongues were heard. A young Welsh evangelist, formerly connected to the Assemblies of God, was present. His name was Bryn Jones and he had caused a 'bit of a stir' in Cornwall by his powerful preaching and healing ministry. (By the late 1970s, this man was to emerge as the most powerful and charismatic leader of the British Restoration movement.)

At the beginning of the 1960s, two more former Brethren members had emerged as leaders in what was still a no-man's-land between the sectarian life of classical Pentecostalism and the Renewalism of the charismatics in the mainstream churches that was to start a few years later. These men were Denis Clarke and Campbell McAlpine. Essentially, like

Arthur Wallis, these men—no doubt due to their Brethren background—were wary not only of the traditional Pentecostals, but also of all denominational structures. Nevertheless, as itinerant preachers, they had considerable influence on Brethren, Baptists, and even some Anglicans. I recall from those days that many church leaders (including Pentecostalists) were suspicious of these itinerants. Denis was not always liked: his sermons tending to be menacing, and his public personality somewhat abrasive. Both he and his wife, Beth, were extremely kind, however, and neither were really sectarian in outlook.

Campbell was already by this time a moving speaker and was seen very much as a godly man. He is highly respected to this day, and has a reputation as a 'confessor' and confidant that would not be out of place in a Catholic or Orthodox tradition. However, though no doubt it was unwitting, there is a sense in which Campbell plays an important part in the early Restoration story. And it takes place not in England, but in New Zealand.

McAlpine arrived in New Zealand in 1959. Throughout that year and the next, he made a considerable impact on Brethren Assemblies in particular and on Evangelicals in general. The Brethren, however, were not aware that the evangelist in their midst was a secret Pentecostal. Soon, the secret got out, and McAlpine was placed in a difficult position. The traditional Brethren approach to the gifts of the Spirit is a dispensationalist one: that the gifts belong to the era of the New Testament canon. McAlpine was so respected by the New Zealand Brethren, that some of the leaders begged him to stay yet keep his Pentecostalism to himself. Through personal contacts and numerous 'cottage meetings', however, McAlpine had considerable influence on Brethren evangelists and full-time workers.[4] By 1961, when he returned to England, Campbell had aroused great interest in the 'baptism of the Holy Spirit' and seen Christian leaders experience the 'second blessing'. He also left behind him a Brethren movement deeply divided against itself.

Before the Brethren had time to lick their wounds, Arthur

Wallis arrived in 1963 at the invitation of the committee of an Easter camp. He was only allowed into a few Brethren Assemblies, but in the twenty-one months he stayed in New Zealand he held many cottage meetings, and attempted to bring together those people of Pentecostal experience who were not in Pentecostal denominations.[5] As he had done with the new charismatics in England, he encouraged them to find their own identity outside the Pentecostal churches. In 1964, a conference was held in New Zealand for the newly 'Spirit-filled Christians'. All speakers but one were former members of Open Brethren Assemblies. This conference is evidence that Wallis had decided to attempt to put into practice not merely a Pentecostalist programme, but to establish a charismatically ordained church on (what he saw as) New Testament lines. 'The time has come,' said a conference circular[6], 'for a larger coming together to share the great vision that the Spirit of God is unfolding . . . the Holy Spirit of God is wanting to work in apostolic power through a fully functioning body, fed and led and governed by spiritual elders, amongst them those with special gifts and callings.' Wallis believed that the conference was prophetic, pointing to what God would do; he said, 'we would not presume to raise a little finger to precipitate anything'.[7]

However, as McAlpine had returned for this conference, many Brethren leaders looked upon this as interference in the internal religious affairs of New Zealand. There is no doubt that Brethrenism in this part of the Antipodes had become bitterly divided (a division that exists to this day). If McAlpine and Wallis could be seen as divisive or even sectarian, then it must be said in their defence that international Brethren opinion considered the New Zealand Brethren to be extremely heavy-handed in their treatment of the new Pentecostals. In the event, after Wallis left New Zealand in 1964, the charismatic issue calmed down in Brethren Assemblies. No new 'restored' church emerged. However, house churches began to appear largely stocked by disaffected Brethren. Twenty years later, when Gerald Coates (an apostle of R2) returned to England after a visit to New Zealand, he told me: 'You're certainly right about Brethren influence on House Churches; over there they're all Brethren.'[8]

The New Zealand episode can be seen as an aborted Restorationism (though it's alive there now), but it does demonstrate that the movement is not the 'Johnny come lately' that some have claimed it to be. Back in Great Britain, Campbell and Arthur found many Open Brethren were now closed to them. They were soon to become caught up in the Charismatic Renewal, but in the spring of 1965 David Lillie, Campbell McAlpine and Arthur Wallis called the third and final of their leaders' conferences. In a sense, this conference is really the beginning of the Restoration story proper; that it is difficult to see it this way is due to the fact that the Renewal movement pushed the embryonic Restorationism to one side. At the very least, the 1965 conference is a link between the 1958 conference and the emergence of R1 and R2 in the 1970s. The theme of the conference was the 'Apostolic Commission'. G. W. North was there. So too were Hugh Thompson (now a leader with Bryn Jones's team in Bradford) and Barney Coombs (the founder of the flourishing Basingstoke fellowships). At this time Wallis's vision was Restorationist but without the discipleship doctrines that were to become such a hallmark of the mature movement. Nevertheless, that vision with its emphasis on New Testament structures and principles was certainly more radical than Renewalist ideology. Ironically, the outbreak of the Renewal prevented the radicality from having any effect.

## Early Charismatic Renewal and Restorationism

The Charismatic Renewal was such a major religious phenomenon in certain church circles in Great Britain in the late 1960s and 1970s, that the rise of this neo-Pentecostalism simply carried Restorationism along with it. From about 1964 onwards, Arthur Wallis, Denis Clarke, Campbell McAlpine and David Lillie were caught up in this new revivalism. At first, I think that most of them saw the renewal as both answer to prayer and proof that the Pentecostal experience could transcend denominational barriers. Both McAlpine and Wallis were closely connected with the Fountain Trust, which was set up in 1964 to promote the Renewal. This organisation until its demise in 1980 was non-denominational and very influential in both Anglican and Catholic churches.

Throughout the 1960s, Arthur Wallis, McAlpine, and Clarke maintained their independent and itinerant status. They maintained links with South Chard, small independent groups, American organisations and mainstream charismatics. There was a great deal of Pentecostal 'jet-setting'; Campbell became one of those rare creatures that are acceptable wherever they go. His gracious manner and genuine openness to new things endeared him to people of widely differing theological opinions.

And yet, none of these men became the leaders of the Renewal in Great Britain precisely because they were outside the traditional denominational structures. British leaders, like their American and European counterparts, were primarily from the historic churches. The thrust of their message was that the existing churches could be spiritually renewed; they had no desire to establish either a new denomination, or create a sort of super trans-national church. The images one remembers from early Renewal are not angry young men nor a Puritan call to re-establish the purity of unsullied Christianity. We remember Catholics dancing in the aisles, and new liturgies (actually unconsciously adopted and adapted from classical Pentecostalism) married uneasily to the old. Hearing Anglicans saying 'Praise the Lord' and 'Thank you Jesus' became as commonplace as Catholics speaking and singing in tongues. But tongues seemed to make nuns click their rosaries more vociferously, and shouting in extempore fashion only appeared to make Anglicans religiously attend the Eucharist. In short, the Renewal created tension and disagreement between the charismatics and their leaders, but for many ordinary Christians it also led to a renewal of their traditional faiths. Perhaps, after all, some sociologists were beginning to say, Pentecostalism does not always lead to schism.[9]

At the very moment that such leaders as Michael Harper, Colin Urquhart, Tom Smail, Peter Hocken, Emmanuel Sullivan, and David Watson were demonstrating that revival could be mainstream, other Pentecostalists were beginning to have their doubts. Cardinal Suenens of Belgium, by virtue of being a Catholic hierarch, alienated many Protestants who felt rooted in the Reformation. The fact that later the Renewal could boast at least one Anglican suffragan bishop in Richard Hare, was proof for some that Charismatic Renewal was Establishment. Certainly, the classical Pentecostals were uneasy from the start. It could be argued, of course, that the Renewal undercut their rationale; no doubt, sour grapes did play some part. However, Richards spoke for many of the older Pentecostals when he pointed out that Renewalist Pentecostalism seemed to be able to hold truck with Modernism, heresy, and papal practices at variance with the Word of God.[10] Quoting Scripture, he claimed that the Holy Spirit was not 'the author of confusion', and yet the charismatics seemed not to give up their errors. Perhaps, after all, the movement was demonic?

Increasingly, classical Pentecostals have become more sympathetic to Renewal (or, at least, less antagonistic). They have taken up a line that I believe Arthur Wallis was already taking in the 1960s. He saw the Renewal as a movement of the Spirit of God, but he also saw its shortcomings. To have the Pentecostal experience without discipline and authority, he thought, was to have power without responsibility. Furthermore, like so many of his fellow travellers who were former Plymouth Brethren, he was a man brought up to believe in 'sound' doctrine. A major weakness of classical Pentecostalism has been its poor theological understanding of its own experience. In so many Pentecostal circles, testimonies of personal salvation and healing have substituted for the more systematic and doctrinal approach that is the hallmark of many Brethren Assemblies. In some respects, however, Wallis was quite happy to be at one with the older style Pentecostals; he was never neutral on doctrinal issues, and he was never at ease with those Anglicans and Catholic charismatics who seemed quite happy with infant baptism.

However, Wallis was hardly a voice being listened to in the 1960s. The stage was taken by the Renewalists, and the emphasis was on co-operation, ecumenism, and being one in the Spirit whilst accepting differences in doctrine. But whilst everyone's eyes were up front watching the performance of the big denominations, slowly but surely house churches began to appear throughout the country. The members of these churches were primarily from sectarian backgrounds. They were suspicious of the mainstream success, yet at the same time they benefited from it. These new dissenters from Brethren, classical Pentecostal, Evangelical Free Baptists, Salvation Army, and various non-aligned churches, were hidden from close scrutiny by church leaders because they became identified with the Renewal. They did not deliberately hide under the skirts of the Charismatic movement: the house churches were neither secret nor subversive; it was just that nobody noticed them until after the Renewal began to slow down from about 1980 onwards. Suddenly, they seemed to be everywhere.

One of the reasons they remained unnoticed was their music and ritual. Many house churches 'plugged into' the Renewal, borrowing its songs and liturgical mannerisms; conversely, the Renewal picked up the new songs of Restoration. By the end of the 1970s, for example, the R2 'Bind us together, Lord' could be found in every type of British charismatic movement. Furthermore, many house church members joined in Renewalist jamborees, and Renewalists attended Downs Week, and The Dales Bible Week. R1 and R2 were separate strands of Pentecostalism, but they did (for a while) become interwoven with the Charismatic Renewal *per se*.

Michael Harper and I have a disagreement concerning the decline of Charismatic Renewal. I believe that it slowed down some five years ago, whilst Michael believes that it has been still quietly growing.[11] However, we both agree that the closure of the Fountain Trust in 1980 left the Renewal without a clear focus. Some of the charismatics eager to go 'where the action is' found that it was happening in house churches and in particular in R1. The Dales Bible Week at the Great Yorkshire showground provided a new focus, and attracted many disaffected charismatics from the mainstream churches. Undoubtedly the Renewal had a profound spiritual effect on thousands of people's lives, but the denominations were left essentially unchanged. Again, I doubt if Michael Harper (or any Renewalist leaders) would agree with me, but I think it possible that hindsight might show us that the Renewal provided the fuel for a new Pentecostalism outside the churches. I offer it as no more than a tentative hypothesis, but could it be that the historical role of Charismatic Renewal has been not to renew the Church, but to aid (albeit unwittingly) the rise of a new sectarianism?

## Nascent Restoration in the 1960s

The 'heyday' of the Charismatic Movement was in fact the 1970s not the 1960s. But from about 1966 onwards it began to accelerate. During this time, throughout Britain, house churches began to appear. John Noble (the leading apostle in R2) started a house church in his front room at Ilford in 1967. He was 'baptised in the Spirit' in 1961 and knew Michael Harper when he was a curate at All Souls, Langham Place, London. During the early days of the Charismatic Movement, he attended meetings of the Fountain Trust. He recalls that Arthur Wallis was an adviser to the Fountain Trust, and that it was Campbell McAlpine who came up with the idea of the 'fountain gate' that led to the adoption of the title 'Fountain Trust'. John Noble's background was Salvation Army, and although he was enamoured with Renewal, he had little in common with Establishment Christianity. Influenced by Watchman Nee's book *Home Missions*—Nee was himself influenced by Brethren missionaries in China—he decided to start his own mission to homes. Soon, he lost all contacts with his former charismatic friends in the Fountain Trust.

About this time in Cobham, Surrey, a young Brethren member, Gerald Coates, and a few others formed a splinter group from the local Assembly. These 'come-outers' met for the next three years in the local Youth Centre. During this time they were visited by a number of itinerants, who were former members of Honor Oak (a neo-Brethren community). The group at the Youth Centre was not initially charismatic.

Indeed, when Gerald Coates went to a retreat at Westwatch, West Sussex in 1967 (organised by Maurice Smith) he thought they were all mad.

Meanwhile, back in Cobham, the splinter group began to have second thoughts about their separateness. 'You can't have two "tables" in the same town,' goes the old Brethren adage concerning Communion fellowship. So, many of the splinter group decided to return to the local Assembly. Gerald Coates, his wife and three friends began to meet in his front room; this was the beginning of the now four-hundred-strong Cobham Christian Fellowship. Gerald's own Pentecostal experience began as he found himself speaking in tongues whilst riding his bicycle. In those very early days, as others joined them and became 'baptised in the Spirit', the Cobham group had no idea that they were only one of scores of new charismatic house groups outside the mainstream denominations. As Gerald Coates put it: 'We were insecure, green as green could be, and felt that we were probably the only people in Britain who really loved the Lord Jesus but didn't actually go to church on Sunday . . .'[12]

What characterised the Cobham group—and many others—during the late 1960s was above all a sense of freedom. They felt released from the dead formalism (as they saw it) of traditional Christianity. No more 'spiritual sandwiches' of prayer, hymn, preaching for them. Sometimes they would sing in tongues for hours, or dance and cry. There was prophecy, and interpreting the *glossolalia*. The new freedom was also experienced as breaking through to 'real' relationships and commitment to each other. None of these groups really knew where they were going during this anarchic and exciting Pentecostalism: the emphasis was on experience, relationships, and free-wheeling liturgies. There was no overt leadership, and those who did minister were known by their first names.

And yet, as the 1967 Westwatch retreat demonstrates, there were conferences going on where Arthur Wallis's earlier vision was still alive although in dormant form. Maurice Smith believes that the 1967 conference (and the earlier one in 1965 organised by Arthur Wallis) was a vital stepping stone to the emergent Restorationism of the 1970s. His own story is worth telling[13] not only because it is interesting in itself, but also because it leads us into the first co-ordinating efforts of early Restorationism.

Maurice was converted in 1955. Then an Anglican, he soon became disillusioned with all types of denominations. By 1956, he was determined to remain Christian but without a church. He remembers praying by the side of his bed: 'Lord, I think your Son is wonderful, and your church is horrible. And I don't want any more to do with it. People in pubs are more friendly than in the churches.' He eventually joined Honor Oak, a neo-Brethren community that was named after the suburb of London. This organisation is an interesting link between the older-style Evangelicalism and the modern house church movements. It was dominated by the personality of T. Austin Sparks, and was greatly influenced by Watchman Nee's writings. Honor Oak was against emotionalism and mass evangelism. It put great stress on self-denial and the corporate life of the Christian community. Maurice Smith became an elder in the community, and remained in the movement for ten years. By 1966 he was desperate to get out. He felt that the community was committed to law rather than grace, and he felt that there was neither great love nor spiritual power. Honor Oak, like most orthodox Brethren Assemblies at that time, were totally against any kind of Pentecostalism. Smith kept hearing of nothing else in the country, so it seemed to him, except 'baptism of the Holy Spirit; baptism of the Holy Spirit . . .'

At that time, he came under the influence of a Methodist called Edgar Trout. Smith was thinking of leaving Honor Oak as a result of Trout's influence, when, driving home to Canterbury through Sussex, 'My car was suddenly filled with light, supernatural light. I was not frightened. I knew that God had separated me to do His work.'

He gave up his job as a sales executive, and in February 1967 came out of Honor Oak with another community member, Ted Crick. Under their leadership 'Canterbury became a little bit of a centre,' and Maurice and Ted began to travel around the country. As they did so, they realised that charismatics and house groups were everywhere; often without leadership, these groups were looking for fellowship with others like themselves. Ted and Maurice also discovered the, by now, quite well developed work of Harry Greenwood and Sid Purse at Chard, and the fellowships of Wally North. Not being from the major denominations themselves, they had little in common with the Anglicans and Catholics (although Michael Harper later became a friend). They began to bump into other itinerants (many of whom had been present at David Lillie's and Arthur Wallis's conferences in 1962/5). Such men as Denis Clarke, Campbell McAlpine, Cecil Cousen, Edgar Trout were ministering to people in the denominations and the new house groups.

The leaders who were invited to Westwatch in 1967, which Maurice organised, were really self-selecting: they were those who had either started house churches, or acted as itinerant ministers to new fellowships. Roger Forster (founder of Ichthus) was there, as were Graham Perrins, Peter Lyne and Hugh Thompson (all former Brethren). Arthur Wallis was in the thick of it all; perhaps by now he saw that the cottage meetings of New Zealand had a greater counterpart in Great Britain. New leaders began to appear such as Terry Virgo (now an apostle in R1), Ian McCullogh (now a leader in my extended usage of R2), and Barney Coombs whom we have already met at the 1965 conference. By 1970, leaders were meeting more frequently, house churches (on an *ad hoc* basis) were continuing to grow, and as the Charismatic Renewal entered its most successful decade (to date), clusters of these new churches began to come together for common worship.

## Notes

1   Editorial introduction to Arthur Wallis's 'Springs of Restoration', Part 1, *Restoration* (Harvestime Publications, July/August 1980).

2 I remember reading this book in the 1950s; many classical Pentecostals, at that time, believed it was a prophetic work. The book is now reissued (and partly rewritten) under the title *Rain from Heaven* (Hodder and Stoughton, 1980).

3 Op. cit., p. 23.

4 P. J. Lineham, 'Tongues Must Cease: The Brethren And The Charismatic Movement In New Zealand', *Christian Brethren Review*, No. 34 (Nov. 1983).

5 Wallis had originally intended to stay only for the Easter camp, but he found that Campbell had laid a foundation on which he felt compelled to build. See 'Springs of Restoratioin', op. cit.

6 Lineham, op. cit., p. 40.

7 Ibid., p. 41.

8 Phone call to Gerald Coates, June 1984.

9 So I suggested in an Agenda article in the *Guardian* newspaper, 'A New Spirit To Light Up The Church' (24 Nov. 1980). However, I feel less sanguine about the Renewal now than I did then. Cf. My 'Pentecostal Power: Charismatic Movements and the politics of Pentecostal experience' in *Of Gods And Men: New Religious Movements*, edited by E. Barker (Mercer University Press, USA, 1984).

10 W. T. H. Richards, *Pentecost is Dynamite* (Lakeland Cox & Wyman Ltd., 1972).

11 This was his view in conversation with me in June 1984. As the empirical work has not been done to establish the truth of our assertions, I can only point to the fact that my impressions are shared by Professor Walther Hollenweger, Emmanuel Sullivan, and Arthur Wallis. (Cf. Chapter 13, note 5.)

12 Gerald Coates, *What On Earth Is This Kingdom?* (Kingsway, 1983), p. 23.

13 The quotes from Maurice Smith in this book come from four hours of interview on 16 May 1984 (and/or numerous letters and phone calls).

## RECOMMENDED READING

Arthur Wallis, 'Springs of Restoration', Part 1, *Restoration* (Harvestime Publications, July/August 1980).
Michael Harper, *None Can Guess* (Hodder and Stoughton, 1971).
Emmanuel Sullivan, SA. 'Can the Pentecostal Movement renew the churches?' booklet (BCC, 1971).

# 3

# THE RESTORED KINGDOM EMERGES

The coming together of scattered house churches was in no sense orchestrated within a predetermined ideological framework. Whilst it is possible by 1975 to look back and see the events that lead up to the establishment of Restorationism, it was not the case that house church leaders in 1970 knew (a) who exactly they were, or (b) where they were going.

The years 1970 to 1974 were heady days of great excitement, and discovery: a discovery of meeting groups all over the country with similar beginnings and common aspirations. Those aspirations, on the whole, were related to 'walking with God' in such a way that the experiential and supernatural became a living grace that seemed to have done away with religious legalism once and for all. The legalism of clericalism, church order, standardised liturgies, denominational certainties, and dogmatic doctrines, were seen to be swept aside by the coming of the Spirit. Certainly, people like Maurice Smith, John Noble, Gerald Coates, and George Tarleton (who became an apostle in R2) experienced those early days as freedom *from* the old religious order; how this new freedom would develop (i.e. what they would become free *to* do) was simply not known.

So anarchic were those days in the early 1970s, that the leading participants find it difficult to recall the events in any logical or chronical way.[1] What does emerge clearly enough is this: from the end of the 1960s to 1974, London became a major focus of the emerging Restorationism. As we shall see, the Capel Bible Week in West Sussex played a part in bringing Bryn Jones into the foreground, but he was already beginning to establish himself and his team in the north of England.

## 'The London Brothers' and the 'Festival of Light'

We can take up the story again with Maurice Smith. By the end of the 1960s he had left Canterbury and moved to a fellowship in Turner's Hall, Chigwell, North London. There, he met up with David Mansell. Mansell, whose 'prophetic' insights and controversial private life have been both sources of wonder and bewilderment for many Restoration followers, is a key figure in the movement. A major leader in the early days, he later became identified with R1 under the apostleship of Bryn Jones. By 1970 he and Maurice were 'into' Community. (I recall that this was a major theme in Catholic charismatic circles at that time.) Maurice is always 'into' something, and usually ahead of the crowd.

By 1969, Maurice had, in his own words, 'a burden for London come upon me'. He wrote to eighteen leaders from different house church movements that included Chard and Wally North. Apparently, Wally North never came, and Lance Lambert of Halford House, Richmond (another small house church that predates the 1960s) came once, did not like what he saw, and never came again. This first meeting which Maurice Smith thinks was in 1970, or possibly 1969, was held in the Leprosy Mission hall. Soon, these meetings became regular, and numbers rapidly increased. By this time John Noble was a major figure by virtue of his strong personality and his success at Ilford and later Romford. Gerald Coates, Terry Virgo, George Tarleton, David Mansell, and Maurice Smith began to be seen—with John Noble—as the core of what became known as the 'London Brothers'.

Chard's influence was strong in the early gatherings which were very similar to the 'Glory meetings'. Sid Purse, however, according to Maurice Smith, saw the thing negatively as an attempt to organise unity. Chard influence petered out, as the London Brothers began to 'do their own thing'. It was the music and worship that marked those early meetings at the Leprosy Mission. Nobody formally led; free expression was the norm, and the sense of freedom itself generated a strong sense of unity. These Leprosy Mission hall meetings were mainly for the emerging leadership, not the rank and file. The fact that there was little formality and a great deal of shouting, praising, leaping and dancing could not mask the fact that leadership was being formed.

Soon, the Leprosy Mission began to attract one hundred or more people; not all, of course, were leaders. The Mission hall organisers asked the charismatic enthusiasts to leave: the noise and threatened structural damage to the floorboards were becoming cause for concern! The emerging leadership continued to meet on an informal basis. Strong personal relationships were formed, and no pecking order had yet arisen. Indeed, in 1970, hierarchical concepts of leadership went against the egalitarian spirit of the London Brothers.

1971 sees the London Brotherhood moving into a different phase. A 'one off' meeting was held at All Souls, Langham Place, but by now house group leaders, itinerant evangelists, and rank and file members were too great in number to get in. It was agreed to start meeting at the London School of Economics.

That year, Peter Hill, who was himself in a house group, organised what Malcolm Muggeridge came to call the 'Festival of Light'. This demonstration against the 'permissive society' began on the 25th of September with a massive rally in Trafalgar Square. It was attended by thousands of Catholics, Evangelicals, charismatics, and some right-wing organisations and Establishment religious figures. Members of the London and south-east house churches came in droves. It must be remembered that although members thought they were 'under grace' and in freedom, most of them came to their new churches with well-conditioned Puritan consciences. The Festival of Light was a battle cry against the 'kingdom of this world' and its Prince, Satan. God's kingdom, they realised, had to be ordered on Biblical principles.

The Festival of Light was a 'call to seriousness' in the Evangelical tradition of the nineteenth century.[2] Even in the 'glory days' of the Leprosy Mission hall, much emphasis had been put on 'kingdom living', the imminent return of Jesus Christ, and discovering the significance of the revival they were all experiencing. Once, some Argentinians who were distant associates of Juan Carlos Ortiz had come to tell the brethren of the need for discipleship and order. The Festival of Light was seen as an attack upon the disorder of a secular world. The fact that the new house groups responded to the call for moral purity in a way that many mainstream charismatics did not, is not very surprising. Many of the latter, being liberal by disposition, were sceptical of the political motivations behind the Festival; they did not share the Puritanism and Evangelical traditions that characterised most house church members.

But if the Festival of Light was a moral crusade and evoked a moral response from house church members, it also had an unintended consequence. Singing and speaking in tongues, free-wheeling worship, fingers pointing high to the Jesus who is king, and cries of 'hallelujah' and 'amen' became a feature of the mass demonstrations. Charismatics were soon able to seek each other out as the Pentecostal signals were self-evident for all to see. And now house church groups found (perhaps for the first time) just how many of them there were. Group leaders had been telling them of an emerging movement of the Spirit, but now they could see for themselves. The Festival of Light did not give birth to Restoration, but it did confirm for many that 'something' was emerging.

That something was still essentially an anarchic animal. The London School of Economics meetings swelled to some five hundred people with leaders bringing their wives and friends. Worship was still free and easy, and no formal leadership existed. John Noble was just plain John to everybody, and Gerald, Maurice, David, George, etc., was the order of the day. Everybody I have talked to about those early days agrees that the 'blessing' was related to friendliness and openness to new things of God. All sorts of charismatic and non-charismatic things were tried. There was 'deliverance ministry' where sickness and sin were rebuked as evidence of demonic possession or oppression. Rebuking was done in the name of Jesus—the usual phrase being 'I command you' or 'I rebuke you, in the name of Jesus to come out.' Sometimes praying for the sick would be a 'laying on of hands ministry' with as many people doing the hand-laying as could reach the sick person. Even in those days, I can find no one who remembers women laying on hands.[3] Demons, miracles, the exercise of spiritual gifts, such as speaking in tongues, interpretation of tongues, prophecy, giving 'words of wisdom and knowledge', were an experienced reality within the context of an overwhelming conviction that Christ was about to return to claim his church.

This strong eschatological thrust was one of the major reasons why early Restorationists began to ask themselves what should be the nature of this Church for whom God is coming? What should we, as redeemed and Spirit-filled Christians be doing to hasten the coming? What does it mean that God is coming to establish His kingdom? What is the kingdom? Anarchic Pentecostalism has no answers to such questions. On the whole mainstream Charismatic Renewal, which was now really taking off in Great Britain, was not concerned with such questions. House church leaders were asking such questions, but even so many of them were still content to bask in the new-found light and warmth of discovered friendships. Finding friends with similar beliefs and practices to yourself is an essential prerequisite to forming organisational structures.

At the LSE meetings anarchy still reigned. There was the curious practice of leg-lengthening: apparently, you stuck out both legs and invariably found one leg longer than the other one. It was believed that lengthening the short leg could improve all sorts of physical ailments. A kind of chiropractice seemed to be the method; massage would be used, sometimes with prayer and sometimes without. George Tarleton was really keen on this—'the odder things were the better George liked them'[4]—but John Noble remained sceptical.

By the end of 1971, John Noble in particular, but also George Tarleton, David Mansell, Gerald Coates, Terry Virgo, Hugh Thompson, Maurice Smith and Ted Crick were *de facto* leaders in the south-east. Graham Perrins and Peter Lyne, who were in association with them, were flying the flag of the nascent Restorationism in the west and south-west of the country. A magazine had appeared in 1970 called *Fulness*. The early editions were not particularly professional in presentation, neither were they dated,[5] but they do reveal that 'a line' was already beginning to emerge amongst the leaders.

The first editions, from 1970 into 1971, are held together by that old duo Maurice Smith and Ted Crick under the editorial direction of Graham Perrins. Guest writers are David Lillie and Hugh Thompson. Discipleship doctrines cannot be found there, but there is already interest in apostleship (re: Ephesians 4). Two strong themes emerge. The first is the call to unity in the Spirit. St. John's gospel, chapter 17 is much in evidence. John Noble remembers that the desire to belong simply to the Church and not a new organisation dominated those early days.[6] This call to unity is seen against the sin of denominationalism. A little book of John Noble from 1971 was entitled *Forgive Us Our Denominations*. In it he writes of denominationalism as disunity and thus sinfulness. (A view also held by liberal ecumenists.) The call to unity is understood not as building a new super church in the sense of a transdenominational church, but a call to repentance and the restoring of New Testament spiritual gifts. Prophetically, John Noble warns of forming a new 'non-sectarian sect' (which in many ways, in my opinion, R2 has become).

This leads to the second theme, for Ted Crick introduces the notion of the remnant church (a theme much loved by Brethren and Pentecostals over the years). This will be the true Church awaiting God's return; the false church is the apostate church of nominal Christians under the direction of liberal and Modernist leaders. There is much talk of 'restoring' the church/kingdom in the power of the Holy Spirit. The belief that God is restoring His Church—and that they are in it—is itself seen as a sign or witness that the world ('this present age') is coming to an end.

The London Brothers, and the emerging southern leadership, continued to have influence for the next few years, but in order to see how Bryn Jones and Bradford come into the picture, I suggest we turn to his work and influence in a new group of leaders. It is this group that takes Restorationism out of its anarchic phase, and turns it into the radical Christianity that it has become today.

## The Rise of Bryn Jones, and Covenanted Relationships

In Arthur Wallis's article 'Springs of Restoration',[7] he seeks to trace the origins of R1 in various 'tributaries' or 'streams' which eventually become the rushing torrent of Restoration. Such imagery is popular in R1 and R2. 'The streams make glad' of Psalm 46 is an ever-popular image used to describe the various strands of the house churches. Like all images, however, they can be misleading. I doubt whether it is strictly accurate to describe early Restoration as having two streams (in the sense of separate ideologies or major differences). However, I think the imagery is helpful if we think of not separateness but different geographical location and focus. Whilst the London Brothers were pioneering the south-east and debating the tenets that were eventually to form the basic teaching of Restoration, Bryn Jones began to establish a well-organised community church in Bradford from 1969.

Since Arthur Wallis first met him in 1962, Bryn Jones had experienced rather a chequered career. He left Cornwall and went to France and later Germany where he worked for three months with the interdenominational evangelistic organisation, 'Operation Mobilisation'. He met his wife, Edna, at the Bible College of Wales. Having married her in 1964, they set off as missionaries to Guyana (then British Guiana). Bryn demonstrated the true evangelistic pioneering spirit in the three years he was there. Sixteen churches were established and there are now eighty-four.

He returned to Cornwall, the scene of his earlier success,

but after the doctrinal squabbles with Chard and others, he moved on to Bradford. By 1970, Bryn was virtually unknown in the south, but his work began to flourish in the north. His brother, Keri, joined him and a flourishing work began. Bryn Jones would not wish it to be thought that the spectacular rise of the Bradford community church (after 1975) and the later establishment of an apostolic team under his direction was simply his doing. He would point to the fact that what I call R1 has other apostolic teams, and that the success of all the teams is primarily due to the Holy Spirit. It would be eccentric, however, to assume that the rise of R1 had nothing to do with the personality and style of Bryn Jones. He is no 'slouch' when it comes to positive action. It is easy to believe that he would have been successful as a trade union leader, or as a director of a large business corporation.

He has two strengths as a leader in addition to his powerful preaching. Not only does he possess vision, but he has the ruthless determination to bring that vision to a reality. Somebody once described him to me as a 'bruiser under anointing'! His critics in R2 and elsewhere would say that he is an 'operator' or a 'manipulator'; they see him as an opportunist who knows a good thing when he sees it, and 'grabs the main chance'. I think that he is also an idealist. The idea that he must either be a saint or a rogue is, I believe, stretching it too far. There is a Russian Orthodox saying that I think might help us in trying to evaluate this interesting man and avoid having to see him as either the greatest saint of all time, or as a man 'on the make'. The saying is that 'great virtues cast long shadows'.[8]

Friends and critics alike admit that he is a born leader. In 1970, with almost no money nor organisation, he set up a summer camp at Pendine, South Wales. 'Two marquees, one for meetings, the other for eating, a team of three volunteer cooks and a set of tents for hire to would-be campers were the total equipment.'[9] These camps were later to become the summer camps at the Lakes, and from 1976 the Dales Bible Week at the Great Yorkshire Showground outside Harrogate. From the outset, they were designed as an interdenominational gathering. Initially, they concentrated on Bible teaching, and Pentecostal ministry. It was not until after 1976 that they emerged as a shop-window for Restoration, and developed a distinctive and highly successful style of worship and song.

During 1970, Bryn developed relationships with American evangelists and religious leaders. He had already developed American connections, however, on his way back from Guyana when he stayed in North America for a while. From the start, the Bradford movement was different in kind from the London and southern fellowships. Biblical and family authority were stressed more than in the south. Members were noticeably more working class than the southerners. Understandably, therefore, leadership was more authoritarian, and followers more conservative than the southern counterparts.

Originally, Bryn Jones's Assemblies of God background showed: the doctrine and the worship were little different from classical Pentecostalism. The first few editions of *Restoration* magazine in 1975/6 have a traditional Pentecostal flavour to them with a little added spice of Renewalism. There was a great expectancy, however, that God was beginning a great work. Bryn was (and still is) an outstanding and clever preacher. He can be folksy Welsh in the best *hwyl* tradition, an inspired expositor of Scripture, and a very funny and witty performer. Added to this talent, he is clearly intelligent (though not intellectual) and thoughtful. He has a reputation for prophetic insight, and miraculous happenings have always been part of his ministry. This obviously looks, in religious terms, like a recipe for a charismatic leadership that is hard to beat. As one of the former leaders of R2 said to me recently: 'If it was just a question of being on the winning side, I'd stick with Bryn Jones.'[10]

Clearly, Arthur Wallis had not forgotten the youthful Jones of 1962. He knew of his outstanding talents and leadership potential, and in 1971 he called together a group of leaders to discuss not Restoration as such, or even apostleship structures, but eschatology. By now, Arthur who had worked hard behind the scenes of Charismatic Renewal, was hankering after a more radical vision: a vision that he had glimpsed in New Zealand years before. What was now fanning the fires of this vision was his eschatological conviction that not only was Christ soon returning to earth to reign, but that He wanted to establish the foundations of His kingdom before He arrived. Wallis wanted to share with other leaders the possibility that the 'end-time' was not to be characterised by total disaster, but the restoration of a glorious church that was itself to signal the 'restoration of all things'.

In a way, Arthur's group got out of hand. What started as a series of meetings to discuss prophecy turned into a workshop to hammer out the principles of the restored kingdom. There was no law or line, or overt leadership during these early meetings, but soon there emerged the conviction that God had separated them to be leaders and apostles in His end-time Church. The first meeting included six people, and they met in February 1972. The Festival of Light was understood prophetically as a symbol —an outward sign of kingdom Christianity; the leadership meetings were the inner or spiritual heart of the kingdom where the rules and order of God's Church would be revealed by the Word (*logos*) of God, and the word (*rhema*) of prophecy. The original six leaders were Arthur Wallis, Peter Lyne (who was in New Zealand until recently), Bryn Jones, David Mansell, Graham Perrins, and Hugh Thompson. After Bryn Jones prophesied: 'Seven shall be your number, and thrice you shall meet', it was decided to add John Noble. Apparently, there was considerable discussion as to whether John Noble was suitable.

The group, who later called themselves jokingly 'the magnificent seven', did meet three times; indeed, John Noble thinks they met more than that. It was then decided to open out the leadership to a broader brotherhood. This has always been a point of controversy. Bryn Jones was away when this decision was taken and felt that it was premature. Years later Arthur Wallis felt that the split of 1976 was caused by not heeding God's advice to limit the number to seven.[11] John Noble does not recall any such advice. In the event, the augmented 'magnificent seven' became known as the 'fabulous fourteen'.

In the first meetings of the seven, what began to emerge as they prayed and fasted together was a strong sense of mutual destiny. As they looked around and saw each other and recognised the work that they had already achieved, they became convinced—under numerous promptings of personal prophecies—that they were already exercising apostolic and prophetic functions. Their recognition of function became the way leadership emerged. So, for example, Graham Perrins could be seen as a prophet and an apostle because he had both the inspired word and had pioneered house churches in Wales. (Before any of the others, incidentally.) Or again, David Mansell was seen as a prophet because of his insights and pronouncements, but he could not be seen as an apostle because he had not established churches. This establishment of churches certainly made Bryn an apostle, but he clearly had gifts of evangelism and prophecy too. John Noble was undoubtedly an apostle because of his 'laying of the foundations' of God's work in the south-east.

These functions were not simply recognised by the word of prophecy alone. They were thought to be confirmed by the Word of God. In particular, they were convinced that Ephesians, chapter 4, verses 8 to 12, were not merely meant for the New Testament dispensation, but were the divine principles on which the Church should have been ordered throughout history. To recapitulate, the key verses 11 to 12 state:

> And these were his gifts: some to be apostles, some prophets, some evangelists, some pastors and teachers, to equip God's people for work in his service, to the building up of the body of Christ. (NEB)

As these men grappled with his startling vision that they now realised was applicable to them personally, they began to also think of what this meant in terms of personal commitment to each other. From this emerged a belief that they should form a covenant together, a belief that was extended to the full fourteen. At one meeting Graham Perrins failed to turn up; the others took this very personally seeing in it a failure of commitment. The new seven that augmented the original group to the full 'fabulous fourteen' were George Tarleton, Gerald Coates, Barney Coombs, Maurice Smith, Ian McCullogh, John MacLaughlan, and Campbell McAlpine. There had been talk of including Denis Clarke, but this nomination did not meet with full approval. (What Denis thought of his exclusion I cannot say as sadly he died two years ago.)

George Tarleton, who was the most liberal and anarchic character in the group, is now amazed that he could have turned his back on the freedom and grace, which he saw as the hallmarks of the London Brothers. However, the workshops were so exciting, and there was such a feeling of God's purposes being worked out in their lives, that he failed to see that they were beginning what he now feels was the beginning of denominationalism. There is no doubt that the 'fabulous fourteen' did take a radical change in direction. Anarchic Pentecostalism was not yet entirely conquered amongst the London Brothers (as we shall see), but from 1974 onwards a firm leadership began to be established both in the south and north. House church fellowships did not seem to want to resist this leadership. On the contrary, scores of independent groups now began to align themselves with the emerging apostles. They wanted to be 'in' on the new thing that God was doing. The language of discipling and submission doctrines were couched in the language of biblical imagery such as 'shepherding' or 'covering'. To be under authority was seen to be in 'relatedness' to apostles and their appointed elders. Both the emerging leadership and the rank and file thought in terms of being 'bound by cords of love', and being released from the bondage of wilful independence. The apostolic doctrines were in no sense worked out at this time, and Bryn Jones and Arthur Wallis were more careful in their statements than a number of the London Brothers.

Nevertheless, by 1974, the self-selection (or God's election) of the 'fabulous fourteen' led to the establishment of a charismatically ordained leadership. This leadership was legitimated by an appeal to members to recognise the *de facto* leadership that had already emerged. Bryn Jones, for example, is an apostle, so the argument went, because he acts like an apostle. Furthermore, house church members were told, the Holy Spirit who had separated Barnabas and Saul in the Acts of the Apostles, was the same Spirit who had separated the fourteen to be leaders of the restored kingdom. This truth was confirmed for the leaders by the inner testimony of personal conviction, and the outward seal of prophetic utterance. In a sense, the 'fabulous fourteen' had ordained each other not in any formal ceremony, but by mutual recognition of ministry, prophecy, and the laying on of hands. In no sense, however, did these men have the delusions of grandeur that led them to believe that they were the only apostles in the world, and that they alone constituted the only true leadership in God's restored church.

The years 1972 to 1974 are not merely the years that saw the gradual establishment of a new leadership structure. They are also the years in which the nascent Restoration movement gives way to a quite different ideological orientation. Now it is held that God's Spirit speaks in a special way through His ordained servants: the vertical relationship with God is now augmented (perhaps even superseded) by horizontal relationships with God via His apostles, prophets, and elders. I think that such an interpretation would be going too far for the majority of R1 annd R2 leaders today. Nevertheless, it was an understanding that some house churches developed. This is particularly true of those groups who stressed the primacy of the prophet. Graham Perrins and John MacLauchlan were to fall out with the rest of the R2 leaders over this matter. In 1974/5, however, the radicality of this change in direction was not fully recognised or understood by many house groups, and the full implications were not even fully realised by some of the 'fabulous fourteen'.

It would seem to me to be unwise to break up our narrative with an analysis of this change of direction. Perhaps, however, we could pause for a parable. Recently, I was sent a cyclostated letter in which the author has an amusing yet thoughtful insight into the adoption of apostolic and discipleship doctrines by the house churches. I include the piece in full:

### Chiefs and Indians

In the not far distant past, the great spirit began to speak to the Indians in the north, in the western coastlands and on the eastern flats. Little bands began to meet in their tepees to rediscover their common life in the great spirit and to make deep friendship. They held pow wows, spoke wisdom and smoked the pipe of peace. Each group a band of equal brothers freely serving and sharing gifts with each other.

After a while each band began to recognise a warrior who seemed to have a deeper knowledge of the great spirit, to whom they would listen with respect, go to for advice and look to for organisation. They gave him a feather to wear and he was soon known as 'one feather'. After three moons 'one feather' ceased to hunt and fish. The others brought him gifts. He told them great spirit's words, how to plan their lives, how to bring up their children. Some Indians found it more difficult to hear the great spirit for themselves, finding it easier to listen to 'one feather'.

It was not long before a One Feather with a larger band than most, was given a pony by his people and began to travel. He met with other bands and eventually called a meeting of One Feathers. 'We need to get more organised,' he told them, 'the present situation is a woolly mess.'

'Didn't the great spirit himself bring it about?' asked one brave.

'Of course,' replied the ponyrider, 'but he has told me that things must change.'

So the One Feathers decided, as leaders, that they themselves should have a leader. So it was that ponyrider became Little Chief Two Feathers with an appropriate headdress and a special tepee. He would not have much time to share with the 'no-feathers' now, but would instruct the One Feathers who would pass his teaching down. Some One Feathers now found it more difficult to hear the great spirit for themselves and found it easier to listen to L.C.T.F.

Some moons later Two Feathers, who now had a horse and travelled more widely holding many gatherings for One Feathers, came across others like himself. They met together in solemn conclave and decided that they too must be 'covered'. (A curious term arising from an ancient writing when a squaw was covered by a famous chief's blanket.) After some fuss and a lot of pow wow, Big Chief Many Feathers emerged. He was given a many-horsed chariot and a team of Two Feathers to travel the country giving input and guidance. Some Two Feathers now found it more difficult to hear the great spirit for themselves and found it easier to listen to B.C.M.F.

Meantime the great spirit began to speak to many no-feathers in the north and in the coastlands and on the eastern flats. Little bands began to gather in their tepees to share their common life in the great spirit and to enter into deep friendship . . .[12]

This parable, whilst pertinent to the new movement, should not be interpreted literally as far as Restorationism is concerned. Indeed, what emerged from the meetings of the fourteen were not only differences of emphasis but competing leadership. Bryn Jones, John Noble, and Graham Perrins emerged as the strong personalities. Ironically, Arthur Wallis who had originally called the seven together, was neither recognised as a prophet nor as an apostle. He has had to be content to watch other people fulfil his vision whilst he has been left in the honorary position of elder statesman; his actual function at the present time is as a member of Tony Morton's apostolic team with an itinerant role as the prophetic teacher of Restoration.

By 1974, I believe the Restorationist movement had become tentatively established with distinctive doctrines, leadership, and liturgical practices. However, there was no formal organisation, and no single leader. John Noble became the leading apostle in the south, and Bryn Jones dominated the north. Graham Perrins was strong in the west, but never established such a strong and wide circle as Jones and Noble. (Although Graham's 'covering' has been accepted outside his Welsh stronghold; Petersfield in Hampshire, for example.)

The primary reason why we can see the years 1973 to 1976 as the years when—although it never had a name—the 'restored kingdom' (however fragile) had arrived, was the mutual recognition of leadership and ministry amongst the 'fabulous fourteen'. These men saw themselves in covenanted relationship, and their work as the fruit of the Holy Spirit. Their vision, at that time, was for a worldwide church founded on the lines revealed to them in their deliberations together. However, even during these years, the 'kingdom' was in no sense a uniform structure. The evidence seems to suggest that it was the London Brothers and their associates who first developed a strong interest in discipleship and apostleship. Conversely, whilst it seems to be the case that Bryn Jones and his colleagues were a year or two behind in fully developing the apostolic/discipling structure, they were certainly ahead when it came to organising successful and rational financial structures. Furthermore, although Bryn Jones and John Noble, for example, were in covenanted relationship in these years, they worked quite separately. Today, Bryn Jones sees the work he is doing as never really a part of what I have called R2.[13] This is not an historical fact: it is a spiritual judgement of hindsight on his part. In the early 1970s, the 'fabulous fourteen' all thought that they were involved in the same work of restoring the kingdom.[14]

## The London Brothers go International, and Capel Bible Week

When the 'fabulous fourteen' came together, the London Brothers had already gone up-market from the LSE, and had begun to hold regular meetings at the Bonnington Hotel. (Hotels seemed to be popular amongst the Restoration leaders.) These meetings became a focal point for many of the ideas that were to be worked out by the fourteen leaders. The fourteen were later to become twenty-eight, but this larger number never had the same prestige as the smaller groups. Significantly, many of the ideas discussed at the Bonnington came from America and many of the guests were neither classical Pentecostals nor leaders from the mainstream Charismatic Renewal. Dennis Bennet, author of a best-selling book, *Nine O'Clock In The Morning*, came to talk. A little later, Ern Baxter who was a member of a group known as the 'Fort Lauderdale Five' made a major impact. These men were involved in similar movements to the English Restorationists, but their vision at that time was far more worked out, and their commitment to 'church growth ministries' much greater. The London Brothers with their grass roots fellowships were somewhat overawed by the idealistic and grandiose plans of these American charismatics. Individual brothers began to make their own contacts with American counterparts. Graham Perrins linked up with a man from Minnesota called Charles Schmitt, and later John MacLauchlan was to 'relate' to a man from Arizona with the unlikely name of Wayne Drain.

But probably it was Orvil Swindoll and other one-time associates of the Argentinian Juan Carlos Ortiz who made the first major impact upon the Bonnington Hotel meetings. Ortiz can claim to be the father of discipling and shepherding doctrines in their modern Protestant form. Indeed, it was the Fort Lauderdale Five who took Ortiz's teachings and established them in North America.

I can imagine some readers leaping to the conclusion that this whole Restoration thing is American; it is important that we distinguish between genesis and form. John Noble and Gerald Coates, for example, were already thinking along discipling lines when Swindoll came into the picture. Of course, unconsciously they may have picked it up from the earlier days at the Leprosy Mission hall when they first met Argentinians there.

Bryn Jones insists too that the apostolic doctrines of Baxter were not the origins of his thinking. Bryn, anyhow, had been influenced in his youth by men of the Apostolic church in Wales which had been ordering its affairs according to Ephesians 4 since the First World War. Former members of that church had already influenced nascent Restoration since David Lillie and Arthur Wallis had started their conferences back in 1958. What I believe Swindoll and later Baxter did do for the London Brothers (and R1, too) was to show them how to conceptualise and think through not only the principles of 'covering', but also the principles that were constitutive of the kingdom of God. The Americans helped shape the formation of Restoration, but the major influence was not upon the London Brothers, but upon the successful emergence of R1 as the major Restorationist movement in Great Britain. This influence was primarily felt at the Dales Bible Week in 1976 and at the Lakes Week the preceding year.

But we are looking ahead, because Bryn Jones's involvement with Ern Baxter commences at an earlier Bible Week. Some of the London Brothers had become involved in this Bible Week at Capel which was the home of the Elim Bible College. Not that Elim had much to do with the whole enterprise. Capel Bible Week was the successor to the Abinger Bible Week of Fred Pride. The Capel Week was run by a committee which was quite independent of Elim. This committee included such names as Harold Owen, Mike Pusey, George Tarleton, and later Gerald Coates and Barney Coombs. These men, whilst sympathetic to the flourishing Renewal movement, were not anxious to turn Capel into a Renewalist shop-window. Most of the committee with their sectarian backgrounds were more sympathetic to the revivalism of classical Pentecostalism and the radicalism of the newer independent groups both in Great Britain and America. In particular they wanted Capel to be involved with men who could 'preach and teach' in a style that belonged to the Holiness, Pentecostal, and Evangelical traditions. People like Michael Harper did not really fit the bill: Ortiz and Baxter did.

They also invited Bryn Jones in 1973. He was such a success that he was invited back in 1974 where he shared the platform with Ern Baxter. Arthur Wallis sees the Capel

Bible Week as a significant 'spring' of Restoration.[15] I think this is far more true for the emergence of R1 than R2. Capel gave Bryn a southern platform. It introduced him to the freer styles of worship and praise pioneered by the London Brothers and other fellow travellers. He saw the potential of Capel-style conventions for providing a focus for the end-time message of God restoring His Church, and establishing His reign and rule in His kingdom. There was no need for him to do so, but he asked the committee if they would mind if he started a northern equivalent to Capel Bible Week. This became the Lakes Bible Week, and for sheer verve and professionalism it soon 'knocked the spots off' Capel Bible Week. The success of the Lakes, and later the Dales, was a major factor in the decline of Capel Bible Week, which soon closed down altogether.

In the south various new jamborees emerged in time, but the London Brothers were never able to set up a rival Restoration week. This was a conscious decision on their part; it was not an inability to get anything off the ground. R1 later on in the 1970s was to start Downs Week under Terry Virgo, and with input by Bryn Jones and his associates. Gerald Coates became involved with Royal Week in Cornwall. Don Double, an independent Pentecostalist, and Peter Lyne of the 'magnificent seven' were involved in this. The mixture there was eclectic: a bit of old-style revivalism, house church, and Renewalism.

Meanwhile, before these southern replacements for Capel became established, the London Brothers continued to be successful in the capital itself. They could fill the Westminster Central Hall, and the Albert Hall even without international speakers. In 1974 fifteen hundred turned up at the Friends' Meeting House. That meeting and subsequent meetings at Westminster Hall demonstrated that the London Brothers had not yet completely abandoned anarchic Pentecostalism. In 1975, when nine thousand people turned up at the Royal Albert Hall, they found no big names, no overt leadership, and no formal programme. At the start, David Mansell stood up and said: 'We've taken the Albert Hall tonight because we couldn't get you all into our front room.'[16]

The fun and frivolity of that night, and the spiritual blessing that many felt that they had received were soon to give way to distress and bitterness in a formal split between R1 and R2.[17] Almost, as it were, before relations between the northern and southern halves of the kingdom had been cemented, Restoration divided.

## Notes

1 Few leaders appear to have a firm grasp of the *overall* picture from those early days.

2 See Ian Bradley's excellent study, *The Call To Seriousness. The Evangelical Impact on the Victorians* (Jonathan Cape, 1976).

3 This is not proof that women were not more evident. Although she provides no specific instances, Eileen Vincent insists that women ministries were around. (Jean Darnell certainly was active in those days both at Capel Bible Week and in London.) See Vincent's exciting version of Restoration written from the inside: *Something's Happening* (Marshalls, 1984), p. 21.

4 There are many wild rumours about George Tarleton. On investigation, however, they turn out to be extremely prejudicial. George is interested in Alternative Medicine, and all kinds of related phenomena. He is a natural anarchist who simply prefers to plough his own furrow. It would seem that the Restoration kingdom is not designed to accommodate deviants like George.

5 This changed when Nick Butterworth joined the editorial staff; the improvement in presentation was quite dramatic.

6 Three-hour interview with John Noble and Gerald Coates on Saturday 10 March 1984.

7  Op. cit. Whilst he is writing for an R1 audience, Arthur would see Restoration as a worldwide movement of the Spirit of God.

8  Enigmatic I know, but simple enough really. For example, total commitment/fanaticism; purity/exclusiveness; will power and determination/bullying; total conviction and certainty/inability to accept criticism. According to the Eastern tradition only limitless love and holiness prevents the shadows from lengthening.

9  Joyce Thurman, op. cit., p. 26.

10  Other people view his preaching differently. An old classical Pentecostal told me: 'Too little of Jesus, and too much of Bryn Jones.' Bryn is certainly a performance preacher, and it is in the nature of that style of preaching that you can never always be up to mark.

11  See 'Springs of Restoration', Part 2, op. cit., p. 8.

12  Alan Halden, 'Barntalk' (undated), 27 Daggs Dell, Hemel Hempstead.

13  Not wishing to distort Bryn Jones's position, he did point out to me, on the phone, that he recognised John Noble and Gerald Coates's ministry as similar to, though more liberal than, his own. Gerald, on the other hand, thinks that the recognition amounts to admitting their existence, but not an acceptance of them as equals; as evidence for this assertion, he points out that he and his associates have never been invited to participate in either Dales or Downs Weeks.

14  As remembered by Maurice Smith, see chapter 2, note 13.

15  See 'Springs of Restoration', Part 2, op. cit.

16  Maurice Smith, op. cit.

17  The split was amongst the leadership; the rank and file did not really notice that much difference, as the leaders had already established separate spheres of influence.

## *RECOMMENDED READING*

Arthur Wallis, 'Springs of Restoration', Part 2, *Restoration* (Harvestime Publications, September/October 1980).

John Noble, *Forgive Us Our Denominations* (57 The Drive, Collier Row, Romford, Essex, 1971), private publication. *First Apostle, Last Apostle* (Collier Row, Romford, Essex, 1973), private publication.

Joyce V. Thurman, *New Wineskins, A Study of the House Church Movement*, chapter 2.

*Fulness*, Vols. 1, 2, 3, 4 (Cairprint Ltd., Keighley, Yorks., undated).

4

# THE KINGDOM ESTABLISHED
# IN DIVISION

I do not think that one could honestly say that Restorationism became firmly established, and then soon after it divided into separate entities. It would be more accurate to observe that the Restoration kingdoms became firmly established during and after the formal split of 1976; firm establishment, in short, takes place in division. Furthermore, too much can be made of the formal breakdown between the northern and southern territories of Restoration. Most official dates of divisions and schisms come some time after *de facto* divisions. Thus, for example, although the formal schism between the Eastern and Western Catholic churches is 1054, real cultural, linguistic and theological differences had existed for centuries; in many ways the Eastern and Western halves of Christendom were never a natural organism.

Similarly, Restoration was never simply a single cell that separated into two organic structures. R1 and R2 were in embryonic form right from the start. Since the formal split, these forms have matured and developed separate existences. The seeds of disunity can be found in the uneasy alliance between on the one hand the London Brothers and Graham Perrins and Peter Lyne in the west, and on the other hand Bryn Jones, Arthur Wallis and possibly Campbell McAlpine.

## The Uneasy Peace
To be strictly chronological, it would be true that R2 precedes R1. It was the coming together of the 'magnificent

seven' and the 'fabulous fourteen' that melded together the two factions into a single movement. This fusion can only be said to have lasted for three or four years. On the positive side, there was the feeling held by most of the members that they were engaged together in God's work, and formed part of a covenanted brotherhood. As Gerald Coates puts it: 'We felt we had seen the nature of the Church . . . we all belong to the same brotherhood, we are all eating at the same altar, we are all sharing the same faith, we all talk to the same Father when we get up in the morning.'[1]

John Noble is quite clear that the brothers in the fourteen were primarily bound together not by doctrines but by the common breaking of bread, and personal commitment to each other. Eucharistic fellowship is not exactly an Evangelical phrase, but if you strip it of its Catholic connotations it conveys the centrality of Communion to a Christian brotherhood. This concentration on the Lord's table as the table of fellowship echoes, as we shall later see, the understanding of church as held by the early Brethren movement in the first half of the nineteenth century. It was not that the fourteen could not share the Lord's table with all God's people, but it was the case that they saw a special significance in sharing the sacrament by the Restoration leaders. This covenanting was taken seriously by the Restoration leaders. As John Noble understands it, 'If I'm working with somebody and committing myself to a Work, I also want to have a particular relationship with someone. That is what binds us together.'[2]

The binding together, however, never hid the clash of styles and personalities that always made for an uneasy peace. The older style Puritanism of Wallis and Jones was in marked contrast to the wit and acid remarks of Hugh Thompson, and the insightful yet seemingly irreverent manner of Mansell. John Noble, with that curious mixture of the authoritarian personality and a generous nature, was inevitably going to lock horns with Jones whose powerful but bull-like approach tended to suggest that he would either win you over or knock you over. From an entirely different angle Jones and Noble were the odd ones out of the seven: all the others were former Open Brethren. Nevertheless, the seven were a tighter and more controlled group than the extended 'fabulous fourteen'.

I am obviously in no position to say whether extending the original group to fourteen was in God's plan or not. However, from an organisational point of view, I do think that five or seven is probably the optimum number you want for a successful oligarchy. If you have a group that has to take executive-style decisions, then fourteen is really too large. Furthermore, as the seven operated on personal commitment rather than company lines, extending your covenant to fourteen is inevitably going to cause strain and greater chance of division. There is no doubt that the 'fabulous fourteen' highlighted personality and ideological divisions more clearly than the original group.

There is a joke about Maurice Smith that he is so sold on teachings of 'grace' that as far as he is concerned teachings on 'law' can go to hell. Smith himself believes that Arthur Wallis and Bryn Jones always saw him as a danger man and a person of instability: a man whose over-emphasis on grace would lead to unbridled licence. I think it not unfair to say that the London Brothers, in particular, were more liberal in their life style and attitudes than some of the others. In many ways, for example, George Tarleton was always the odd man out. He did not come from recent sectarian movements, but was a former minister in the Congregational church. His politics and theology were anarchic, and his general views more liberal than his colleagues. He welcomed women in the ministry, for example, which was enough to give some of the former Brethren apoplexy. He insisted on Christ alone being designated the term *Logos*, and on this count refused to call the Scriptures the 'Word of God'.

What with that other strong character, Graham Perrins, insisting on the supremacy of the prophetic ministry over all others (a view shared by John MacLauchlan), Hugh Thompson's jokes 'often close to the knuckle', and Mansell's informality—'let's chat a prophecy'—the fourteen were never dull but not always clear as to what they were doing. After a hard day's prophecy and prayer, sometimes held at Fairmile Court in Surrey, many of the group would go off to the pub for continued fellowship. George Tarleton saw it as 'all of a piece—part of being in the Lord'. Campbell McAlpine, who, like Arthur, was from an older generation of charismatics, found this hard to take. Whilst he no doubt felt privileged to be on the early sessions of the workshops, his heart seemed never to be really in it. George Tarleton recalls that he did not approve of mixing Spirit with spirit. In fact Campbell soon quietly withdrew from the fourteen, and plays no further direct part in the British Restoration story. Proof of his low profile and lack of participation is the fact that a good number of the 'fabulous fourteen' could not remember that he was one of their number . . .

Perhaps the most enigmatic aspect of the division between R1 and R2, is that when it takes place, there is not a straight north-south divide, nor a split on personality lines: when the schism comes it is those who are with Arthur Wallis and Bryn Jones, and those who are not. From the south, Terry Virgo, Hugh Thompson, and David Mansell enter R1. The rest of the leadership in R1, such as Tony Morton, David Tomlinson, Keri Jones, and Tony Ling, were never members of the fourteen.

Apostleship and discipling emerge more firmly in the south at first. Gerald Coates recalls that Bryn and his colleagues admonished them for overemphasising these doctrines in 1974/5. Looking through the early numbers of *Restoration* magazine in 1976, when Bryn Jones was editor, there is virtually no emphasis on apostleship at all. However, if the London Brothers were quick off the mark with the new teaching, they were fairly haphazard in their methods. Discipling was never established with a crack of the whip or in any formal and legalistic way. House groups increasingly—through their self-elected elders—related to John Noble, or Graham Perrins and later Gerald Coates. Many of the groups that joined R2, and R1, were already established autonomous churches when they asked for 'covering' by the new apostles. Later, apostles would choose their own elders or approve those elders already established in leadership on the local level. Nick Butterworth, George Tarleton, John

MacLaughlan, Peter Lyne and others continued to be seen as leaders. Whether they saw themselves directly as apostles in 1975 seems unlikely; moving towards apostleship, or taking on apostolic functions might be a better way of understanding their roles at that time.

By as early as 1974, Maurice Smith was prophet to John Noble's apostleship. This teamship, which was to last ten years, was an interesting and fruitful partnership of opposites: John Noble very much the 'father in God', strong—sometimes 'heavy'—always concerned, and Maurice all quicksilver and effervescence; if he led John a merry dance, they managed to keep in step for a remarkably long time.

By 1975, R1 was not really firmly set on the path of Restoration in its fully doctrinal sense, but it was already organising itself into a powerful movement. You may call him opportunistic if you will, but Bryn Jones understood the importance of organisational structure, sound management, and financial security that is necessary to putting a big outfit on the road. The London Brothers never doubted this. They felt at the time that Bryn Jones with his Assemblies of God background was an institutional creature. For their tastes, he was too conservative and denominational in outlook; too bound by structures and rules. Judging from his reaction in 1976, Bryn Jones saw the Brothers and their associates as too frivolous and woolly-minded. If he was thought to question nothing by some of the Brothers, they also felt that Bryn was convinced that they questioned and doubted too much. I do not think it true that Bryn Jones does not have doubts and uncertainties, but he does not allow them to impede his course of action which he believes is right.[3] He seems to me to be essentially a man of action, not a man of reflection.

Given these tensions, personality clashes, and differing style of working, it is not surprising that 1975 and 1976 saw the emergence of public differences and a series of quarrels that was to end in bitterness and disception.

The specific issues involved in the split were the publication of *Restoration* magazine in 1975, the debate over law and grace that centred around the practice of masturbation,[4] the

David Mansell problem, and the 'spirit of deception' letter that came from Arthur Wallis and Bryn Jones to the southern and western leaders of the 'fabulous fourteen'. Whilst these are separate issues, there are connecting factors; in particular the nature of grace and holiness. In order to enter the complicated controversies that led to the division of the 'kingdom' almost before it was established, I think we could do worse than start with the powerful influence of an American, Ern Baxter.

## The American Connection

As we noted in the last chapter, Bryn Jones and Ern Baxter met at the Capel Bible Week in 1974. Both men were attracted to each other's ministries. Ern Baxter is a much softer personality than Bryn Jones; a number of people have told me that he is also an insecure personality.[5] He certainly does not appear insecure, however, and his public performances are masterful and inspiring. An older man, Ern Baxter has a long track-record of charismatic activities that go back to the days after the Second World War when he was a Bible teacher with possibly the most controversial and interesting of all America's Pentecostal preachers, William Branham. I remember as a boy listening to Branham's raucous Southern voice and hearing his amazing diagnostic talents when he claimed that he could see colours (or auras) that helped him correctly to diagnose illnesses. Professor Walther Hollenweger, who is not given to exaggeration, believes that whilst Branham's claims to healing are sometimes questionable, his ability to correctly diagnose illness was phenomenal.[6]

Baxter is the elder statesman of the group known (or formerly known) as the 'Fort Lauderdale Five'. Their basic teachings are taken from Ortiz of Argentina, and they are responsible for establishing in North America chains of followers who submit to their apostolic authority. They have been in existence since the early 1960s. Baxter and Mumford are probably the most liked of the five: their personalities are attractive, and their manner gracious. Derek Prince is an intellectual and a former fellow of King's College, Cambridge.

Despite his erudition and obvious scholarship, he seems to have a predilection for extreme Biblical interpretations. In more recent years, he has become associated with a passionate Zionism, and Israel seems to dominate his interests. Basham is well known in America for deliverance ministry. A leading British charismatic told me that he was 'dead keen on demons and dead against masturbation: he thought the former were responsible for the latter'. Charles Simpson seems to be the least liked of the five because of his aggressive personality and what many people see as bullying tactics concerning submission and discipling doctrines. An indication of his personality can be picked up by the comment of a former London Brother: 'Charles Simpson makes Bryn Jones seem like a "wet".'

All of the five are intelligent men. In the American religious context they are somewhat of an enigma. They are conservative in their theology and politics, and yet they are not typical of 'Bible-belters'. They are not exclusivists, and number among their friends and associates Roman Catholics from within the Charismatic Renewal. They have attempted to introduce their doctrines and 'covering power' inside and outside the traditional denominational structures. Their discipling doctrines, which have flourished in some of the Catholic covenanted communities as well as Protestant churches, split the American Renewal movement down the middle at the very time that Restoration was springing up in Great Britain. Indeed, when Baxter was in England in 1975 and 1976, the American Charismatic Movement was attempting to heal its wounds over this matter.[7] Unlike Britain, therefore, the American experience of the 'shepherding movement' has been far more mainstream; many Anglican and Catholic charismatics in England have never even heard of, or at least experienced, these controversies.

Clearly, we can see from an international perspective, that the British Restoration movement is part of a much larger phenomenon. Admittedly, there is no international organisation, and many of the groups have nothing to do with each other—and are sometimes opposed to each other—but they all adhere to a kingdom/apostleship/discipleship nexus. Like so many apparently indigenous religious movements in Britain, we are able to note firstly the international dimension, and secondly the domination of this internationalism by North American Pentecostals. Noting this is not only to recognise the importance of the American connection, but also to realise that the tale of British Restorationism is only one chapter in a much larger story. Bryn Jones has never claimed to be the leader of the Restoration movement *per se*. It was he who pointed out to me that similar work to his own is going on in South Africa, North and South America, Africa, and Europe.[8] To my knowledge, R1 has working relationships with people in all of these places, and also in India.

As I mentioned in the previous chapter, I do not think that Ern Baxter introduced Restorationism to Britain; nor did he first outline the doctrines of discipleship and shepherding. What he did do, however, was to mould the thinking of the 'fabulous fourteen', and even help Restoration One on its way.

Although Bryn Jones made great use of Ern Baxter in the years 1975 and 1976, R2 was also involved with its new-found American friends. Members visited Florida, as did Bryn Jones, and talked with the 'Fort Lauderdale Five'—and their friends—in their homes. But it was at the Lakes Week in 1975, that Baxter first made a real impact. David Tomlinson, who was an apostle with R1 at that time, recalls[9] that Baxter's influence was sensational; the audiences went wild every time he appeared. As a result of his teaching on the need for 'covered' relationships, many groups attending the Bible Week joined themselves to Bryn and his fellow apostles. During the first Bible Week at the Great Yorkshire Showground in 1976, Baxter was the great attraction and as in the previous year excitement was at fever pitch.

Interestingly, Ern Baxter's preaching style is not in the American Pentecostal tradition at all. There is no ranting, no table-thumping, very little overt emotionalism, and no shouting. He relies heavily on notes, and in small gatherings favours the blackboard and other visual aids. His methodology is building up strong arguments by means of Biblical exposition and original hermeneutics. Like most of the five, there is an elaborate usage of typology and Old Testament incidents which are then read into the New Testament and the present day. The most effective typology that was used in those years was to compare the kingship of Saul and David with the state of leadership in the Church. It was pointed out that Saul was not ordained by God but chosen by the people. Democratic methods were compared unfavourably with the theocratic arrangements of God. The Lord, for example, chose David as the anointed of Israel. Today, he is anointing with His Spirit men who are charismatically chosen to be the apostles of the kingdom. Baxter warns of forming a new sectarianism, and insists that the only unity of the Church is in Jesus Christ.

Ern Baxter may have helped R1 on its way, but he and the rest of the American group had already become aware of the tensions within the British Restoration movement. They were concerned at the lack of real unity, and were convinced that the covering situation was failing at the top. It is difficult to resist using Old Testament typology in helping us to explain their understanding of the situation. Israel, as we know, was bound together by the tribal structure, which itself can be seen as a form of covenanted brotherhood. However, the nation was divided into the ten tribes of the northern kingdom, and Judah and Benjamin in the south. During Solomon's reign, his power and kingship held the kingdom together, but after his death the old tribal conflicts reasserted themselves: the kingdom was divided between Jeroboam in the north, and Rehoboam in the south.

In bringing the 'magnificent seven' together, Arthur Wallis was also potentially healing a north/south divide. The fourteen might have been bound together by covenant like some ancient tribal system, but the kingdom that emerged under their tutelage never found its king: no Solomon or David was chosen. Given the hierarchical or theocratic nature of Restoration ideology, the system of relationships that developed demanded headship. Even apostolic collegiality requires a 'first amongst equals'. The American five felt that the problem lay in the personality clash between John Noble and Bryn Jones. Their solution to the problem was to ask both Bryn Jones and John Noble to submit to Arthur Wallis.[10] He, in turn, would be covered by an American apostle. I do not think that one need be too cynical to realise that this was also a method of bringing the English operation under their control. If that was their intention, then they picked the wrong men in John Noble and Bryn Jones.

Initially, Bryn Jones accepted this solution, but John Noble refused it. John's view was simply that Arthur was not a strong enough personality for the job, nor was he an apostle. (Certainly, on this latter point, according to the understanding of the fourteen, Arthur was not an apostle because he had not established and nurtured churches.)

Problems were beginning to brew up within R2 at this time too, and John Noble and Graham Perrins were to be at loggerheads over the primacy of prophecy and who should submit to whom. At the same time and into 1976, the London Brothers had discovered that David Mansell's private life 'was not totally glorifying to the gospel'. There were problems of mutual trust here, and the Brothers found that Mansell would accept no sanctions from them.

It was in the light of this that John Noble and Maurice Smith went to see the Lauderdale Five in Florida. Ern Baxter promised, according to Maurice Smith, to 'bust the whole David Mansell thing open' when he came to England in the summer of 1976. The major purpose of the meeting, however, was to see if John Noble would agree to submit to Arthur Wallis. Maurice Smith remembers being overawed by their wealth—the swimming pools, the discussion of many thousands of dollars, the glancing at watches like bank managers giving their clients moments of their valuable time. The notion of 'double honour' has a long history in American Pentecostal circles: the idea is that Christian leaders should be apportioned more of the wealth than their followers by virtue of their leadership. Certainly Maurice

Smith began to realise, what many Restoration leaders were to realise, that great things can be achieved through the tithe! But let Maurice tell the story his way:

They were exasperated with John Noble because he was such a strong man and would not submit to Arthur. John went out to the loo on one occasion. And he had no sooner gone out to the loo when Bob Mumford leant forward and said to me: 'Look, quickly Maurice, while John's in the loo. Obviously, you're not as clear as John about all this.'

So I said: 'No. I'm open to the fact we might be wrong.'

But he said: 'You see you're not one with him in this. We're all one.'

'Yes,' I said. 'But our oneness does not depend on agreement of doctrine.' (So all this was tearing Bob apart—I like Bob, he's a warm and friendly guy.)

So he said: 'Look Maurice: let's put it like this. Do you think a woman should submit herself to her husband?'

I said: 'Yes. I think there's safety in that.'

'Do you think she should only submit herself to him when he's right?'

I said: 'No. That is not submission; that's doing what you want to do and calling it submission.'

'And what would happen, Maurice,' (because he's a very clever fellow, Bob) 'what would happen, Maurice, if a woman submitted herself to her husband who was often wrong?'

I said: 'I think that she would help to lift him into his place of authority' (because that's how I used to think then) 'in the family. By not undermining his authority she would put him into authority.'

'Exactly!' he said. 'And that is our solution for your country. As God is moving in this House Church way, if John and Bryn will submit it would help to put Arthur Wallis into his authority; even though he has not got that gift, it will help to bring it about and he will bring these two men together.' So he said: 'Maurice, you see it?' (John is still in the loo.)

So I said: 'No. No. No!'

So he said: 'What's the matter, Maurice?'

So I said: 'I can't agree with it because the woman fell in love with the man—that it was organic: something happened between them which meant she wanted to willingly let go of some things at some times so the thing would work out. But this isn't happening now. It's a shotgun marriage, Bob. You're forcing this issue.'

'Oh!' (And he clapped his hands in exasperation.)[11]

John Noble and Maurice Smith may have come away from Florida without having resolved the submission issue, but they felt that Baxter was on their side concerning the Mansell trouble. By this time, Bryn Jones was arguing with the Brothers that they were being too judgemental in their attitude to David Mansell and offered to take over the 'covering' role himself. (To this day the Brothers have never understood Jones's attitude over this matter.)

Baxter's arrival in England certainly had a dramatic effect on the Restoration story, but not the one that John Noble and Maurice Smith were expecting. At the Dales Bible Week, which was a tremendous success, Baxter's presence and contributions were seen as an endorsement for Bryn Jones and his fellow apostles David Tomlinson and Terry Virgo. Tomlinson recalls that the drama between Bryn and the rest of the fourteen hardly effected him personally. He was never a member of that group, and when the division came he automatically sided with Bryn Jones because he knew him and was involved with him; in no sense can he remember making an objective analysis of the situation at that time.

Although I have not been able to uncover the exact sequence of events, it is clear that Ern Baxter, after meeting and working with Bryn and Arthur, took their part in their handling of the Mansell row, and in their general disagreement with R2. What so alarmed the London Brothers and Graham Perrins was Ern Baxter's attitude when he came down from the Dales to attend a smaller convention at Bath. Maurice Smith felt 'there was something terribly wrong'. Baxter was uneasy, and on the first night made, the Brothers thought, an appalling contribution that was neither up to his usual standard nor seen by them to be conducted in the spirit of charity. In an earlier chapter, I mentioned Graham Perrins as being a strong personality. This crisis brings this out clearly. Baxter, apparently without any apology or explanation, asked the members of R2 what they would like for the next night. 'Never mind the next night,' Perrins said, 'we want an explanation for tonight, Ern.'

Under pressure to 'come clean' and explain what was going on, Ern Baxter protested that he did not need this kind of aggravation. His wife was seriously ill, and perhaps, he suggested, he would just pack his bag and go right back to America. In the event, he did stay another night, but the Brothers that I have spoken to about this episode claim that he was preaching against them on the platform and not preaching to the congregation.

Arthur Wallis, the architect of Restorationism, and the man who had tried so hard to bring the factions together, was heartbroken at this open show of discord.[12] Maurice Smith remembers him walking and praying all night ('Arthur always prayed until he felt he had an answer'), and in the morning had come to see—along with Baxter—that the R2 section of Restorationism were deceived. If I have understood this correctly from John Noble and Gerald Coates, this idea of deception was not a psychological form of deception; they were seen to have been led astray by demonic forces: a 'spirit of deception'.

After this incident, Ern Baxter left England, and he plays virtually no more part in the story after 1977. His contribution, however, is vital. It was he, and his colleagues, who helped the theological formulation of early Restorationism. His personal ministry was a major boost to the establishment and success of R1. His intervention at Bath was a significant factor in the hastening split between R1 and R2 in October of 1976. Ironically, Ern Baxter's influence with Bryn Jones was also coming to an end. Bryn Jones recalls that Arthur Wallis felt that there should be an input from some other source in 1978. The Dales Committee decided to ask Bob Mumford to come. He came, and was very much liked. Like Baxter before him, he too was a great success, but he did not have the pioneering influence of his colleague. In 1979, the link between R1 and the American five was severed. It was decided no longer to invite them, and they have not been back since.

David Tomlinson feels[13] that the Fort Lauderdale Five, and in particular Ern Baxter, felt that they had a stake in the British scene. They had, after all, made such a contribution to the initial success of R1. Morally, Tomlinson thinks, Baxter believed that Bryn Jones owed it to him to submit to American authority. Neither Tomlinson nor Noble, however, think that the Americans were thinking improperly of a 'take-over': it was simply that they thought God wanted to extend His kingdom through them. If there had been an American operation, it would have probably involved the mainstream denominations; one wonders if they approve of the separated direction of R1? Tomlinson also wisely points out that if you look at it from Bryn Jones's perspective you get a different moral picture. The American guests were outstaying their welcome. They had come to the Dales as a result of an invitation by the Bible Week committee. In effect, they were 'hired servants': it was not their place to talk about rights or privileges.

This perspective seems reasonable, and certainly it can be morally defended. I discussed this issue with Bryn Jones, and he confirms that all of his team—and the associated teams—felt that whilst they were eternally grateful to the Lauderdale group for their input, Restoration was primarily a British affair. Bryn was anxious that the work he was involved in should not be written off as merely the satellite of American interest. In short, you can believe that Bryn Jones used the Americans and then dumped them, or you can accept that he acted in both a patriotic and proper way.[14] Whatever the case, the Americans eventually found out, as they already had with John Noble, that Bryn Jones was neither a man to manipulate nor one to submit to their ultimate authority.

# The Rending of the Kingdom

Gerald Coates sees October 1976 as the date of the formal split. This was the month when Arthur Wallis wrote a letter to the brothers in R2 disassociating himself with a number of their attitudes and practices. Without exception the members of R2 saw this as a letter written by Bryn Jones and signed by Arthur. They were both deeply hurt and furious at the accusations made against them in this letter. The letter, as they saw it, was tantamount to being 'disfellowshipped'; in older times the language of anathemas and excommunication would have been used. The letter was, in effect, the straw that broke the camel's back. From that time onwards the 'magnificent seven' and 'fabulous fourteen' ceased to exist; the uneasy peace between the north and south was shattered.

However, from R1's perspective, October 1976 does not loom as such a major catastrophe. Their show was now well and truly on the road, and doing very well. The fact that they felt uncomfortable with members of R2 inevitably meant that they would prefer to work on their own, and with their own. Furthermore, a number of leaders in R1 had been brought in outside the original fourteen leadership. The historical problems did not effect them so personally. Therefore, although the division was regretted—very deeply by a few—the split was not quite the tragedy that it was for R2.

I think it is not difficult for us to understand how John Noble, Gerald Coates, Graham Perrins, George Tarleton, Maurice Smith and others felt. They saw themselves as the pioneers of the kingdom. It was they, so they believed, who had developed the doctrines of apostleship and discipling within the British context. They saw themselves as first not in terms of honour, but in laying the foundations of a charismatically ordained church. Then along came Bryn Jones—a 'Johnny come lately'—borrowed from them, improved on them, out-manoeuvred them, and then gave them their marching orders.[15]

It was during one of the many meetings at Fairmile Court in 1975 that Bryn Jones announced to the assembled

Brothers that R1 was publishing a new journal, called *Restoration*. Those involved in *Fulness* were furious. It seemed to those Brothers that a betrayal had taken place: Bryn was going into competition against them. It was as if, some of them thought, Bryn Jones was running up the flag of his own empire. By publishing *Restoration* magazine he was declaring UDI.[16]

UDI or not, by 1976, thanks partly to Ern Baxter, R1 had suddenly come from nowhere not only to rival R2, but to emerge as the major vehicle for Restorationism in Great Britain. Although I think we can see the announcement of *Restoration* magazine as the beginning of the end, and the Wallis/Jones letter as the end of the generic Restoration movement, these two events are only historic markers in what was really a fundamental difference over the nature of grace. I am not personally so convinced that this was the real underlying problem, but it was perceived to be by many participants. Here, I believe, some personal interpretation is necessary. R1 and R2 have had virtually no contact with each other over the last nine years. Consequently, their perceptions of each other are coloured by historical events and disagreements of the past. Bryn Jones, for example, wonders if they were not always as different as chalk and cheese, but he does not know, in any personal or empirical sense, what the leaders of R2 are like today.

Conversely, as Gerald Coates and John Noble have not met Bryn Jones for a long time, they have never been really able to clarify exactly what went wrong between them. Restoration ideology acclaims confrontation as a means of healing, and yet the leaders of both R1 and R2 have chosen not to take that path.

David Tomlinson, however, can claim knowledge of both sides of the divide because he has crossed over from R1 to R2. What he has found is very instructive. On beliefs and doctrines, there is virtually no difference (though there are a number of minor points that are undergoing change in R2). He primarily notices a difference in style and atmosphere. For his money R1 was too structured, and R2 is not structured enough. R2 is more relaxed than R1, and far less intense; there is less pressure to conform to an organisational 'line'. R1 is now basically set on its path. R2 is still fluid and changing.

Such differences of style and *modus operandi* help us, I think, to see a little more clearly what the law and grace debate was about in 1975 and 1976. At Fairmile Court, and other places, there was an attempt to thrash out the permissible actions open to Christians. How, in short, do children of the King behave? What did it mean to be no longer 'under law but under grace'? Christians are free in the Spirit, but what was the nature of that freedom? Maurice Smith took the line (which he takes even more strongly today) that living in the Spirit meant that you had been made free from the Old Testament dispensation of law. This was, on the surface, in line with Honor Oak and Brethren teaching; most Evangelicals could declare with St. Paul that the shackles of law had been broken when sin itself had been destroyed. It is not typically the case, however, that the Evangelical world has understood this to mean that the law (the Ten Commandments, for example) was no longer operative; Christ came to fulfil the law, not to destroy it, they would claim.

None of the London Brothers ever claimed that Christians could murder, steal, or commit adultery. However, John Noble and Gerald Coates did think that masturbation could be a neutral act, and was not necessarily a sin. Gerald had written a little booklet on 'Law And Grace', and Arthur Wallis and Bryn Jones saw in this an invitation to licence (so John and Gerald recall). The booklet is not a call to 'situation ethics' nor an invitation to immorality, but I think it not unfair to say that it could be open to misinterpretation.

Joyce Thurman, probably unintentionally, gives the impression in her book that this controversy took place at a distance,[17] but the masturbation issue was discussed face to face between the various leaders. Its discussion reveals the underlying difference of style between R1 and R2. Gerald wanted everybody to admit that they masturbated sometimes. One can only imagine what Arthur Wallis and Bryn Jones thought when they were asked about this openly! I recall from my own Pentecostal background what would have been the reaction if such a topic had been raised. (As a matter of fact, you could not raise this particular topic as a teenager, because such practices were not admitted to exist.) Perhaps Gerald's question was an impertinence, prurient, or simply lacking in decency? However Bryn Jones and Arthur Wallis saw it, they did not wish to condone it as a Christian practice.

But too much can be made of this already well publicised dispute. It was only one of a number of issues. Drinking alcohol was also a major bone of contention. Most of the brothers drank alcohol, but Gerald and John counted it as a virtue to declare it openly. Bryn and Arthur were not exactly secret drinkers, but neither did they declare it from the rooftops. Gerald and a number of the London Brothers liked the cinema, theatre, and pop music. Others thought this worldly. Gerald believed that most of the leaders enjoyed doing the things that he did. As there was nothing wrong with them, he thought, you should not hide these practices: you should declare them as desirable. In the older Pentecostal tradition emphasis had always been put on not doing anything that might cause your brother to stumble: 'remember the weaker brethren' was often taken to mean not doing things that were lawful in themselves but were not necessarily expedient. To personalise this and put it into extreme form: Bryn Jones thought that Gerald flaunted his permissiveness, and Gerald thought that Bryn was a hypocrite because he did the same things in secret.

Some of the differences between the leaders of the 'fabulous fourteen' were partly differences of class and culture, and partly differences of moral understanding. Clearly, both Gerald and Bryn's positions can be morally defended, and I do think there is a tendency for the two sides to exaggerate the *substantive* disagreements between them. John Noble does like to drink, and Gerald Coates is 'flashy' and uninhibited in his talk as extroverts often are. Neither, however, are liberal in their moral beliefs, and their personal lives have attracted no scandal in recent years. Perhaps Gerald's 'flashiness' (does he still have the yellow canary suit?) and 'froth' were taken by Bryn Jones to be the substance of the man? His friends inside and outside R2 know that Gerald is unashamedly a showman, but they also know that he is generous, kind, totally honest, and always open to correction and improvement.

Conversely, I think it likely that the London Brothers did not fully appreciate the older-style Puritanism of Wallis, nor did they fully understand how their liberality would be seen by the people with whom Bryn Jones originally associated and still has a great love for: namely, the classical Pentecostals. Having lived in the Welsh valleys and attended chapel three times on a Sunday, I know from that 'neck of the woods' how alien the London Brothers, Peter Lyne, and Graham Perrins looked. Graham, for example, was not only good-looking, but was always dressed in the latest fashions. Gerald's clothes tended to be idiosyncratic bordering on the outrageous. What with the enjoyment of some aspects of modern culture, the risqué jokes and alcoholic chatter,[18] these modern-day charismatics would look like agents of hell to some classical Pentecostals.

This being so, it is understandable that Bryn Jones is cautious in this area. Wishing to be all things to all men—being careful not to offend—can be a positive Christian virtue; hypocrisy may very well be too strong a charge. These issues are still alive today between the older-style Pentecostal denominations and the new independents. Chatting with Bryn Jones in his office recently, I saw a bottle of excellent quality French wine on his filing cabinet. Pointing to it he remarked, regretfully, that some members of Elim and Assemblies of God still found it difficult to accept somebody as 'sound' if they indulged in alcohol. The 'demon drink' belief in these denominations is very similar to the Salvation Army.

This issue, more than the disagreement over masturbation in my opinion, highlights what I have called the difference in style between R1 and R2. Bryn Jones drinks moderately, and admits it if he is asked. Gerald Coates drinks moderately, and proclaims it on the radio and in print. The same can be said in investigating the events and issues leading to the split in 1976. R1 have hid nothing from me but have volunteered no information. R2 have been willing to tell all without the same feeling of reserve.

It remains a curiosity, however, to see why Bryn Jones should want to take David Mansell under his wing. The London Brothers felt, that at the moment they were being indicted for turning grace into licence, Bryn Jones was telling them that they were being too judgemental with David Mansell whom they thought had gone too far. Whatever David Mansell's 'problems' were they are of no concern to us, but in 1976 he agreed to be 'covered' by Bryn Jones and as a result left R2 for R1 where he has remained as an important member of Bryn's team, and a significant contributor to *Restoration* magazine.[19]

When the letter was sent to the leaders of R2 in October 1976, it was in effect a list of the disagreements between them. There were references to theological issues as well as the law/grace row. For example, Arthur Wallis felt too much was being claimed, at that time, for apostolic authority; he was not happy, either, with the 'Remnant' eschatology that was favoured by Ted Crick (who had already left R2) and Graham Perrins. The serious charge, however, was the suggestion that they were falling into licence with a hint that they were being led astray by demonic forces. Apparently, this tendency to licence was supposed to include 'associations with hairies'. (Ernie Baxter seemed to have strong views about long hair at that time.)

To an untutored ear, all this may sound like the breaking of covenant, but I suspect that this is not so. From what I know of Arthur Wallis, I doubt very much whether he saw the parting of the ways as synonymous with breaking covenant. John Noble certainly does not: 'I made a covenant with Bryn which as far as I'm concerned still stands . . . There was an issue of conscience. (This puts your working relationship into parenthesis for a time.) I'm actively working in my own heart to see how this can be resolved so we can get back together again.'[20]

The failure to hold the Restoration kingdom together was a personal tragedy for many of the leading apostles and elders. Whilst, for us, no doubt it is fascinating and certainly an essential part of the story of this radical Christianity, it is worth remembering that for those whose story it is, the split remains painful if not shameful. Not all the leaders thought that the split was a disaster. We have already seen that R1 was not so badly effected as R2, but George Tarleton now thinks that the split was God-ordained. He believes that it helped prevent the emergence of a new and large denomination. This is a minority view, but I think that most leaders are convinced that much has been learned by these mistakes.

By 1976—despite the division—a new radical Christianity had become established in Great Britain. Since that time, to the present day, there has been a steady growth of the Restoration movement. No other Christian grouping, outside the mainline denominations, can boast such a rapid rise in size and popularity. To accurately chart the course of R1 and R2 over the last few years would take a full book in itself. Before we look at Restoration teachings, practices, sociological complexion and historical antecedents, we can at least catch up with the major developments within the two movements. Such a brief look will not only bring us up to date, but demonstrate in what ways R1 and R2 have continued to diverge.

## Notes

1  Interview with Gerald Coates and John Noble, see chapter 3, note 6.

2  Ibid.

3  Remarks made to me by Bryn Jones in his office on 21 March 1984. As I did not have my tape-recorder on, I'm relying on memory. (David Matthew and Goos Vedder were also present at the meeting.)

4  See Joyce Thurman, op. cit., p. 98.

5  I have never met Ern Baxter, so I have nothing to go on but hearsay.

6  Professor Hollenweger was an Assemblies of God pastor as a young man, and was responsible for translating Branham's words for continental readers (so he speaks with more than just academic knowledge).

7  Michael Harper alludes to this in *Charismatic Crisis*. An early editorial in the May/June copy of *Restoration* 1976, comments on it.

8  Conversation with Bryn Jones, see note 3.

9  Taped conversations over the weekend 16–17 March 1984.

10  Bryn Jones confirmed over the phone in June 1984 that this was *a* solution to the problem, but left unsaid what the alternatives might have been.

11  Interview with Maurice Smith, see chapter 2, note 3.

12  I have it on good authority that, radical though he may be in his beliefs, Arthur Wallis has a good record for bringing together people who have fallen out.

13  See note 9.

14  Bryn Jones's enemies would obviously go for the first one, and his followers for the second one. I feel inclined to take his part in this matter.

15  This is not, of course, historically true, but I think that is how many of the leaders of R2 felt *at that time*.

16  They cannot all have been so furious, for I notice that Gerald Coates was on the editorial board of the new magazine until he was removed after the split.

17  Op. cit., p. 98.

18  They are in good company here. Bawdiness, beer, and tobacco

were characteristic of C. S. Lewis's circle. (Tobacco seems to be universally decried in R1 and R2.)

19   Whilst David Mansell is seen as a prophet, I don't wish to give the impression that he is 'way-out' or an unruly person. He sees his prophetic task as intellectual as well as intuitive. A university graduate, he has knowledge of Classical Greek, and speaks modern Hebrew.

20   See note 1.

## RECOMMENDED READING

Arthur Wallis, 'Springs of Restoration', Part 2, *Restoration* (Harvestime Publications, September/October 1980).
Roger William Curl, 'Three Communities: A Sociological Study' (unpublished D.Phil. thesis, Oxford).
Eileen Vincent, *Something's Happening* (Marshalls, 1984).
Joyce V. Thurman, *New Wineskins, A Study of the House Church Movement* (Verlag Peter Lang, 1982), chapter 6.

# 5

# EXTENDING THE KINGDOM

After the failures and disappointments of 1976, the Restoration kingdoms grew amazingly quickly. Despite further serious divisions (as we shall see), the two movements continue to attract new members, and form new churches. By 1980, evidence that they had really arrived on the religious scene can be found in the growing opposition to them in some mainstream charismatic and Evangelical circles. Much of the criticism at that time was somewhat muted by the lack of information concerning the new movements, and in particular the failure to distinguish not only R1 from R2 but both of them from other house church movements. The British Council of Churches consultation on the Renewal in 1979[1] was typical of much denominational reaction: something was happening that was clamouring for attention, but few knew what that something was, or what its significance could be. In the absence of clear information, that was not helped by R1 and R2 refusing to identify themselves in any clear way, rumours about this new movement began to proliferate. The rumours have not stopped since, and despite the fact (or, perhaps because of the fact) that R1 sets out its doctrinal position very clearly in *Restoration* magazine and the writings of Arthur Wallis, this has not prevented controversy concerning the nature of Restorationist religion.

It is easier to discern a shape and pattern to R1 than to R2. In many ways, they seem to have done a great deal more than R2 to determine the direction in which they are going. This being so, and because R1 is clearly larger and more insistently Restorationist than R2, we will first look at how they have developed since the division.

## Restoration One

Exactly one year before the split of October 1976, and following the successful summer Bible Week at the Lakes, Bryn Jones became leader of a Pentecostal community that consisted of his own congregation from the independent Holiness Assembly, a former Brethren Assembly, and a charismatic house church. This new and enlarged church has become the home base (R1 does not like the idea of headquarters) of Bryn Jones's apostolic ministry. It was in Bradford that *Restoration* magazine was first started in 1975 as an expression of that new community church. By the end of 1977, *Restoration* expresses not only the work of Bryn Jones, but also his newly 'related' apostles, Terry Virgo and David Tomlinson. Terry was pioneering in the south-east, whilst David Tomlinson was working in the north-east and the Midlands. The three apostles spent very little time in those days outlining apostolic doctrine, or announcing their work with a great fanfare. What they were doing was actually working out in practice Restoration principles, and building together their fellowships.

The amount of work and territory they covered in those days was phenomenal. Charismatic groups, small house churches, and sections of Baptist and Pentecostal denominations were eager to come under their 'covering'. Even before they had properly established their British churches, they had become involved in missionary work that has been a hallmark of R1 ever since. Visits to Norway were started as early as 1975. In 1976 David Tomlinson, Terry Virgo, David Mansell and others went to Spain where they worked in both Protestant and Catholic communities. David Tomlinson recalls the cultural shock of seeing a Catholic charismatic priest with cigar in mouth, glass of wine in one hand, whilst his free hand was dispensing Pentecostal blessings![2]

1977 was both a year of missionary expansion and home consolidation. Bryn Jones and David Mansell went to Kenya where they pioneered a new church, and the following year on a return visit came into contact with the new President following the death of Jomo Kenyatta. The missionary work there resulted in many reported miracles of healing. Feeling that they had some entrée into Kenya with their relationships with government officials and the President himself, R1 decided to raise money in various projects designed to help the Kenyan tribes be self-supporting. That same year, Arthur Wallis, Peter Paris, Alan Vincent (now a member of Terry Virgo's team) and Hugh Thompson visited India where they established contacts and preached Restoration principles. Contacts were also made with South Africa, and later Bryn Jones, David Mansell, and David Tomlinson went to Argentina where they worked with Orvil Swindol for a time.[3]

The most significant event in 1977, however, was the purchasing of Church House in Bradford. This was formerly the Anglican diocesan headquarters. Purchased in January of 1977, the building was in a terrible condition. Over the next few years the building was first gutted, then reshaped, and refurbished to a high professional standard. Many members of the new community have given not only their money, but also their time and talents.

Today this Victorian gothic building is an impressive centre for the Church House Community Fellowship (to give the Bradford church its full title). It houses not only worship and recreational facilities for the five hundred or so members, but also boasts administrative offices, a coffee lounge, a bookshop, and the gift shop of the Harvestime organisation. Harvestime was set up as a commercial enterprise to raise money to support the growing needs of Bryn Jones's team. R1 has often been called 'Harvestime' in the absence of a more suitable religious title. This organisation of religious free enterprise has grown in importance for the whole of R1 over the years. In the past, it primarily concentrated on tapes, gifts, and stickers. Now, it concentrates on more quality products. 'School of the Word', a correspondence Bible course, is the latest and most ambitious project to date. (The plastic throwaway goods still exist, but they are now augmented by quality leather gifts.) Run efficiently and professionally—including the latest micro-computers, word-processors and other software packages—this self-supporting business now has an annual turnover of around three quarters of a million pounds.

Much of the Harvestime work is done on a separate site from Church House. This site, which also houses the *Restoration* magazine, radiates calm and efficiency, but it invokes an atmosphere of cottage industry rather than big business. Since the Harvestime shop was opened in late 1977, and the Granary coffee lounge in 1980, Church House itself has become a popular centre in Bradford. In the basement is a full-size basketball and sports arena surrounded by a gallery. This is sometimes used for plays, and musical shows. The shop, coffee lounge, and bookstore are on the ground floor. On the first floor (up a wide and commanding staircase) there are various offices housing three secretaries, elders, and administrative staff. The showpiece, however, is the main hall next to these offices which seats up to three hundred and fifty members for the regular weekly meetings. For those who cannot get in to the services, there is an overflow room where an internal televised relay can carry the message and blessing to a further hundred members.

The success of the Church House enterprise has led to similar projects in other parts of the R1 kingdom. Terry Virgo in Hove has bought an old dilapidated church in Clarendon Villas. When I visited it, it was just nearing completion. The vast and plain hall, rectangular in shape and holding five hundred people, dominates the pine-stripped utilitarian offices and anterooms. Bath, Southampton, Leeds and Leicester are also developing large centres. At the time of writing, R1 is negotiating for an old Odeon cinema in Leeds.

The growth of such 'plant' are only the major examples of many church buildings and halls now owned by R1 house churches. Many churches are still rented, but church purchase is the goal. In addition to churches, there are private houses that have been bought for the leaders; I know of no houses that have been bought outright, but Restoration members have made significant financial contributions. In

Hertfordshire a school has been started, King's School, the building for which is on lease from the County Council. In 1980 Riddlesden College was formed and housed in a converted barn. This college, just a few miles from Keighley in Yorkshire, is open to students other than members of R1, but it is very much a Restoration college. Its curriculum is designed for leadership not for academic success.

This impressive growth rate of church buildings and other supportive organisations has been accompanied by the proliferation of house cell groups. Churches are broken down into such cells, and the house group leaders regularly meet with the elders, who in turn report to the apostles. The house groups are considered an essential component of R1 as members are not encouraged to live outside the fellowship; they are expected to interact with each other on a regular basis outside the church services. Not that these house cells are indispensable: the Bradford groups were suspended in 1984 because people were becoming too attached to them at the expense of the larger church.[4]

From 1978 onwards, *Restoration* magazine began to major on the central doctrines of the new movement. It is not until 1980/1981, however, that whole issues were given over to discipling and apostleship. By this time, the Dales Bible Week was running not only without visits from the Fort Lauderdale five, but was topping eight thousand residents a week. This made it a larger Christian convention than any other weekly residential event of any denominational or inter-denominational gathering. Indeed, except for the Christian rock festival, Greenbelt, and Spring Harvest, it has been larger than any form of residential Christian event in Great Britain. The Dales, not surprisingly then, became the shop window for Restoration teaching and worship. Its music has had far-reaching effects outside its own circle. All the Pentecostal denominations, and many Baptist and charismatic mainstream churches can be found singing 'songs of the kingdom' that originated at the Dales. I visited a large independent Pentecostal church in the Easter of 1982, which I have visited on previous occasions when in the north-west of England, only to find that the old hymns of Elim and

Assemblies of God had been largely replaced by Restoration songs.

The Dales also became a successful recruitment office for R1. Many fellowships and congregations (mainly from Baptist, Elim, and Assemblies of God churches) became Restorationist after visits to the Dales; a good number went on to join R1. The success of the Dales owed much to the preaching power of Bryn Jones, but the continual growth of R1 during the years 1978 to 1983 is proof that it was not a one-man show. During this time, except for his visits to the Dales, Bryn Jones was living in America. He had moved to St. Louis, Missouri, where he pioneered Restoration churches. Whilst there he oversaw one thousand five hundred people. Whilst it has always been true that Bryn Jones is very much the man at the top of his particular segment of R1, he has shown shrewd judgement when it came to delegating functions. He has not concerned himself, as some leaders do, with every little item of administrative and bureaucratic detail. Because he is an apostle, he has not assumed that he is therefore an entrepreneur, a manager, or an administrator.

In June 1983, Bryn Jones, somewhat unexpectedly, returned to Bradford 'for good'. Rumours surrounded his return, but rumours attach themselves to Bryn Jones with the same persistence as records of miraculous happenings. In the face of stories I had heard concerning disagreements of practice, personality clashes, and the accumulation of personal wealth whilst he was in America, Bryn Jones was able to dispel one rumour that stated that he owned a house in St. Louis worth £250,000. He pointed out that he did not own a house in America.[5]

During 1981 and 1982, criticisms were growing within the mainstream churches and Pentecostal denominations that R1 was 'stealing sheep' from existing churches instead of obtaining converts from amongst non-Christians.[6] Similar claims existed against R2 also; both groups tended to see the issue not as one of 'poaching', but of simply growing greener pasture. (A rather unfortunate choice of image given the connotations of what happens to people who think that

the 'grass is always greener on the other side of the hill'.)
Whether this criticism is valid or not, from 1983 onwards, R1
showed a definite change in direction: they dismantled the
massive Dales Week organisation by halving its size and
moving into the regions with smaller residential weeks and
weekends; they commenced, following this reorganisation,
the beginnings of evangelistic campaigns in the large provin-
cial cities.

In preparation for these new changes, which had always
been envisaged by Bryn Jones, the apostles formed around
them teams to help a more effective Restoration ministry.
These men were prophets, evangelists, teachers, and pastors
who assisted the apostle. However, at this stage, these
teams do not seem to have been a formalised deaconate surrounding the apostle, which would be an episcopal model,
neither do they seem clearly to have fitted the ministries
which R1 sees stemming from Ephesians 4 (which would
be a charismatic apostolic model). Suffice it to say, that
the teams consisted of leaders of the movement, whose
functions were sometimes, and sometimes not, clearly
defined.

The year 1983 saw the first new-style Dales Bible Week,
and also the first Welsh Bible Week. These were repeated in
1984, and with the Downs Week still running at Plumpton,
Sussex, some twelve thousand people were resident at
Restorationist camps; several thousand day visitors attended.
In addition to these massive camps (the whole combined
might of the British Council of Churches could not produce
more than a thousand people at its Youth camp in Lincoln),
there were residential weekends held in Cheshire, Shaftesbury,
Bury St. Edmunds, and Chelmsford.

In 1984, evangelistic outreaches were held in Birmingham,
Leicester, and Leeds. This first organised assault by the
'restored kingdom' upon the secular world, what Bryn Jones
calls the 'other ninety-five per cent', was begun only when
leaders felt that the kingdom base was now secured: in the
heart of enemy territory (i.e. the Devil's world, or Babylon)
the foundations for the restored kingdom had been laid.
Initial results from these short campaigns have been

encouraging rather than spectacular. For example, two thousand people turned up to hear Bryn Jones on the 10th of March 1984 at Leicestershire's De-Montfort hall. After the subsequent 'follow-up', it is believed that there were a hundred and fifty converts. A further three hundred and fifty converts were claimed during a four-month period in Yorkshire.[7] These results, though modest by the standards of Billy Graham and the George Jeffries of fifty years ago, must be seen in the context that Bryn Jones is starting off as a virtual unknown as far as the British population is concerned. Even if these Restoration evangelistic campaigns are primarily designed to bring new converts into R1, the very fact that they exist has encouraged many from the Evangelical constituency, whose major criticism against R1 is that it has not evangelised. A well-known charismatic leader felt that if Bryn Jones could keep this up, he hoped that there would be 'more power to his elbow'.

At the time of writing, R1 would seem to have around fifteen to eighteen thousand committed members and their children, and several thousand other people interested in Restoration principles but still in their churches.[8] This is a phenomenal achievement making them, in only ten years, marginally smaller than the Elim Pentecostal churches. R1 is well organised, financially secure, and led by thoughtful and powerful leaders. They would seem to be poised to make a major breakthrough in British life. However, we need to keep a sense of proportion. R1 is still a tiny fraction of the religious population of Great Britain, which is itself only some ten per cent of the population of over sixty million people. R1 has done very well, growing even more quickly, probably, than the West Indian Pentecostal churches which easily outstrip the church growth of conventional denominations. Restorationism needs also to be seen against a meteoric rise in the number of Mormons over the last few years. Although they have been in this country since the nineteenth century, it is only the last ten years that has seen a rapid rise in membership. Today, the Church of the Latter Day Saints, has well over a hundred thousand members (and the leaders would put it much higher). Unlike the House

Church Movement, the Mormons have received very little attention by either the media or Christian churches.

Not only is R1 still small by the denominational standards of the mainline churches, but it has yet to demonstrate that it can remain stable without wholesale defections. Splits of various kinds have occurred ever since the division took place in 1976 between the leaders of R1 and R2.

Peter Paris, who left Wally North to join Bryn Jones in Bradford, fell out with the Welshman in 1978. He moved to Little Rock, Arkansas where he came under Ernie Baxter's 'covering' for a while. Part of the problem was that Peter Paris maintained relationships with Maurice Smith and John Noble. After Paris fell out with Jones, his name was removed from the editorial board of *Restoration* magazine. From 1978 to the present time, a considerable number of individuals and families have left R1 complaining of too much rigidity, legalism, and heavy-handedness.[9] A number of these people ended up in R2.

The most serious division, however, that significantly depleted the numbers of R1 and weakened the leadership, was the defection of David Tomlinson and his churches to R2. At the Dales Bible Week in 1982, I noticed that David Tomlinson was absent from the leaders' platform for most of the time: he was being sanctioned for his dissent with Bryn Jones. Soon afterwards, David Tomlinson decided to withdraw from R1 (and his name was removed from the editorial associates of *Restoration* magazine).

David Tomlinson had been a genuine pioneer in the north-east and Midlands. Those under his pastoral care were very loyal to him, and most of them chose to stay with their shepherd. In many ways Tomlinson's disagreement with Bryn Jones repeats the division of 1976. Differences with Bryn Jones were more a question of style, method of leadership, and emphasis of doctrine, rather than major doctrinal disagreements. David Tomlinson is almost the opposite in personality to Bryn Jones. Bryn (to use psychological terminology) is the classical convergent thinker. He presses on regardless of opposition and set-backs, running a tight ship all the way. David Tomlinson is a divergent thinker. He is always rethinking his position, always seeing new angles and aspects to doctrines and practices, always learning and changing. Despite the absence of a formal university education, he has a first-class mind, and appears able to be constantly open to self-criticism and yet continue in his work. He was the perfect foil and check to Bryn Jones, and Jones's incisiveness was the counter-balance to Tomlinson's caution. The attraction of opposites, however, so easily leads to opposition, and the same power that attracts becomes the power that repels.

The absence of David Tomlinson has caused, many would argue, a serious imbalance in the life of R1. Many people there still miss him, and he is still greatly respected by such people as David Matthew (the respect is mutual) the present editor of *Restoration*. David Tomlinson is glad to be free of R1. He had felt, for a number of years, that R1 was already a denomination. In its desire to be the kingdom—to be truly the place of God's people—he felt R1 had adopted a 'fortress mentality' and was turning its back on not only the rest of Christendom, but also the whole of modern culture.

## Restoration Two

If, on following R1 since 1976, despite the defections and clouds of rumour, we can discern purposefulness and firm direction, a first glance at R2 seems to reveal partial disintegration and a perpetual running around in circles. First impressions are always useful, even if they are at best superficial. The collapse of the 'fabulous fourteen' seems to have caused no more than a hiccup in the life of R1, but its effect on R2 was traumatic. For a long time there seemed to be no unity of purpose. The firmest decision that seems to have been taken, was consciously not to try and ape R1 by setting up a bigger and better Dales.

The split had brought some relief. David Mansell was gone, and with the absence of Bryn Jones and Arthur Wallis, some of the London Brothers thought the atmosphere lighter. Perhaps the 'good times' of the Royal Albert Hall would return?

In the event, although the anarchic animus was still at

work in R2, it was experienced more as a twitch and a stretching than a full flowing of power: R2 was alive but creaking. Morally and spiritually the leaders gave each other support, but co-ordinated efforts seemed to be difficult to sustain. This was partially due to the way apostleship worked in R2. Once churches were established, covenanted relationships assured, and 'covering' arrangements understood, both house churches and house groups were expected to get on with it. John Noble, for example, organised his own team, set up churches, and left elders to run their own affairs. His was the ultimate authority, but he did not see it to be his place to delve into the minutiæ of everyday kingdom life. Father in God he might have been, but he did expect his children to grow up and have enough independence to run their own lives.

Not that nothing went on in Collier Row, Romford in Essex, where he had his stronghold. Up on the hill—the fellowship held to the image of kingdom light shining forth from the mountain top—members moved into the same streets and became neighbours. Similar formations (which later Nick Butterworth was to characterise as ghettos) took place in Petersfield, Cardiff, Cobham, and Yeovil. Gerald Coates started up 'Kingdom Life' in Cobham where praise and worship reflected the glory days of the Royal Albert Hall. Gerald's sense of drama and style developed in those meetings, and many hundreds of people attended. Some Evangelicals found the meetings shallow, emotionally manipulative, and lacking in traditional evangelical content. 'It was just religious show biz,' someone reported to me. Another saw it as a platform to promote Gerald Coates. The majority of people, however, found the meetings liberating and stimulating; fun but spiritual. There is no doubt that by 1981, Gerald Coates had more friends than enemies. The success of Cobham was parochial in the sense that it reflected what Gerald was doing, with support from John, rather than influencing R2 as a whole.

It is very difficult looking back to the late 1970s and seeing R2 as an entity at all. In discipling terms, Gerald looked to John Noble as the senior apostle, but other leaders were less submissive. Gradually, and without much of the drama that took place in R1, relationships began to weaken. John MacLauchlan had a disagreement with John Noble as to who had the primary responsibility for the flock in Yeovil. He also, along with Graham Perrins, began to develop ideas of the primacy of the prophet in the end-time kingdom. By the end of the 1970s, R2 no longer formed a unity based on an alliance between the London Brothers and the western leaders. Peter Lyne departed for New Zealand, Ian McCullogh went off on his own and ended up with one community relating to no one except some obscure American shepherd. John MacLauchlan and Graham Perrins decided to work together and no longer 'relate' to John Noble and Gerald Coates.

Up until 1979, *Fulness* magazine had been the major focus for the, by now, damaged kingdom of R2. With the departure of Graham Perrins into his Cardiff stronghold, *Fulness* ceased. Nick Butterworth valiantly tried to edit a new journal in the early 1980s. *Dovetail*, as it was called, did not really live up to its name. There seemed to be little editorial co-ordination, and it was a bits and pieces magazine compared to the earlier *Fulness*. George Tarleton was still around, but remained, as he always had been, a law unto himself. ('George was around but not with us.') By 1981/82, R2 now had two faces: what was left of the original Restoration movement was really no more than a weakened London Brothers (Terry Virgo and David Mansell now being in R1). For the rest, there were isolated pockets of Restorationist-style groups, which included Graham Perrins and John MacLauchlan who related together and with Wayne Drain in America, the Basingstoke fellowships that were led from America, Ian McCullogh's church, and a few floating communities that flitted from apostle to prophet. None of these disparate groups formed any kind of co-ordinated movement, and only Basingstoke in my extended use of R2 can be said to have really flourished. A feature of the extended R2 churches, is that they were more authoritarian and demanding then the churches under John Noble and Gerald Coates.

Unlike R1, until the present moment, R2 has been little interested in plant. They primarily rent their churches and halls. In 1980, John Noble did start an independent school which has always been difficult to finance. A number of Christian business ventures were tried, but they did seem to have the habit of going off half-cock. The *Rainbow* company was started by John Noble in 1983. After a very poor start, it seemed to be finding its feet by late 1984. There seems to be genuine optimism this time, but I think it not unfair to say that R2 has not been the efficient business machine that characterised R1 in the same period of time. (George Tarleton finds this one of the most endearing qualities of R2.) By 1983, Graham Perrins and John MacLauchlan had fallen out. Reports that Graham Perrins had 'gone off the rails' began to filter through to the London Brothers. It appears that Graham Perrins has been man enough to admit mistakes have been made, and the communities under his direction have reportedly stabilised. This cannot be said of John MacLauchlan's churches, where there have been recent defections, complaints of false prophecy and undue heavy-handedness.

Remarkably, whilst R2 can neither boast co-ordinated efforts nor a clear-cut programme during these years, it continued to grow. Landmarks are difficult to find, but there were significant events and interesting experiments. For example, in the two years that Graham Perrins and John MacLauchlan worked fruitfully together (the end of 1979 to 1982), they produced a remarkable journal that I think will become a collectors' item. Perrins has always had a reputation for wide readership, and John MacLauchlan's Greek and historical scholarship has been a byword in Restoration circles for years. The magazine they produced, *Proclaim*, not only contains shocking and radical views concerning the nature of prophecy, it also contains a level of genuine scholarship that cannot be found in any other Restoration publication that I have read.

Gerald Coates joined the Evangelical Alliance, and with his interest in media and pop culture became instrumental in the 'Spring Harvest' and 'Banquet' organisations which promote Christian music and gospel in modern form. This move of Gerald Coates, coupled with John Noble forming links with Catholic charismatics from 1982, demonstrates a desire to relate their style of Restorationism with the rest of neo-Pentecostalism.

By 1983, with the arrival of David Tomlinson and his churches, R2 recovered its nerve and its sense of direction. Indeed, David Tomlinson's appearance heralded the emergence of R2 in its new and mature form. The old London Brothers, Peter Lyne, Graham Perrins axis having shattered, what remained was a remnant of the London Brothers and refugees from R1. There was a celebration and dedication of commitment in 1983 with R2's first attempt at a Dales-style camp. 'Festival 83' was held for a week at Staffordshire Showground, and although it was not a financial success, it succeeded as a demonstration of identity and spiritual seriousness. 1983 was a good year for Gerald with the publication of his book, *What on Earth Is This Kingdom?*, and his subsequent appearance on Radio 4 and local radios. To the many churches under the newly constituted leadership,[10] there was no sense that there was a going back on Restoration principles, but there was a feeling that there was a moving on to a new phase.

In the event, 1984 turned out to be as significant and as traumatic a year for R2 as it was for R1. By now David Tomlinson, John Noble, and Gerald Coates (and Peter Fenwick who formerly worked with Peter Paris) were working closely together whilst remaining autonomous and publishing their own house magazines. There was a new searching for how kingdom principles can be applied to a more evangelistic and pioneering effort. David Tomlinson took a bold step—to move into the inner London areas and establish new churches. There was an eagerness to learn from past mistakes, holding onto the essentials of Restoration revelation but disregarding what they saw as exclusivist and legalistic tendencies.

'Festival 84' was held at Stafford, and it was a huge success. It was attended by over four thousand exuberant people. The format was similar to the Dales, but its workshops and seminars were far broader in content and more controversial and provocative than Dales teaching. Dales Bible Week is like a spiritual pressure-cooker, but Festival like a spiritual Butlins. Certainly the R1 refugees felt they had escaped into a holiday camp: women could and did say that they did not always want to stay at home. Some of them showed an interest in leadership, and issues of racism, unemployment, and peace were discussed by many groups with a seriousness and interest that would not have shamed the British Council of Churches. And yet at the moment when, for the first time for years, the newly rejuvenated (and admittedly partly reconstituted) R2 was emerging as a more united force, it suffered its own defections.

1984 had not started well for Collier Row, with a bad school report by Her Majesty's Inspectors. It was not a damning report: the community spirit and primary provision were praised. It did suggest, however, that the school had bitten off more than it could chew; the secondary schooling curriculum and teaching was not up to scratch.[11] More seriously for John Noble, Maurice Smith decided to break with him, and also Nick Butterworth pulled out his churches from the covering umbrella of John Noble's leadership. A number of other members from the Essex fellowships decided to leave. One of the issues revolved round a greater financial commitment that John Noble wanted, to help both *Rainbow* and more concerted team work. Complaints were made by some that John had become too authoritarian. This is a charge that John denies. Perhaps it was the case that he was the victim of leaving his followers too much to their own devices; they had become used to the status quo, and did not seem prepared to offer any greater commitment. Nick Butterworth believes that Collier Row and his fellowships had become a ghetto. He claims[12] that he woke up one day and realised that he did not know anyone in his street except kingdom people. It was time, he thought, to quit what had become a 'holy huddle'.

Both he and Maurice Smith feel that the discipling doctrines are wrong, and that the whole psychology of Restoration (both R1 and R2) is based on insisting that there is always something within people which needs improving. They have decided, for now, to abandon such principles, and preach that Jesus is happy with people just the way they are. Influenced by Norman Grubb (who is an old friend) and the American 'Union Life' movement, Maurice is nevertheless insistent that he has not joined that movement, and has no intention of doing so. He appears to be launching out on his own in a new full-time ministry, which he jokingly told me might become known as 'the leader of the nebulous church'.

George Tarleton, on the other hand, has decided to throw in his hand completely, and retire not only from R2, but full-time Christian work. He loves many of the brethren, and in particular John Noble, but feels that there has been too much delusion in what they are doing. He feels that R2 is itself already taking the road to denominationalism. This is, of course, a great temptation for them now. Despite the defections and setbacks, R2 is stronger and has a more settled base than it has had for years. They look set, at the very least, to consolidate. But there is a wind of change in the air, and it is by no means clear where that wind will lead them. They could create a more liberal version of R1 based on the new Festival venue and the new triumvirate of Noble, Tomlinson, and Coates. Indeed, they may have already started that process. To withstand such a direction may be impossible for them in their desire for identity and unity. R2 may, of course, break up against its will (it has already happened to it once), but to disband R2, or attempt to break down the loose-knit structure into even more autonomous and atomistic fellowships would not only take an enormous act of will, it would be flying in the face of Church history.

R2 has not had the spectacular success of R1, and yet it is not surrounded by the same clouds of rumour and scandal as the larger Restoration kingdom. My extended version of R2, including the Basingstoke communities and non-aligned independents, probably number some sixteen thousand. The Tomlinson, Noble, Coates axis, which is at the core of my strict usage of R2, numbers some eight to ten thousand. This is similar in size to the Apostolic church in Great Britain. Such a size is clearly vulnerable to either outward attack or inner defections. Leadership is strong, however, and member commitment is high. The real question for them, at the moment, is not how big or small will they become, but which direction will they take: away further from the mainstream into a sectarian enclave, or back into the central flow of British religious life and culture?

There is a limit to how far an interpretive narrative can take one into understanding a new phenomenon. It will have been obvious that whilst I have not denied the importance of seeing Restorationists as living members of the kingdom of God, I have used the notion of 'kingdom' as a metaphor to describe the new movements. Having used this metaphor in an extended way to see in what manner the kingdom of Restoration was established, I wish now to extend it further to see how we can understand and evaluate its significance. My central contention is that Restoration is a radical kingdom. An examination of its doctrines, an investigation into its historical antecedents, and a look at its sociological complexion will help us establish the nature of this radicality.

## Notes

1   See chapter 1, note 2.

2   See chapter 4, note 9.

3   I am indebted to Joyce Thurman for this information. Op cit., pp.28–29.

4   Discussion with Bryn Jones at Church House, see chapter 4, note 3.

5   Ibid.

6   This was the thrust of my report on the Dales Bible Week for Radio 4's *Sunday* programme, 8 August 1982.

7   Information from Bryn Jones in telephone conversation in June 1984. (A former member of R1 claims that many of the crowds at these evangelistic campaigns were Restorationists 'bussed in' from Bradford.)

8   David Pawson is recorded in the *Methodist Recorder* on 9 February 1984 as claiming that there are a hundred thousand fellowships meeting in homes. Taking all kinds of house churches, inside and outside the denominations, this figure is fairly accurate. Restoration *per se* is much smaller. None of the leaders of R1 and R2 have tried to augment their figures for media presentation, but I have overestimated the numbers myself in previous publications. Not clearly making a distinction between those attending the Dales and Downs Weeks, those pro-Restorationist but not yet committed members, and the members themselves, I have tended to see the overall size of R1 and R2 as seventy thousand. Now, I feel with greater confidence, that thirty thousand is a more accurate number.
   As I pointed out to Peter Brierley who edits the *UK Christian Handbook*, the handbook's figure of 180,000 house church members is wildly inaccurate. He promised to look into the whole matter.

9   I say complaining, but few have been willing to talk in specifics. We could find nobody willing to talk for *Front Room Gospel*, on Radio 4, 23 March 1984. In researching this book, I have been presented with little firm evidence, and few people who were willing to give their names. My own view is that if such stories exist in any great numbers it will be only a matter of time before they surface.

10   There is no formal constitution, or officially established leadership. What has emerged is a *de facto* leadership.

11   The *Havering Post* headlined on 14 July, 'Shock report slams school'. This is typical media hype. The report by H.M. Inspectors on 'Acorn Independent School, Romford, Essex' is available from the Dept. of Education and Science, Publications Despatch Centre, Honeypot Lane, Stanmore, Middx. HA7 1AZ.

12   In interview on 11 May 1984.

## *RECOMMENDED READING*

'The Dales Dilemma: Church Splitters Or Kingdom Builders?',
   *Buzz* magazine (August 1984).
*Pioneer* Bulletin, Vol. 1, Issue 3 (Pioneer Enterprises Ltd.).
Ross Peart, 'The House Church', *Methodist Recorder* (9 Feb.
   1984).
Gerald Coates, *What On Earth Is This Kingdom?* (Kingsway,
   1983).
Eileen Vincent, *Something's Happening* (Marshalls, 1984).
*Word to the World*, Voice of the Harvestime Team, Issue 1, 1984
   (Harvestime Publications).

*Part Two*

# THE RADICAL KINGDOM

# THE RADICAL PRINCIPLES OF
# RESTORATION (Part One)

## On Radicality

It was the philosopher Wittgenstein, who claimed in his later works that the meaning of words are related to their usage; to know what a word means, he felt, it was not sufficient to use lexicon or dictionary: terminology could only be understood by examining the ways people used it. Whilst such a theory has its difficulties, its certainly a useful insight when we come to investigate idiomatic language used by religious movements (or the jargon of social scientists for that matter!).

It is useful also when we examine words and phrases in our culture that have extended usages and multiple meanings. The word 'radical', for example, is particularly problematic. Ever since the word became associated firstly with the Whigs, then later with Liberalism and Socialism, it has become very difficult to disassociate it from politics of a reformist or revolutionary kind. In calling Restorationism 'radical Christianity', I want to make it clear that I am invoking no political meaning. Indeed, politically speaking, Restorationism is neither radically left wing nor right wing; like so many enthusiastic religious movements, Restorationism tends to be apolitical.[1]

Another extended usage of 'radical' is to make it synonymous with 'liberal' and apply the term to either morality or theology. If we take this to mean against tradition and think of such examples as 'situational ethics' and demythologising theology, then Restoration is clearly not radical at all in this sense. On the whole its moral and theological positions are conservative, and as we shall see, the majority of its doctrines clearly belong to the conservative Evangelicalism of classical Pentecostalism.

So far my use of the term 'radical' is in harmony with the Restorationists themselves. Arthur Wallis, however, in his book *The Radical Christian*,[2] discusses radicality in a far more ideological and comprehensive way than I shall be able to do. I feel it more useful to define and 'operationalise' the notion of radical in a way which I can then apply with some certainty and explanatory power. (Another way of understanding this is to realise that Arthur is writing from the inside; my perspective is that of the outsider.) Let me, at least, start with Arthur's usage.

Arthur points out, correctly, that the word radical has its origins in the Latin *radix*, or root. He sees the radical Christian as one who returns to the origins, roots, or sources of pure Christianity. The radical Christian, then, is not one who turns away from the tradition, but is one who returns to the pure tradition. This tradition he sees as totally committed Christianity both in personal and corporate terms. For Arthur the true Christian by definition is one who stands absolutely for truth and eschews compromise. 'Or to put it differently, when it comes to important issues he refuses to sit on the fence or adopt a "wait-and-see" policy. It's right or it's wrong. It's true or it's false. It's light or it's darkness. He cannot go along with those who, for personal considerations, are content to live in the twilight.'[3] In the kingdom of God, Wallis claims, 'radicalism means unswerving righteousness'.

This return to pure Biblical Christianity, in Wallis's understanding, is radical in a twin sense. Firstly, it is radical because it is a turning round (*metanoia*) and going back to a Christianity of the New Testament. This, as we shall see, entails going back to a Christianity that precedes denominationalism in order to go beyond denominationalism. Secondly, it is radical because the true disciples of the Jesus of the New Testament are seen to treat the *root* problem of all social and political ills: the wickedness of the human heart. Put together this twin notion of radicality leads us to see a Christian who is committed to eradicating sin, error, apostasy, and compromise. He is also one who stands for righteousness, truth and unswerving commitment to God's reign and rule(s) in His kingdom.

Restorationists' claim, that they have restored the pattern of New Testament Christianity, is certainly radical enough. Personally, I find the claim less than convincing,[4] but the problem with Arthur's definition is not that I cannot personally give wholehearted assent to the claims inherent in it, but that his understanding of radical is too comprehensive for me to operationalise in a strictly defined way. I propose, therefore, to limit and narrow my understanding of radical, so that I can use it in a non-theological way.

I believe that an examination of the doctrines and practices of both Restoration One and Restoration Two demonstrates that we can usefully apply the term 'radical' if we keep in mind this Kingdom Christianity entailing a comprehensive degree of social control by leaders, and a strong personal commitment by members not normally found in Christianity. Restoration religion circumscribes the lives of its followers to a far greater extent than is typical not only in the mainline denominations but also in the majority of Pentecostal churches.

In the typical Evangelical churches, believers are expected to 'give their hearts to Jesus', and there is an expectation that some demands will be made on free time. Restorationists, however, are prepared to give their all to the kingdom whether it be time, money, personal possessions, or skills. Being an Anglican or a Baptist can be a part-time pursuit (almost a leisure activity). To become a Restorationist is to adopt a total way of life.

For this reason, it is not enough simply to lump R1 and R2 with fundamentalism and dismiss them as yet another addition to Protestant sectarianism. In the United States there has been a considerable rise in fundamentalism in the last ten years. There is strong evidence to show that it is gaining political muscle.[5] But being a fundamentalist or a 'Bible-belter' does not necessarily lead to a radical alternative to the American way of life. All too often it is seen as synony-mous with it. A particularly interesting aspect of Billy Graham's 'Mission To England' in 1984, was the way in which he confided to Christian leaders that many of the new conservatives in American religion were blind to the evils of American society. R2 is still working out its relationship to British secular culture, but R1 are quite clear that they belong to an alternative society.

The fact that Restorationism circumscribes the lives of its adherents every bit as much as the Salvation Army is not only sociological evidence of its radicality: it is a demonstra-tion that its theological claims are radical too. Salvation Army control is related to its hierarchical organisation which is self-consciously modelled on the secular army: orders are given at the top, and passed down the line. In the Restora-tion churches, claims are made not only to belong to the Lord's army, but also to be subjects of the King in a theo-cratic state. Theocracy is not unique in Protestant history, but it is rare in the modern world.

To recapitulate: whilst it is not my intention to disprove the thesis that Restorationists have restored New Testament Christianity, neither do I intend to substantiate that claim as evidence of its radicality. I shall discuss Restorationist Christianity as radical in two interrelated ways. Firstly, against the conventional wisdom of denominational Christ-ianity, it insists that the charismatic gifts of the early Church have been restored and that God has re-established His control over the kingdom through a theocracy of apostles. Secondly, a belief in the restored theocracy has led to an ordering and control of believers' lives not typically found in conventional Christianity.

Restorationists claim that the Christianity which they practise is to be seen as the New Testament norm both in terms of church government and individual commitment. By contemporary denominational standards, their beliefs and practices clearly deviate from the normative behaviour of most mainline Christians. In this narrow sense they are indisputedly radical. I do not mean this to be seen as a polite way of saying that Restorationism is sectarian. It is that too—from a sociological standpoint at least—as I shall later argue. But even from a sectarian perspective, Restoration makes claims and demands upon its members that are not typical of many such movements. It is clear, then, that Restoration is neither 'run of the mill', nor just another Pentecostal movement. Its beliefs are radical in its claims, and its organisation is radical in the effect it has on believers' lives. Whether it can also be said to be radical in its effects upon Christendom and society as a whole, is a question best left to the end of our study of its beliefs and practices.

## The Christian Context of Restoration

To locate the principles of Restorationists is to recognise that they belong firmly to Evangelical Protestanism. Furthermore, most of their beliefs and practices are identical to classical Pentecostalism. Both R1 and R2 resemble the traditional Pentecostal denominations more than the Renewalism of neo-Pentecostalism. This is true because their theology of the 'baptism of the Holy Spirit', and their total commitment to adult baptism is no different from their classical counterparts. Their eschatology too has its origins in Pentecostalism (and to a certain extent Brethrenism).

Classical Pentecostals pioneered lively and spontaneous liturgies. The coupling of informality with serious ideological content has been taken over by the Restorationists and revamped into their own style.

So similar in many ways is Restorationism (as indeed have been the aspects of the Renewal) to classical Pentecostalism, that a first glance fails to notice the difference. Many of the members of Elim and the Assemblies of God who have attended the Dales Bible Week felt immediately at home. If anything they felt more at home than in their own churches because the Dales generated greater expectations of God's blessings, more excitement, and a real feeling of revival.

I think it important that before we concentrate on the few distinctive and radical doctrines of Restoration, we realise how close they are to their older Pentecostal cousins. Restorationists accept the Bible as the inerrant Word of God in all matters of doctrine and religious practice. They are literalists in matters of interpretation whether it be the miraculous stories of the New Testament, tales of Old Testament heroes, or understanding the Creation story of Genesis as an historical account.

They not only reject the scholarship of modernist theologians, but they are not, on the whole, versed in issues of hermeneutics, historical criticism, or demythologising tenets. I think it not unfair to describe them as 'fundamentalists' (though they do not like the term) rather than 'conservative Evangelicals'. This distinction is a vital one because whilst the former—within Protestanism—will be the latter by definition, a conservative Evangelical might well be able to accommodate some forms of higher criticism and evolutionary theory whilst remaining committed to the essential truths of the incarnation, life, death, and resurrection of Christ.[6] Many Evangelicals, also, would not wish to identify themselves with a firm commitment to a particular eschatological theory.

Restorationists, like all fundamentalists, counterbalance their literalness with wide use of typology, analogy, and ingenious speculations concerning the end of the world. Adventism dominates all forms of Pentecostalism and a commitment to and expectation of the imminent return of the Lord Jesus is the backdrop against which the drama of Pentecostal life is played. Restorationists are by no means in agreement on all interpretations of the Second Coming and in that they are no different from other Pentecostal groups.

Like all Pentecostals, Restorationists believe that one becomes a Christian by the regeneration of the 'new birth'. Christian life can not begin until Christ has been accepted as Saviour. This acceptance, based on the belief in the vicarious death and resurrection of Christ, is the passport to the Church which consists of born-again believers. The same issues of faith and grace, are debated in Restoration as in the rest of Pentecostalism. The majority of Restorationists are tacitly Arminian in the sense that like many of the early Methodists self-will and personal faith are stressed more than doctrines of grace and electionism. (This would not be true of Hove where the leading pastor there—under Terry Virgo—has a strong Calvinistic emphasis which stems from his earlier days in the Baptist Union.)

Restorationists are aggressively Baptist. I say 'aggressively' because Restoration leaders are anxious to stress that believers' baptism is not an option for Christians but an essential part of the restored church. Whilst I have met two vigorously argued cases against infant baptism,[7] and heard many vehement sermons against it from R1 leaders, I have never seen any evidence that they know what the Biblical and historical defence of the traditional practice could be.[8] The proselytising attitude to believers' baptism has clearly divided Restorationists from many Catholic, Anglican, Presbyterian, and Methodist Renewalists. I have seen Anglicans rebaptised at the Dales. The fact that this takes place is evidence of the strength of feeling that Restorationists possess over this issue. It is another example of how they are closer to classical Pentecostalism than the Charismatic Renewal *per se*.

It could be argued that their Baptist views owe as much to Brethrenism as Pentecostalism. The same could be said of their general attitude to sacraments. The doctrine of the Lord's Table seems to be identical to Brethren usage. Like all Brethren and Pentecostals they abhor ritualism and sacramentalism of any kind.

Their view that the 'baptism of the Holy Spirit' is a second experience quite separate from conversion is taken from classical Pentecostalism. They believe that the 'baptism' is the initiation into the power of the Holy Ghost. Most Restorationists believe that the initial sign, or evidence, of the baptism is speaking in tongues. There is no dogmatic ruling on this, however. Following other Pentecostalists, Restorationists have emphasised the gifts of the Spirit as outlined by St. Paul in 1 Corinthians 12. Great emphasis is placed on divine healing and the deliverance of people from the possessive and oppressive power of demons. In this respect,

Restorationists can be said to major on demons and 'deliverance ministry' far more than Elim and the Assemblies of God. There has been considerable input from America in this area; both in terms of the older-style revivalist Pentecostalism and the newer independents. R2, in my strict use of the term, are less committed to exorcisms than R1.

Most classical Pentecostals are nominally trinitarian in belief, but few groups have a developed doctrine of the Trinity. This applies also to Restorationists. It is not even clear that the old dispute, that we earlier noticed in regard to Chard concerning the correct formula for baptism, is yet resolved. I have heard the Holy Trinity invoked at water baptism, but reliable informants have told me that some baptisms use the name of Jesus only. An interesting feature of classical Pentecostalism and Restorationism is that despite the emphasis on the Spirit, most theology tends to be Christocentric. Prayers are rarely addressed to the Holy Spirit, and never at all to the Holy Trinity. (Tom Smail, Professor Colin Gunton—and many Reformed theologians—would see this as a general failure of most Protestant churches; not a peculiar feature of Pentecostalism.)

It might seem that given the close similarities between themselves and classical Pentecostalism, Restorationists see themselves as belonging in that camp. This is not so. Restorationists admit to a filial relationship, but that is all. They think that the classical Pentecostals fell into the error of denominationalism on the one hand, whilst on the other hand they failed to see the full implications of the restoration of the charismatic gifts. Restorationists believe that God is saying something new to Christians and something more radical even than the Pentecostal belief in revival.

They see the great revivals of classical Pentecostalism as the first phase of restoring the supernatural gifts of the Holy Spirit to the Church. The second, short phase, was the Charismatic Renewal, when God demonstrated that Holy Ghost power could not be contained within the sect or denomination. The third and final phase, was the restoration of the kingdom of God, which has been absent in its full power since New Testament times. This restoration of the kingdom is to be the final chapter in the history of the Church in preparation for Christ's bodily return to earth, and the establishment of a new heaven and a new world: '. . . the time of universal restoration . . .'

## The Restored Church as an Eschatological Imperative

The key to understanding the emergence and significance of the Restoration movement, as Restorationists understand it themselves, is eschatology. Following Edward Irving and the early Brethren movement, a section of the Evangelical world has inherited a fascination with certain interpretations of the last things. In America under the influence of the Millerites and the early Mormons and Jehovah's Witnesses, eschatology became a burning topic amongst many non-Christian sects too. Today, Christadelphians, Seventh Day Adventists, and most Pentecostal movements share with these sects a concern to understand history in the light of an eschatological doctrine.[9]

John Nelson Darby, perhaps the most dynamic of early Brethren leaders, believed that the Second Coming of Christ would be preceded by 'wars and rumours of wars'. Following Darby a considerable concensus developed in non-conformist Evangelicalism that the end-time would be characterised by such wars, but also moral depravity, natural disasters, and religious decline. In recent years, with the arrival of 'the bomb', and a growing concern with ecological problems, this thesis has continued to thrive.

One of the central controversies has centred around the issue as to whether Christians would be whisked away from all the troubles and tribulations of the last days. (Perhaps, in a secret rapture—as Darby and Irving thought—in the air with Christ and the saints of history?) The role of the anti-Christ (seen either as an actual person or an evil system) has been just one of the many enigmas in a prophetic jigsaw that few have claimed to fully understand.

Against the 'doom and gloom brigade', who have tended to hold onto a remnant eschatology where only a few true

Christians would be saved, have arisen the countervailing groups who emphasise the 'latter rain'. This was a movement that gained prominence in classical Pentecostal circles, and the central idea was the belief that a worldwide revival would herald the return of Christ. The 'first rain' was interpreted as Pentecost and the beginning of the Christian dispensation. The 'second rain'—latter rain—was understood as a restoration of Pentecostal power to the Church before the end of time. There was a latter rain movement in American Pentecostalism in the late 1950s, which no doubt influenced Arthur Wallis. In Great Britain today, the charismatic leader, Colin Urquhart, belongs in this tradition.

The early Restorationists, like many Renewalists, saw the Charismatic Movement as a sign of the latter rain. As the movement developed, however, they saw the Renewal as just a few 'showers of blessing' before the real deluge. The nature of this deluge began to take on an interesting and concrete expression. God, it was claimed, would not let His Church be swamped by sin, or the forces of the Evil One. On the contrary, He would restore the Church to her original splendour. But this would entail not only revisiting her with charismatic gifts, but also equipping her with the government and ordinances of God's kingdom.

This kingdom would be not of this world (Babylon, the whore city, is the image often used for world), but would exist in this world as an alternative society run according to God's rules, and staffed by His devoted followers. Graham Perrins has tended to emphasise the people of the kingdom as a prophetic people both pointing to and in part realising the eschaton. The majority of Restorationists, however, especially in R1, see God's people as those fulfilling God's original plan for Adam. This plan was to populate the earth with men and women made in His image. Since The Fall, and since the failure of the Old Covenant with Israel, Christ—the new Adam—has initiated the covenant of the New Israel. Henceforth, the people of God—both Jew and Gentile joined to Christ as the head of the Church—have continued God's plan to populate the earth. In the last days,

God will make it possible for His people to multiply, fill the whole earth, and become rulers in His kingdom.

Despite the apostasy of the Church, then, the kingdom of God is destined to be restored. Denominations will be abolished and the new Church will establish a substantial and glorious witness to the power and holiness of God. His people, in the last days, will prosper and become victorious over their enemies. The rest of the world, which will begin to disintegrate during these last days, will look on in wonder.

God's kingdom is to be understood as 'the stone cut out without hands' of Nebuchadnezzar's famous vision of the kingdoms of the earth. In this vision of the image composed of gold, silver, iron, and iron and clay (representing historical epochs) the stone was dashed against the image, which was smashed to pieces. The stone became a great mountain and filled the earth. Daniel interpreted the stone in this way:

> And in the days of these kings shall the God of heaven set up a kingdom, which shall never be destroyed: and the kingdom shall not be left to other people, but it shall break in pieces and consume all these kingdoms, and it shall stand for ever.[10]

As the great restored kingdom begins rapidly to grow so it will meet great opposition. The so-called Great Tribulation is to be endured by the saints in the Restoration schema before the Second Coming. Most Restorationists believe that the secret rapture of the Church, which allows the saints to miss the Tribulation, is an unfounded biblical inference. They believe, however, that the kingdom of God, which will be attacked by the anti-Christ and his forces, will withstand all opposition. Indeed, the very establishment of God's alternative society, they believe, will inevitably polarise the world into the forces of Good and Evil.

All this is not quite as black and white as it seems. Those not in the kingdom will recognise it for what it is: the dwelling place of the people of God. David Matthew, the editor of *Restoration* magazine, can foresee the day when the

politicians and workers of the world will come to kingdom
people cap in hand.[11] Conversely, all those living within the
shadow of the kingdom are not necessarily in the Church.

On first meeting kingdom people, I thought that 'kingdom' and 'church' were interchangeable terms in Restorationist circles. Apparently, this is not so. The kingdom of
God is to be understood not as a place, but as the rule of
God. God's laws and precepts are to be written in the hearts
of men and women, and adhered to in practice in a corporate not merely an individual way. God's alternative society
exists wherever God's rule(s) is obeyed. The kingdom enters
the world through the Church which acts like a portal or a
door. Once established, this kingdom derives its spiritual
authority supremely through King Jesus but also through
'His Body': the Church.

In one image Restorationists use, the Church is seen as
the cutting edge of the Kingdom. Another image is the
hardened tip of the arrow. In short, the Church leads and
the kingdom follows. I assume the logic of this position is
that members of the Church are *ipso facto* members of the
kingdom, but that members of the kingdom need not necessarily be members of the Church. (Children would fit this
category, for example, in Restorationist churches themselves; this is one of the consequences, as Edward Irving
saw, of conversion experience not infant baptism being the
initiation into the Church.)

The Church, then, is to usher in the kingdom of God prior
to the historical return of Christ to earth. The return of the
King completes the full restoration of the kingdom on earth.
Some Evangelicals will no doubt see this as pre-empting
God's sovereignty: 'How can Jesus come like a thief in the
night,' they might ask, 'if the kingdom has to wait to be
properly established?' Others might see this as tantamount
to saying, 'Even so, come quickly Lord Jesus, but not yet
because we haven't finished the job.'

Restorationists do not claim that God is bound by their
eschatology; they are merely demonstrating their commitment to the promises of God's Word, as they understand
them. Furthermore, they insist that God is merciful and

wishes, if possible, for all to be saved. At the very least, therefore, the Church should be seen not as a little band of the faithful huddling together like some little sect awaiting their final release from a hostile world: it will be powerful and strong awaiting the return of the king. The Church militant and defiant is the message of Restoration; not the Church defeated:

> We are the army of God
> As a church we stand in God's armour.
> The pow'rs of darkness are trembling
> As Jesus our captain goes before us.[12]

The Restorationist adventism is essentially pre-millennial but millennialism is not an essential theme in their vision of the last things. Christ will return when the Church is perfect (the Bride without blemish) and the kingdom restored. He will come as king and take his rightful place; 'And every knee shall bow, and every tongue shall confess to God.' Whether He will then reign with His saints for a thousand years, or whether Christ's historical return heralds the end of time seems less clear. I think most Restorationists think there will be a gap between the return of the king, and the full 'restoration of all things' in eternity. The essential thrust of their adventism, however, is the establishment of a mighty kingdom of God prior to the return of Christ.

Not all Restorationsts hold to such a strong eschatological position as outlined above; but despite disagreement over details most members of R1 and R2 hold to some version of it. I would describe the version that I have outlined as the classic Restorationist vision. It is not only the dominant eschatology of R1, but it is the vision with which Arthur Wallis inspired the 'magnificent seven' and the 'fabulous fourteen' in the 1970s.

Graham Perrins and John MacLauchlan have increasingly, since those days, veered away from the idea of doing prophecy to becoming prophetic. One consequence of this would seem to be a concentration on the prophetic role and the bringing forth of prophecy. The extreme version of this, is that the prophet declares it, and it is! This prophetic emphasis has replaced the more traditional Pentecostal concern to piece together a correct interpretation of the end things. Members in R2 seem less caught up with eschatology than R1. I suspect that David Tomlinson, for example, is wary of insisting on too strong a Restorationist eschatology. (Both R1 and R2 tend to see eschatology in terms of adventism rather than a theological doctrine of the final judgement *per se*.)

The significance of Restoration eschatology is not that either R1 or R2 has a 'correct' line which everybody holds dogmatically. Its significance lies in the vision of Church life and kingdom order that the eschatology inspires. The eschatological vision has not been added to Restorationism after it became established: it preceded the movement and provided the motivating force for the establishment of the Restoration kingdom(s).

The vision of a powerful and resplendent church standing high on the mountain like a beacon offering, paradoxically, both hope and warning to a lost world, is also seen as a judgement on the Church. Or to be more accurate: it pronounces a judgement on what men have tried to do to God's Church. The eschatological view of the fulfilment of God's plan, therefore, has also provided Restorationists with a means for both interpreting and judging Church history. Reading the eschaton back into history led the Restorationists to the conviction that the original glory of God's Church had been dimmed; consequently the power of the kingdom had been virtually switched off. The restoration of that power was a gradual process culminating today in the reappearance of a re-energised and charismatically ordained church.

## Denominational Apostasy, and the Reunification of the Church

Whether one reads the history of the Remnant church in the early *Fulness* magazines, the prophetic history of the *Proclaim* journal, or the nine-part 'Church Adrift' series in *Restoration*, one will not find an account of Church history that accords with conventional scholarship. Neither is there anything to cheer the heart of anyone from an Orthodox or Catholic tradition. Many Protestants too will be unable to identify with the way in which the Church has been presented.

It might seem as if the writers are unaware of the Greek fathers, and have certainly not read their Kelly.[13] Perhaps they do not know that Calvin and Charles Wesley were saturated in the theology and spirituality of the Chalcedonian thinkers? Perhaps too, the writers do not really know their Catholic history? Whether they do or do not, it is a mistake to understand the interpretation of Church history by Restorationists as an intellectualist exercise.[14] They are concerned with discerning the survival and gradual restoration of the true Church—amidst the apostasy of denominational history.

Looking at Table 1, it can be seen that Restorationists believe that the Church took a nose dive at the end of the New Testament canon. After a brief attempt at rousing itself under the Montanists, it hits rock bottom by AD 600, and stays there until the Reformation. The failure of the early church is seen primarily as an abandonment of the sacred and inviolable rules of Scripture for the maintenance of normal (i.e. charismatic) Church life. In a short time after the death of the apostles, extra-biblical doctrines concerning the nature and power of the Church began to circulate. Beliefs in ritualistic and sacramentalist theologies (seen by Restorationists as magic or superstition) and ecclesiastical systems of episcopacy began to distort the Gospel. In short, the Church fell into error, and the power of the Holy Spirit was withdrawn.

Restorationists see the Reformation as recovering the supremacy of Scripture over church traditions. They also see with the emergence of the Anabaptist movement, the recovery of believers' baptism (which they see as a New Testament practice). The recovery continues and accelerates with the outbreak of Puritanism, religious enthusiasm and the growth of Evangelicalism. A milestone in this recovery is seen to be the Methodist movement. It is particularly interesting that the Salvation Army and Brethrenism are highlighted as stepping stones to Restorationism.

The twentieth century is primarily seen as the century of the recovery of the gifts of the Holy Spirit, and latterly the restoration of apostolic ministries. Watchman Nee is cited by all Restorationists as a genuine apostle and precursor of both the House Church Movement, and Restoration *per se*. (Watchman Nee was no Pentecostalist: he has also been claimed as a mentor by the Exclusive Brethren!) Billy Graham is praised too for his mass evangelistic efforts.

Throughout this Restorationist view of Church history, a consistent theme is the apostasy of the historic denominations and the failure to adhere to New Testament principles. Although the Reformation is hailed as the beginning of the recovery, Protestanism is indicted for failing to return to a unified Church. Protestant denominations are viewed as churches perpetuating their own distinctive doctrines and failing to repent of the sin of divisiveness.

It is significant that the religious movements most admired in the past are the movements of enthusiasm. David Matthew firmly places himself in that tradition: 'Personally, I like to think that, had I lived in a bygone era, I would have been an enthusiastic Montanist, Clunyite, Reformer, Anabaptist, Wesleyan or Pentecostal.'[15] Many members from R1 and R2 have told me of their 'radical roots', and they all see these roots in the sort of movements described by David Matthew.

John Noble pointed out to me[16] that the emergence of new denominations that encapsulated new truths (or rather recovered old ones) was a sin on the one hand because these movements gradually established new and divisive church structures; on the other hand these churches—in bits and pieces—brought back the forgotten truths of the Gospel. God the Holy Spirit, in other words, revealed Himself to men in small portions according to the faith of believers. Now that the truth is out for all to see, however—now that the full power of the Holy Spirit has been returned to the Church—denominations are not only no longer necessary, but they are a hindrance to the work of God. The new wine of the Spirit cannot be contained in the old denominational

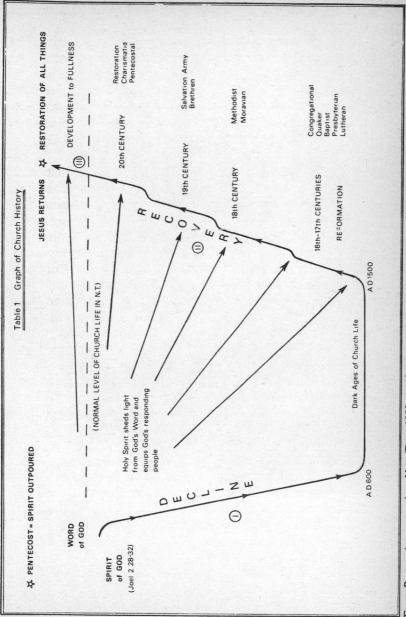

Table 1   Graph of Church History

☆ PENTECOST = SPIRIT OUTPOURED

WORD of GOD

SPIRIT of GOD (Joel 2 28-32)

JESUS RETURNS ☆   ☆ RESTORATION OF ALL THINGS

DEVELOPMENT to FULLNESS

(NORMAL LEVEL OF CHURCH LIFE IN N.T.)

Holy Spirit sheds light from God's Word and equips God's responding people

20th CENTURY

Restoration
Charismatic
Pentecostal

19th CENTURY

Salvation Army
Brethren

RECOVERY

Ⓘ

18th CENTURY

Methodist
Moravian

16th-17th CENTURIES

RE-ORMATION

Congregational
Quaker
Baptist
Presbyterian
Lutheran

A D 1500

Dark Ages of Church Life

A D 600

DECLINE

Ⓘ

From *Restoration* magazine, Nov./Dec. 1983, p. 40.

structures. New flexible and biblically principled structures need to emerge to contain and mature the new wine.

The attack upon denominations really has a twofold movement. Firstly, it is insisted, denominations have perverted the teachings of the New Testament. Secondly, it is pointed out, many churches are made up of people who are not Christian at all. Infant baptism is seen not only as pernicious because it is seen to be unbiblical, but because it allows people to be in denominations and participate in Communion without having to be regenerate. The Church, as Restorationists understand it, is not a social structure surrounding declared articles of faith: it is the 'Body of Christ', and only those who are born-again belong to that Body.

Not only the historic denominations are seen to be in error, all denominations fall short of being what was in 'God's heart from the beginning': a people of God linked organically to the new Adam, Jesus Christ. God wants only the Church. He does not want denominational expressions of it.

Brethren readers will find much of this familiar territory. In many ways the Restorationist thesis is an updated and Pentecostal version of E. H. Broadbent's *The Pilgrim Church*.[17] In this work, Broadbent attempts to trace the faithful witnesses down the centuries; witnesses who have carried aloft the torch of the Gospel. The general image of the Church is the spluttering candle kept alight amidst the blackness and perfidiousness of denominational Christianity. For Broadbent, the Brethren movement—in the words of another Brethren classic—is the 'great recovery'.[18] Restoration sees the torch taken from the Brethren by the Pentecostal movement. By now the spluttering light has become as bright as the Olympic flame. With the coming of Restoration, the flame ignites to become the white heat of pure Pentecostal power.

That Restorationist churches (not only R1 and R2, but international counterparts in the 'shepherding movement') are seen as the foci of God's final chapter in the history of His people—and thus the whole world—can be seen in the list of recovered truths of the twentieth century as declared in *Restoration* magazine.

(1) The baptism in the Holy Spirit. (2) The return of the gifts of the Spirit for both corporate and individual life. (3) A belief in a worldwide end-time revival. (4) The restoration of apostolic and prophetic ministries as a major means of bringing about the unity of the Church. (5) The establishment of apostolic teams to supplement and complement the work of apostles. (6) The growth of discipling practices, under godly leaders, in the local churches. (7) A recognition that denominations are not in God's plan, and are ultimately unrenewable. (8) New freedom in worship and praise.[19]

'A plague on all your houses' declare the true radicals of Restoration, who wish to shake off the dust of conventional Christianity from their feet. Their desire is to replace denominations by the Church. Their radicality springs from their zealous concern with truth and purity. If, for example, David Matthew's 'Church Adrift' series sounds strident, it is because it is written with the deliberate aim of shaking people out of their complacency. The series is not so much an historical overview of the Church as a prophetic denunciation of heresy, betrayal, and 'luke-warmness' in the Church. Burning conviction is a phrase that aptly characterises both David Matthew and Arthur Wallis.

Restorationists declare themselves to be not a new denomination, but the alternative to denominationalism. They wish to be simply the Church. The Church is understood as operating on two levels, or possessing two modes. The universal Church is simply all those who are born again who together make up the Body of Christ. The second mode is the operative one: it is the local church. The local church is the place where people who are related to each other organically by their shared membership in the Body, share a common life according to the precepts of the New Testament. Locality ranges from the 'house cell', local community church, to a celebration event such as the Dales Bible Week.

Restorationists believe that it is possible to be a member of the Body of Christ (as are all people who have experienced the New Birth) but not be moving in the vanguard of

God's people. Kingdom people do not constitute all those who are 'saved', but are God's shock troops. For them the only Church worth belonging to is the Church militant. They often like to see themselves as a battleship ready for war; denominations are viewed as luxury cruisers. Restorationists are convinced that Christians who are willing to listen to 'what God is saying to the Church today', will recognise that He desires all men and women not to be passengers in the Church, but enlisted warriors.

To revert to kingdom language: members of the Church are not destined to be slaves in the kingdom of God, but rulers. To rule, however, is also to learn to obey. Personal sin and denominational sin are the result of rebellion. Rebellion has no place in the ordered life of the kingdom, or the king's army. To be kingdom people is to learn to follow only God and His anointed leaders. A truly united Church can only exist on the voluntary principle of covenanted relationships under God. To become a Christian of the kingdom, therefore, means voluntarily abandoning individualism and self-interest, and freely choosing to become subjects of King Jesus and accountable to His chosen apostles and leaders.

The way forward to Church unity, Restorationists are convinced, is through the re-establishment of charismatically ordained apostles. Only such an anointed leadership can ensure that Restoration will unite the Church. As far as R1 and R2 are concerned, denominationalism has had its day.

## Notes

1   George Tarleton thinks that most leaders in R2 tend towards Conservatism politically. However, I met a number of persons at Festival 84 who were Labour, Liberal, and SDP supporters. Bryn Jones expressed admiration to me for Arthur Scargill's fight to save miners' jobs and communities. (Bryn's father was a leading member of the Welsh Communist party.)

2   Kingsway, 1981.

3 Ibid., pp. 15–16.

4 It is not so much because it offends my Eastern Orthodox sensibilities, but more a question of scholarship. For example, Arthur Wallis's attempt to bring alive the New Testament church in *The Radical Christian* looks, to me, not how I understand (imperfectly) the New Testament church to be, but like the modern Restoration movement read back into the canons of Scripture. Cf. Wallis's version of the New Testament church with Professor James Dunn's 'Models of Christian Community in the New Testament' in *Strange Gifts? A Guide to Charismatic Renewal*, edited by D. Martin and P. Mullen (Blackwell, 1984).

5 See Samuel S. Hill, 'NRPR: The New Religious Political Right In America', in *Of Gods And Men*, ed. E. Barker.

6 The head of the BBC radio religious broadcasting, David Winter, has recently spearheaded this distinction. See his *But This I Can Believe* (Hodder and Stoughton, 1980).

7 Wallis and E. Vincent, op. cit.

8 Ironically, one of the better ones comes from an old friend of Ern Baxter. See Larry Christenson, *What About Baptism?* (Minneapolis, Bethany Fellowship, 1973).

9 As they are often purportedly based on scholarship, then they can be called 'historicist'. See C. S. Lewis's scathing criticisms on 'Historicism' in *Fern Seed and Elephants*, edited by Walter Hooper (Fontana, 1975).

10 The Book of Daniel 2:44 (AV).

11 In conversation with me on 11 September 1984.

12 Song 63, *All Hail King Jesus* (Harvestime Press, 1982).

13 J. N. D. Kelly: *Early Christian Doctrines*, Adam & Charles Black, 1977.

14 David Matthew has written a very good article against purely intellectualist approaches. I am sure he feels it should have been

read more carefully by me! See 'It's All In The Mind', *Restoration* (May/June 1983).

15 'Church Adrift' series, Part 8, *Restoration* (March/April 1984).

16 Interview on 10 March 1984.

17 Pickering and Inglis, 1931.

18 D. J. Beattie, *Brethren: The Story Of A Great Recovery* (John Ritchie Ltd., 1939).

19 'Church Adrift' series, Part 6 (*Restoration*, Nov./Dec. 1983), p. 40.

## RECOMMENDED READING

Arthur Wallis, *The Radical Christian* (Kingsway, 1981).

E. H. Broadbent, *The Pilgrim Church* (Pickering and Inglis, 1931).

D. Matthew, 'The lessons of Church History', Part 8, *Restoration* (March/April 1984).

D. Matthew, *Church Adrift, Where in the World are we Going?*, Marshall Pickering, 1985.

# 7

# THE RADICAL PRINCIPLES OF RESTORATION (Part Two)

## Restorationist Ecclesiology: the Kingdom as a Theocracy

Ecclesiology is often seen as a minor adjunct of theology. The doctrine of church order, however, not only has major implications for the status of ecclesiastical structures; it has been a major cause of schism in Christendom. The understanding of papal authority, for example, and its relationship to the inspirational and governing power of the Holy Spirit, is, perhaps, the primary conflict between the Catholic West and the Eastern Orthodox churches. Within Protestantism, episcopal, congregational, and presbyterian structures have developed as a result of fundamental differences in ecclesiology.

Restorationists, having declared that denominations are not in the plan of God, and having insisted that the Church is now entering its last phase when it will be 'as it was in the beginning', have attempted to reintroduce what they believe was the apostolic structure of the New Testament. Their system could be described as a charismatic episcopacy. Leadership does bear some similarity to bishops and priests in the way in which Restoration elders relate to apostles. There is, however, no hint of apostolic succession: apostles are ordained, or anointed, solely by God. For this reason, I think Restorationist leadership can better be described as a theocratic apostolate.

The decision to reintroduce apostles was not an intellectualist one. As we have seen in Part 1, apostleship emerged in the early 1970s when leaders recognised that God had anointed and sanctified what was already a *de facto* apostleship. However, the establishment of apostles and prophets by Restorationists has not been purely inspirational and mystical. Because Restorationists are Bible people and because scholarship is not despised when seen to be God-inspired, they have presented their case as an apologia.

Restorationists recognise, along with most Church scholars, that the issue of religious orders is extremely complicated. It is difficult to know, for example, from the New Testament texts alone how exactly the orders of the diaconate and the presbytery (or elders) worked in conjunction with apostles. Many scholars think that the Early Church during or soon after the Scriptural canon developed an episcopal system where bishops became the overseers of districts or dioceses. Bishops came to be linked with apostleship (in the sense of delegated authority from original Apostles; St. Paul appointing Timothy, for example). Elders became identified with priesthood. Religious orders also included deacons, deaconesses, and readers. The relationship between these orders, and the exact status of the presbyterate as a second order of clergy—as distinct from a third order of laity (deacons/readers)—still taxes and fascinates Church historians. It would seem from the Scriptural canon and the Early Church records that there was a fluidity of leadership and a certain interchangeability of roles. (Women, however, whilst being in the deaconate, seem never to have been members of the presbyterate.)

Restorationists show no interest in the first few centuries of Church history. They insist that the pattern for Church order can be, and must be, discerned from Scripture alone. For them, the foundational Scriptures for Church order are to be found in the epistle to the Ephesians, chapter 4, verses 8 to 12. The key verses, as we have noticed twice already, are 11 and 12:

And these were his gifts: some to be apostles, some prophets, some evangelists, some pastors and teachers, to equip God's people for work in his service, to the building up of the body of Christ. (NEB)

Sometimes referred to as the 'fourfold ministries', Restorationists are convinced that this is the only correct New Testament pattern for Church leadership. Strictly speaking, they do not like the idea of a priestly order because they are not happy to make too much of the distinction between clergy and laity. They prefer the idea of function in the Body of Christ—stressing the priesthood of all believers. But whilst they do not use priestly terminology, they do believe firmly in authority in a constituted hierarchy. The ministries in Ephesians 4, for example, are understood as being under the apostle. The apostle is God's delegate, or anointed one.

Restorationists are well aware that not only is it controversial to claim that this pattern for the Church has been restored, but also that apostleship in the New Testament itself had different meanings. Firstly, and supremely, they claim, Christ is the first apostle: He is unique; the sent one of God. The writer to the Hebrews declares that Christ is 'The Apostle and High Priest of our confession' (Hebrews 3:1). Secondly, they identify the twelve disciples of Jesus as the unique band of Apostles who witness to the life, death, and resurrection of the Lord. These Apostles (who, of course, do not include Judas Iscariot but do include his replacement, Matthias) are identified as the 'twelve apostles of the Lamb' (Revelation 21:14). Because of their unique relationship with the Lord Jesus, these men will be the foundation stones of the New Jerusalem interlocked with the cornerstone who is Christ.

Restorationists claim that Ephesians 4 refers to neither of these usages: there is a third group of apostles who are God's appointed gifts to His Church. First amongst these was Paul. James, the brother of Jesus, Barnabas, and Timothy, are all cited as examples of this group. These men are seen as apostles that were appointed after Pentecost as charismatic delegates from the ascended Christ. The twelve were commissioned in Christ's earthly lifetime, but the third group of apostles are Pentecostal appointments. The gifts of the Spirit as outlined in 1 Corinthians 12 are not the only charismata therefore. The offices of apostles, prophets, evangelists, pastors, and teachers are themselves 'gifts of the ascended Christ'.[1]

Having identified the apostles of Ephesians 4 as a distinct group from the twelve, and Christ Himself, Restorationists then ask, what is an apostle's function in the Church? The answer they give, in the words of St. Paul is that he is a 'skilled master builder' (1 Corinthians 3:10, NEB). By this they mean that the apostle is one who lays the foundations of a church—a local community—and is ultimately responsible for ensuring that the stones of the 'building' are put together in the correct manner according to the will of the divine architect (God). This foundational and overseeing ministry and the extended metaphor of the building clearly lends itself well to the image of the kingdom. Apostles are master builders of the kingdom.

God uses multiple charismatic ministries, however. Evangelists are needed to challenge people with the gospel. Apostles ensure that the kingdom is being properly constructed. Teachers are needed to teach and impart the correct understanding of kingdom principles. Pastors, or elders, are men who will care for, or shepherd, the flock in each locality. Prophets bring the inspired word to the whole Church. Citing 1 Corinthians 12:28, Restorationists point out that within the kingdom, prophets are to be second only to apostles (close as they are to the 'heart and will of God'). It is difficult to find an adequate analogy to express this relationship. Shall we say that the apostle is the chief executive, and the prophet the advertising 'whiz kid'?

I feel a more appropriate image would be to see the apostle as king, and the prophet as court jester or 'holy fool'. From my brief conversation with David Mansell, who is a prophet in R1, I think he would prefer the more intellectual notion of adviser/wise-man to the king.

Restorationists point out that the New Testament clearly reveals apostles as men who missioned, travelled, and founded new churches. Their responsibility in the Church, therefore, was trans-local. Elders were men, who worked at the local level and were accountable to the wider responsibility of the apostles. In practice, New Testament apostles sometimes acted as prophets and teachers in addition to their primary function as overseers. Restorationists also feel that apostles were surrounded by a team of helpers.

This is a more recent interpretation by Restorationists who in the mid-1970s tended to stress simply the function of an apostle, a prophet, teacher, etc., without much emphasis on a team of charismatic leadership. The restoration of apostolic teams, they believe, gives the lie to the criticism that apostolic leadership is a one-man ministry. This emphasis on the team is a major development in Restorationist thought. They understand the team as a flexible instrument: people will join and leave the team according to the needs that will arise. The team, as it were, takes on the mantle of the apostle and becomes endowed with his anointing. To be in Bryn Jones's or Tony Morton's team is to exercise apostolic authority in some sense.

Restorationists do not see teams as something they have invented. They claim that the epistles of Paul are full of examples of team membership:

'I have sent Tychicus to you . . .', Eph. 6:21–22.
'I hope to send Timothy to you . . .', Phil. 2:19.
'I thought it necessary to send Epaphroditus . . .', Phil. 2:25.
'I have sent Onesimus . . .', Col. 4:9.
'Make every effort to come to me . . .', 2 Tim. 4:9.
'Pick up Mark and bring him . . .', 2 Tim. 4:11.
'When I send Artemas . . .', Titus 3:12.[2]

A charismatically ordained Church is, then, for Restorationists a Church established and run according not only to the teachings of the apostles of the New Testament, but also governed by present-day apostles and their related ministries. The leaders of the New Testament were men who were anointed and sent by God. Qualification for leadership, today as then, is neither intellect nor training, but Christian character and charisma (in the Pentecostal sense). God does not despise learning, as evidenced by His choosing Paul, but it was not a condition of his calling. To be leaders, men should be able to run their own households, and be full of the fruits of the Spirit. The man who exercises proper authority over his family is obviously fit, with God's anointing, to oversee churches (cf. 1 Thes. 2:8–11).

Apostles were not optional for the Early Church: they were the master builders of God's master plan for His kingdom. Nowhere, Restorationists proclaim, does Scripture ever suggest that apostles were meant to cease with the death of the twelve. On the contrary, all the internal biblical evidence points to apostolic structure as being the norm for Christian life. Part of the apostasy of the first-century Church was to abandon God's plan for successfully building His kingdom. Unbiblical ecclesiastical structures go hand-in-hand with extra-biblical doctrines of sacramentalism, infant baptism, and ritualism.

It is possible, Restorationists agree, to be a Christian in a church without apostles and prophets, but it is not possible for that church to become what God would have it to be. The master plan is that the kingdom shall grow and fill the whole earth. Only a kingdom built on kingdom principles, and run by God's appointed men can achieve such a goal. In the words of Robert Brow: 'If the true church of Jesus Christ is to grow faster than the population explosion, we will need to produce, recognise and use Pauline apostles.'[3]

Restorationists recognise that apostles do not fit into the spirit of the age. Modern man has become accustomed to consensus agreements and democratic methods as a means of reaching corporate decisions. Whilst they accept that such methods have their place, in politics for example, Restorationists do not see them having any place in God's kingdom. A kingdom run on divine principles, and ruled by God's delegates is by definition a theocracy.

God alone is sovereign. It is He who chooses apostles. Authority in the kingdom has its source in King Jesus, who until His return to reign victoriously over His restored kingdom, has delegated authority to apostles. It is precisely because denominations have abandoned apostles—the guardians of the gifts of the Spirit—that Christendom has been almost overcome by the Evil One. In the absence of Holy Ghost power, churches have been swayed by 'every wind of doctrine'. The rot can only be stopped by a 'structure of authority directly from the throne of God'.[4]

Jesus, declared Ern Baxter,[5] never set up a system of government or church order: 'he poured His life into twelve men.' In their turn, the Apostles did not initiate a set of rules for the Early Church: they established relationships within the Christian community based on mutual submission and a voluntary denial of selfhood for the sake of the brethren. In short, they made disciples too.

## Spiritual Authority and the Nature of Discipling

The idea that the spiritual authority of the apostles and elders can reach right down into the minutiæ of everyday life, affecting Christians' personal and social lives, may not seem to be necessarily entailed by an apostolic structure. In Restorationist thinking, however, what have become known as 'discipling doctrines', 'relatedness', or 'shepherding principles', are so directly bound up with apostleship doctrines that they do not distinguish between the two.

As an outsider, it took me quite a long time to realise this. To me the doctrines look quite separate. You can have a strong shepherding movement without having to have apostles. You can certainly have doctrines of apostles without any commitment to Restorationist submission teachings. In the other apostolic structures of recent times, such as the Catholic Apostolic Church and the Apostolic church, apostolic rule has never carried the comprehensive authority which can be found in Restorationism.

Terry Virgo thinks[6] that the restoration of apostles is the most important and distinctive feature of Restoration. With respect, I think that what makes Restoration more distinctive—and certainly more radical—is the way that the theocratic apostolate has gone beyond simply restoring apostolic structures to establishing a far more complex and interwoven system of relationships. The reason, I think, that most Restorationists do not divide apostleship from shepherding, is because historically apostleship was taught to them through the writings and personal exhortations of American leaders in the shepherding movement. That movement has taken doctrines of apostleship and theories of radical discipleship and blended them together into the form now dominant in all Restoration movements whether in England or other countries.

As these theories are analytically distinct, I have decided to deal with discipling doctrines separately. This is solely for the sake of clarity and exemplification. Clearly, Restorationists see these doctrines as one set of principles not two. Though they are not logically connected, they can, as we shall see, be understood as one coherent system.

The aim of discipleship is not to bring everybody into line, or impose ideology from the top onto those below. The aim is to make sure that everybody in the Restoration movement (including apostles) are open to correction and admonition within the context of loving relationships. 'Those whom the Lord loves he chastises' is extended or projected into the context of Christian personal relations.

However, the notion of admonition or chastisement is not to be understood as bondage, or authoritarian domination. Such methods, declares Restoration teaching, are the devilish counterfeits of the cults. The very idea of correction is possible precisely because it is in the nature of a Christian to be a disciple. A disciple is a learner: a follower of a master, or one spiritually more mature. Restorationists in R1 and R2 often say, 'one who is a little further along the path'. The true disciple desires to become like the teacher; ideally, like Christ Himself.

Restorationists believe that a Christian who is not prepared to be a disciple is no Christian at all. The word disciple is mentioned two hundred and sixty-nine times in the New Testament, Ernie Baxter told the Lakes Bible Week in 1975. He went on to say that the meaning of discipleship is made clear by the Lord Jesus Himself: 'If anyone comes to me and does not hate his father and mother, wife and children, brothers and sisters, even his own life, he cannot be a disciple of mine.' (Luke 14:26, NEB) And again: 'If anyone wishes to be a follower of mine, he must leave self behind; he must take up his cross and come with me.' (Matthew 16:24, NEB)

To be a disciple, then, from the ultimate authority of Christ's own lips, is to love God above all else. This is the radical heart of the gospel for every believer. Jesus demands nothing less than that a follower becomes like Him not only in His glory but in His suffering and sacrifice. 'Take up the cross.' This radical sense of following, this discipleship, is designed 'not to manipulate people but to mature them spiritually'.[7] To be under anointed and God-constituted authority is to be a learner. Only learners, those in obedience, can reach the sort of spiritual maturity where they can cease drinking the milk fit only for babes, and partake of the strong meat of adulthood: become leaders of the kingdom.

In the United States, discipling doctrines have found their way into some lay Catholic communities. These covenanted and charismatic communities have recognised, more readily than many Protestants, how close discipling is to their own tradition. This is so, because in many ways such a radical discipleship is not usually associated with the lives and homes of ordinary people: it is usually seen as belonging to monasticism. Whether one thinks of the harsh asceticism of St. Anthony of Egypt, or the spiritual exercises of the hermits and desert fathers, or the kenoticism of the early Franciscans, one thinks of all these people as under a rule of obedience. Reading the *Philokalia*,[8] for example, one can see that it is permeated with practices and spiritual exercises designed to break the 'spirit of rebellion', foster total obedience—often through a spiritual master—and break the iron hold of egoism.

Restoration writers do not invoke such practices. (One leader in R2 felt that leaders in R1 were overweight, and could do with a dose of asceticism!) They do not like the distinction between the committed dedication of certain clergy and monks, and the lives of ordinary Christians. All believers, they feel, should be saints. In this respect, Restorationists fit, far more closely, the Puritanism of early Calvinism than the asceticism of Catholicism. To a certain extent, it could be argued, enthusiasm and Evangelicalism—from the eighteenth century onwards—did not always show the unswerving attachment to righteousness that we find in so many of the seventeenth-century Puritans. The corporate sense of covenant with God certainly disappeared. I think it not stretching it too far to see Restorationists as modern-day Pentecostal Puritans.

The belief in a corporate covenant between God and His people is a dominant theme in discipleship doctrine. Gerald Coates rarely uses the terms 'discipling' or 'shepherding', but often refers to the work in R2 as one of 'covenanted relationships'. A disciple is one who shares a common life with others of like mind and heart. This community of committed Christians, who are all disciples 'under authority', is expressed by the sharing of the bread and wine of the Lord's Table. Covenant implies a solemn oath, and discipleship is not to be entered into lightly. When a new member of Restoration submits himself to one who has authority over him, this submission is to Christ Himself.[9]

We have already seen, in looking at the theocratic apostolate, that apostolic authority and its concomitant ministries are modes of authority established by God's anointing. This being so, discipleship doctrine sees such authority as sacrosanct; only the God who has raised up this authority can bring it down. Disciples should submit to those set over them. This has echoes of similar arguments in favour of the divine right of kings. Many Restorationists have tried to demonstrate the anointing of apostolic and eldership appointments as a parallel to the anointing of King David in the Old Testament. We have already encountered this comparison between apostles and David, in our earlier narrative section. Suffice it to say here, that David is the key figure in Restoration hermeneutics and typology. His life is followed in minute detail and used as a model for apostolic leadership.[10]

Some Restorationists insist that delegated authority should be obeyed because it is God's authority, not because the delegate is always right. The Basingstoke communities, in particular, stress this, but so too do most leaders in R1. We have already seen, in Maurice Smith's discussion with Bob

Mumford,[11] that it was thought that a woman should submit herself to her husband because a husband is God's delegate for the wife and family, regardless of whether he acts rightly and fairly or not.

In discipling doctrine generally, God's delegated authority goes further than the supernatural authority of apostles. Husbands are seen as the head of the family, including his wife. Parents are God's delegates over children. Political authorities too are seen as God's delegates. The State, in short, should be obeyed. In conversation with Restorationists, it is clear that the distinction between Caesar and God applies to the State. There is no question, therefore, of having to submit to a Hitler without a murmur. It is clear, however, that political and social action do not figure highly on a Restorationist list of moral imperatives.

A great deal of Restorationist understanding of authority, especially spiritual authority, comes from Watchman Nee. Whilst Nee could not be described as a Restorationist or even a Pentecostalist, his influence upon both the American and English discipling movement is considerable. Nee was a controversial figure in Chinese religious life between the two World Wars. Greatly influenced by Western missionaries, Nee nevertheless pioneered a house church movement throughout China. Violently opposed to Communism, even today the movement that he founded, the 'Little Flock' is still *persona non grata* with the authorities.

Nee's style in translation is turgid, and not altogether clear. Most Restorationists seem well versed in his book *Spiritual Authority*,[12] but seem unaware of many of his other works. The fact that his theology is Docetic, and his spirituality appears gnostic—with his unusual belief that spiritual regeneration results in the physical death of Christians—seems to be unknown amongst people in R1 and R2. Neither do many of them seem to know that his spirituality is far closer to Darbyism (Exclusive Brethrenism) than their own. It is ironic, that one of the seminal thinkers of early Restorationism, David Lillie, has been the one to point out that the 'Little Flock' developed into an authoritarian denomination after the death of Nee.[13]

There is no denying, however, that Watchman Nee is one of the most interesting and remarkable religious figures of the twentieth century. His life is shrouded in mystery and intrigue, and we still await a major biography on his life and teachings. *Spiritual Authority* is replete with 'hard sayings'. On the question of whether people should trust and follow wrong authority, Nee says:

> . . . If God dares to entrust His authority to men, then we can dare to obey. Whether the one in authority is right or wrong does not concern us since he has to be responsible directly to God. The obedient needs only to obey; the Lord will not hold us responsible for any mistaken obedience, rather will He hold the delegated authority responsible for his erroneous act. Insubordination, however, is rebellion, and for this the one under authority must answer to God.[14]

In a more telling aphorism he remarks; 'All who are insubordinate to God's indirect authorities are not in subjection to God's direct authority.'[15]

Two themes develop out of Nee's conception of authority which are fundamental to Restorationist discipleship doctrine. Firstly, as in the above quotations, we see that rebellion against God's delegates is rebellion against God Himself. Rebellion is understood by Nee, and Restorationists, to be the essence of sin. Secondly, Nee as a counterbalance to the power of God's delegates, insists that (at least in the case of Christian leaders) spiritual authority carries with it not only enormous responsibilities but dire consequences if mistakes are made. I think it important that we examine each doctrine in turn.

The 'essence of salvation is subjection', said Ernie Baxter at the Lakes Bible Week in 1975. By this he meant that without submitting to Jesus Christ, and without admonition and correction being accepted from God's delegates, true discipleship cannot be achieved. Pride and rebellion are masked behind the secular virtues of an independent and individualistic spirit. Rebellion is the hallmark of the world, but an anathema in the kingdom. The marks of that kingdom are harmony, love, and doing the will of God.

'Brokenness' is a term used frequently in Evangelical circles. It means allowing God to take over your life after He has broken down your wilfulness and egoism. There is a Russian Orthodox saying that says: 'God will bring you to Himself by either breaking your heart, or every bone in your body.' Whilst this is, hopefully, not to be taken too literally, it captures the essence of being broken in a spiritual sense; for it means that God will eventually bring his disciples to a place where there is no more rebellion or resistance to the Divine Love. Brokenness is that moment in spiritual experience that allows the next step of total surrender to God.

Restorationists see that brokenness is hard for the average Christian to accept because he has been weaned on doctrines of self-sufficiency and such notions as 'standing on your own two feet' and 'being your own man'. Furthermore, and fundamentally more problematic, the childish petulance that refuses to accept parental and school authority becomes the adult wilfulness of self-reliance. Discipleship, therefore, stresses the need to break rebellion in the child so that character can be built. Breaking down bad habits, unsocial traits, sinful ways and a rebellious heart is a necessary prerequisite for building up characters to be fitted into the kingdom of God.

To discipline children into the precepts and rules of God's kingdom is not seen as enough by Restorationists. Many of the Christians who join a Restorationist church are seen as having practised rebellion all their lives. Restoration principles have to be imparted through teaching. Just as a Protestant receives instruction before embracing Catholicism, so converts to God's restored kingdom must undertake a commitment course. As Eileen Vincent puts it:

It is not assumed that those coming into the churches automatically know how to bring up their children or how to have successful marriages. These practical topics are carefully taught and, through close discipling, the new understanding is woven into the fabric of a new style of living.[16]

It is at this juncture that the other side of the discipling coin needs to be looked at in order to avoid a distorted picture. As Nee made clear, spiritual authority carries with it a fearful responsibility. He is very careful to insist that the husband acts towards his wife with love and respect; that parents treat their children with justice; and spiritual leaders discern truly the will of God. Apostles and elders are considered in Restoration circles—at least in principle—to be servants of the people, not dictators over them. Much has been given them by God, and much will be asked of them in return.

Nee, even more so than present Restorationists, pays great attention to the qualities necessary to enter leadership. Many of these qualities are the spiritual fruits outlined in Galatians 5:22, 'Love, joy, peace, patience, kindness, goodness, fidelity, gentleness, and self-control' (NEB). Nee lays particular emphasis on self-control. Nee and Restorationists have both agreed that no man may set himself up and say: 'I am your leader: submit to me.' Spiritual authority has to be recognised.

Both R1 and R2 are very clear on this point. Authority has to be accepted voluntarily by church members, otherwise it has no validity nor power. Both groups also agree, following Nee and the Fort Lauderdale Five, that all leaders must themselves be under authority. Even apostles must be judged by their peers. This is, of course, the same in principle as the collegiality of bishops. It was the claim by the Latin West that the Bishop of Rome held a unique position amongst the ancient sees—greater even than *primus inter pares*—that broke up the order and unity of the ancient Church.

Restoration apostles are under an authority greater than collegial correction. The Scriptures are to remain the ultimate authority in matters of doctrine. All prophecies, statements of doctrines by apostles, and discipling instructions by elders, are to be submitted to Scripture for authentication.

David Tomlinson adds another safeguard, which I have not found in Nee, Trudinger, or Prince's seminal document on discipleship. He states: 'No-one has such authority that he cannot be questioned or challenged. Even children should be allowed the privilege of dialoguing about an issue provided they do it in a right attitude. It is important that those being discipled feel that they will be seriously heard in their misgivings, and not merely swept aside. True men of God are aware that God does speak "through the mouths of babes and sucklings".[17] 'And little old ladies', I know Gerald Coates would want me to add.

The overall context within which discipling operates, so Restorationists feel needs to be constantly stressed, is loving relationships. To be shepherded, or 'covered'[18] cannot be done through a cold unfeeling covenant. Covenanted relationships are not legal contracts: they are personal commitments.

Restorationists do not find the image of hierarchical relationships helpful. They feel that a shepherd is paternal. A father in God is a quite different creature from an executive, or a general, or even a scout master. Military men give orders, but apostles, prophets, and elders, bring conviction. Disciples cannot be corrected from above; they can only be corrected from within.

One of the ways in which disciples can express their love and support for the leadership, is to support them financially. Tithing has a long and controversial history in Pentecostalism, and as a doctrine it does not belong to discipling *per se*. But just as Restorationists do not divide apostleship from shepherding (as I have done for the sake of explication) neither do they see tithing as a separate issue from good discipleship. Again, this may well be because historically tithing was introduced into Restorationism as part of the discipling package received from the Fort Lauderdale Five. I would not want to insist on this, however: tithing was around in the House Church Movement long before Ern Baxter arrived at Capel Bible Week.

Under the Judaic law, Derek Prince points out, tithing was the means for supporting the priestly orders.[19] Restorationists assume that tithing was a practice in the New Testament. Certainly it was the case that St. Paul taught that shepherds were entitled to material support from their flocks

(1 Corinthians 9:7). Prince takes this to mean financial support. (He does not mention that Paul claimed the right, but refused to take it!)

Tithing, then, is the means for supporting full-time ministries and part-time leaders. Tithing should be given to leaders to administer as they see fit. But tithes in themselves will not be enough to meet the full needs of the flock. Money for new buildings, new methods of communication, computers for God's businesses, musical instruments for His praise, etc., will need to come from special offerings. Tithing is a demonstration of commitment to kingdom leadership. Special offerings, and the profits from business ventures, are proof of commitment to the kingdom as a whole.

Prince puts up a case for ruling elders to receive 'double honour'. 'Let the elders that rule well be counted worthy of double honour, especially they who labour in the word and doctrine. For the scripture saith, Thou shalt not muzzle the ox that treadeth out the corn. And, The labourer is worthy of his reward.' (1 Timothy 5:17–18, AV) These texts have a long and notorious history in the American Bible belt. They have been taken to mean that leaders have the right to considerably more money than their followers.

On the whole, however, this interpretation is not favoured in England (where it has no history). If it exists in print from within either R1 or R2, I have not seen it. I believe that a more typical understanding of financial support for leadership is that they should be properly supported financially; kept comfortable, but not made wealthy. Restorationism does not preach a gospel of poverty,[20] but it has not yet started preaching a gospel of personal prosperity.[21] (Kenneth Copeland in North America would be a contemporary example of someone who teaches what is—in fact—an old Pentecostal chestnut.)

## Kingdom People on the Move

The problem with looking at doctrines analytically, is that they take on a static and unchanging quality. In reality, Restorationist principles—whilst remaining *basically* the same as I have outlined them above—are constantly undergoing minor changes and modifications. Restorationists also differ a great deal over details despite holding a common core of distinctive doctrines. John Noble has been particularly anxious to keep moving on, making adjustments, checking Scripture, and if necessary being prepared to bring in sweeping changes in the future. Restorationism is, after all, supremely a movement of the Spirit. As such it cannot be nailed down too firmly to a fixed position.

In my view, the eschatological vision and the distinctive principles of kingdom theocracy and covenanted relationships have transformed what might have been a fairly typical (though middle-class) form of Pentecostalism into a movement that claims a more radical cutting edge.

If, however, I have given the impression that Restoration in being so serious and Puritanical is glum and boring, then I had better correct that impression by highlighting another principle of the kingdom: folk (to us a favourite Restorationist term) are expected to have a good time. It is not only kingdom doctrines that show some signs of movement. Kingdom people spend a good deal of their time jumping, dancing, and leaping. What is known as 'body worship', or free expression in worship is seen as a sign of the kingdom. David, that great Restorationist archetype, 'danced before the Lord'. It is expected that the Holy Spirit will effect the body and emotions too, not only the mind and will.

I think that in R1, the style of worship is seen not as cultural, or optional, but as a fruit of the Spirit. As God is working to restore His ministries of apostles, so too He is restoring true praise and worship. Many people in R2 feel the same way, but a number of leaders would not want to make Restorationist worshipping-style into a cardinal Restorationist principle. It is a cherished principle, however, both in R1 and R2, that God's people are a worshipping people. There is a great deal of emphasis on celebration and adoration. The Church itself is seen to operate on three local levels: the house cell, the local church, and the coming together of churches for celebration (Dales, and Festival, for example).

The moving, feet-tapping people, are caught up in the eschatological vision with which we started. Restoration is seen as essentially a movement of the people of God. It has no headquarters, and no earthly head. King Jesus is the lord of the kingdom, and He has delegated His authority to the apostles, prophets, evangelists, teachers, and elders. When such anointed authority is established, and covenanted relationships adopted, the New Testament order of the kingdom can begin. But this new wine cannot be contained in the old wine skins (denominations): it demands new and flexible structures founded on old and inviolable New Testament principles.

Each local church that becomes established on kingdom lines is a microcosm of the whole Church. If it is established aright, and the foundations are truly laid, the building will be both the place of, and witness to, God's alternative society. Apostles with their translocal responsibilities will recognise other apostles when they arise under God's anointing. In the future, what started off as isolated and unconnected churches will become a mass movement. Just as the house cells and front-room churches sprung up overnight, so shall that mycelial structure be repeated on a larger scale.

Within the great cities of the world, large communities will be set up as an offence to Babylon and an apostate church. Because of sound Christian principles in business, and stewardship, Restorationist enterprises will flourish. Modern communications, such as video, cable, and satellite television, will beam God's end-time message around the world. (This is a much greater theme in R1 than R2.)

As a dying and decaying world sees the health, vigour, and security of the kingdom, people will flock to the Restoration standard in increasing numbers. The kingdom will not be a sanctuary: it will be a mighty fortress. The image of Nehemiah restoring the broken walls of Jerusalem towers over Restoration thinking. Jerusalem the city is itself a biblical image of kingdom. Everywhere the little microcosms of the kingdom, and the larger communities, businesses, and enterprises, will grow up together, become more closely knit (jointed together is another favourite image), until the kingdom reaches its full and perfect structure. The microcosms become the macrocosm—the mountain fills the earth—and the King returns to lead His powerful and holy army against the final battle with the Evil One.

That is what kingdom people are moving towards, insists the Restorationist vision. God's disciples are to be essentially pioneers not settlers. Denominations breed rigidity into Christians: they can no longer move on. Anointed leaders, committed and 'covered' relationships, and flexible church structures all denote a mission people; not wandering aimlessly like the children of the Old Covenant through the desert, but towards the last battle of the end-time.

> The church of God is moving,
> The church of God is moving.

People on the move are not restless because they are people with a mission; they are in harmony with each other and under the clear direction of the King. Restorationists want to move on with the whole of God's people. They believe that they are in the vanguard of God's purpose for this (the final) generation. In that sense, paradoxically, they are a people set apart calling Christians to themselves. They fervently believe that as their numbers swell, and the growing ranks show that they have the discipline and formation to qualify for God's army, denominational Christians will desert their demoralised barracks and join the crusade.

Restorationists want to teach Christians and new believers their principles. But most of all they want them to catch their vision. 'Christians unite!' sounds the battle cry. 'We have nothing to lose but our institutions!'

## Notes

1   These are the words of Paul, but their meaning is expanded and put into apostolic context by Arthur Wallis in 'Apostles Today? Why Not!', *Restoration* (Nov./Dec. 1981).

2   David Tomlinson, 'Some Burning Questions About Apostles', ibid.

3   'Voices', ibid.

4   Ern   Baxter at the Lakes Bible Week, 1975.

5   Ibid.

6   In interview, 23 November 1983.

7   Herbert Harrison, 'Voices', *Restoration*, Nov./Dec. 1981.

8   A collection of texts of the spiritual masters of the Orthodox Church. Volume one of the complete text is now available in English, translated and edited by G. E. H. Palmer, Philip Sherrard, and Kallistos Ware (Faber and Faber, 1979).

9   Derek Prince, *Discipleship, Shepherding, Commitment* (D. Prince, Pub., 1976), p. 19.

10   See, for example, Ron Trudinger's *Built To Last* (Kingsway Publications, 1982).

11   See Part 1, Chapter 4, *The American Connection*.

12   Christian Fellowship Publishers, 1972.

13   David Lillie, a key figure in the early days as we have seen, has pointed this out in *Beyond Charisma* (Paternoster Press, 1981), pp. 49–50. Lillie's book is both sensible and intelligent.

14   Op. cit., p. 71.

15   Ibid., p. 72.

16   Eileen Vincent, op. cit., p. 166.

17   David Tomlinson, 'Is Discipling Biblical?' *Restoration* (July/August 1980).

18   Meaning protecting, or watching over. The origin of this term is the concern Japheth demonstrated in covering Noah's nakedness (Genesis 9:20–27). David Tomlinson of R2 hates this term because he thinks it smacks of animal husbandry (emasculation of rams in the north of England, for example).

19   Op. cit., p. 23.

20   So Bryn Jones told me at Bradford.

21   Though I believe such doctrines are dangerously close to Bryn Jones's segment of R1.


## RECOMMENDED READING

D. Prince, *Discipleship, Shepherding, Commitment* (D. Prince Pub, 1976).

R. Trudinger, *Built To Last* (Kingsway, 1982).

A. Wallis, 'Apostles Today? Why Not!', *Restoration* (Nov./Dec. 1981).

D. Tomlinson, 'Is Discipling Biblical?', *Restoration* (July/August 1980).

T. Virgo, *Restoration in the Church*, Kingsway, 1985.

# 8

# THE STRUCTURE AND SHAPE OF KINGDOM LIFE

As early as 1974, Bryn Jones circulated a cyclostated letter, warning many of the house churches not to get carried away with thoughts of the Second Coming. The Church's job, he pointed out, is to build the kingdom until the king chooses to come. Since that time, whilst it remains true that Restorationists expect the coming of Christ to be imminent, their response to the return of Jesus is to establish—as quickly as possible—the kingdom as an alternative society to the secular world.

Putting kingdom principles into practice, however, has inevitably led to a certain amount of adaption of those principles: the obduracy of reality has a habit of cooling visionary fire. One of the major differences that now exists between R1 and R2, is that R2 is self-consciously coming to terms with its adaption, whilst R1 feels itself still to be on course and is not consciously aware that maybe things are not going according to the master plan.

Both R1 and R2 admit that they still have a long way to go. The Church, as they envisage it, has not grown in size and power to become a 'mountain' to fill Great Britain let alone the whole earth. What has happened is that Restorationism has become a significant religious movement in Britain in just over ten years with its own organisational shape, practices, successes, and failures.

To say that Restorationism has a clearly defined shape needs some clarification. Both R1 and R2 are still in the early stages of formation. There is a fluidity of organisational structure that has not yet hardened into a fixed mould. We should keep in mind the image of a kaleidoscope: peering through it presents us with a clear pattern and order. But with a twist of the scope the pattern dissolves and a new picture emerges. In short, I believe that Restoration's organisational structure can be understood, but the structure is volatile. What I can describe as the structure and order of 1985 will probably have changed in ten years' time. To predict what the new structures will be is as difficult as guessing what new shape will emerge from the movements of coloured glass in the kaleidoscope. (I shall later argue, however, that we can make some rational—though not infallible—predictions.)

## Ephesians 4 as an Organisational Model

Restorationism by adopting the ecclesiology of Ephesians 4, adopts with it an organisational pattern. To put it this way is not to present it as Restorationists would do themselves. They would say that to accept God's theocracy is to enter into a series of covenanted relationships with those leaders that God has ordained should rule in His Church. To talk of organisations or structures leads one, very soon they feel, to talk of denominations. R1 still rigorously denies that identification. If we are a denomination, they say, where is our headquarters? R2 also insists that they have no centrally ruling body. The Apostolic church, like the Restorationists, also bases its organisation on the ecclesiology of Ephesians 4, but clearly has a headquarters situated in Penegroes, South Wales. Restorationists see this as evidence of denominationalism.

To resist being labelled 'a denomination' is understandable because, as we have seen, Restoration is motivated by the desire to go beyond denominations. Denominations are not in God's plan: He wants Christians of this last generation to restore the kingdom. An essential, if not the essential, ingredient of this restoration is the re-establishment of apostolic ministries.

There are really two different questions here. Firstly, is

Restorationism a new denomination? And secondly, can the two groups that I have identified as R1 and R2 be said to have an organisational structure? Put this way, I do not believe that Restorationists would wish to (or be able to) deny that their work has a structure, but they would still resist the notion that they have become denominationalised. I do not think that we can fairly assess Restorationism as a denominational formation until we have explored the way in which—in practice—Restoration works. For the rest of this chapter, therefore, whilst I will be attempting to identify the structure and practices of Restorationism, I shall for the time being put the question of denominationalism on one side.

To recapitulate: the full list of ministries outlined in Ephesians, Chapter 4, are apostles, prophets, evangelists, pastors, and teachers. In practice, the foundation of the Restoration kingdom has primarily been laid by apostles working on a regional basis, and elders working on a local level. Since 1980, both R1 and R2 have built up apostolic teams.[1] These are groups of men, as we noted in Part One, who work with the apostle on a regional or translocal basis. It is by no means clear how the membership of teams coincides with the ministries of Ephesians 4.

## Apostles

Of all the various ministries that have been established, the apostolic ministry seems to me to be the most clearly defined. R1, for example, consists of groups of churches who are all accountable to a rubric of apostles who either founded them from scratch, or took over the senior 'covering' role when asked. Each apostle is responsible for a chain of churches. Whilst each chain is separate, they are linked together at the top by a mutual recognition of ministry amongst the apostles. The apostles, then, have separate areas of responsibility, agreed territorial boundaries, and considerable—though not total—autonomy. (Churches from the different chains sometimes meet together at such celebration events as Dales, Downs, and the Welsh Bible Week.)

Apostles are easily identified because of their role, and

because they are so few. In R1 (at the time of writing) the apostles are Bryn and Keri Jones who are based in Bradford (with some fifty to sixty churches under their direction);[2] Terry Virgo, who is based in Hove (and responsible for some forty churches or more); Tony Morton is a more recent apostle. He is based at Southampton (and has some seventeen to twenty churches under his direction). The number of apostles are by no means fixed and will vary according to need, as well as defections (remembering that David Tomlinson was once an apostle in R1).

There is talk that Tony Ling may be a future apostle. But apostles are not names conjured out of a hat; they have to prove themselves as *de facto* apostles before they become recognised formally as apostolic leaders. A number of people have asked me whether Keri Jones fits this model. One person thought that Keri was a sort of suffragen bishop to Bryn Jones. Others have seen Keri's position as nepotism: climbing to power on the back of Bryn. This, I think, is unfair. Keri Jones may not, so far, have had the same impact as his brother, but he did come to his position by right. He pioneered a number of churches in his native South Wales. I think it not unfair to say that his authority and work seem to be clearly linked to Bryn's authority.

In this respect, Bryn and Keri Jones are merely carrying on a long tradition in Welsh Pentecostalism where brothers have often worked together. Before the First World War, the Williams brothers were instrumental in the founding of the Apostolic church. A little later one thinks of the Jeffries brothers and the beginnings of the Elim and Assemblies of God movements. Stephen, the eldest brother, had all the fireworks, but George eventually emerged as both the most stable and the most able leader. I am not suggesting that history will repeat itself in the case of Restoration. Nevertheless, Keri Jones is a very thoughtful and warm personality. Whereas Bryn seems to attract either total loyalty to him, or distrust, everybody seems to like Keri Jones. At the very least, in my opinion, he is a leader to watch for the future.

The apostles in R1 are very much the men at the top. They deal not only with matters of policy and finance, but also matters of discipline and excommunication. Apostleship operates through mutual recognition in a framework of covenanted relationships. All the apostles' names appear as editorial associates of *Restoration* magazine, and they support each other in joint ventures, and sometimes travel abroad together. In practice, Bryn Jones appears the senior apostle and would appear to 'cover' the others.

The fact that Dave Tomlinson could be sanctioned by Bryn, suggests that Bryn is *primus inter pares*. Dave Tomlinson does not know who, if anybody, disciplines Bryn.[3] Too much can be made of Bryn's authority, however. Neither Terry Virgo nor Tony Morton are facsimiles of Bryn; nor do their churches run on exactly the same lines as the Bradford churches. Indeed, the covenanted relationships between the apostles are tentative as the defection of David Tomlinson demonstrates.

Apostleship works in a similar way in R2. John Noble and David Tomlinson are clearly apostles in the R1 sense. Gerald Coates is too, but whilst he works on a translocal basis and has an input (as he puts it) into many house groups and fellowships, he also works in many non-restored churches.[4] I mention this because whilst Gerald is happy to be associated with the House Church Movement and its leadership, he is actively involved outside it. This looks to be the way that John Noble and David Tomlinson will also work in the future. R2 has, at the moment, no focus ideologically in the sense of a magazine. The apostles meet regularly, but mainly on an *ad hoc* basis.

Looking at my extended use of R2, it is noticeable how very close Basingstoke is to R1 in its organisational structure and its ideological base. Barney Coombs, for the time being, is apostle in charge, but under the covering umbrella of American leaders. Graham Perrins and John MacLauchlan are very much the leaders of their small groups, but they have tended to conflate the roles of apostle and prophet.

## Elders

In practice, eldership has become the combined role of pastor and teacher. Usually, but not always, elders are responsible for shepherding the flock in the local church. Occasionally, leaders of house groups are seen as elders, and some elders join apostolic teams without their new role being clearly defined. But on the whole, elders are pastors of churches. The Early Church of the first three centuries AD tended to identify eldership with priesthood. The contemporary 'Restored Church' identifies elders with pastors. This, so it seems to me, is increasingly the picture that has emerged in the last five years; it was not so clear in the second half of the 1970s.

Elders in both R1 and R2 regularly meet together with their respective apostles. They can wield considerable power in their local churches, but they are overseen by apostles (and sometimes members of apostolic teams). They implement the policy and ideas of the apostles in the locality, and also constantly report back on developments and problems in the local church. Elders meet with the apostles in retreats, and there are usually special seminars for these leaders at the Dales, Downs, Festival, and other Restorationist residential gatherings.

The eldership is the backbone of the Restoration movement. They are the ones who shepherd (discipline and exhort) the flock, and feed (teach and promote kingdom principles) the sheep. I have come across a number of examples where elders have engaged in activities not really approved of by the apostles. Apostles in both R1 and R2 are busy men, and are often ministering in other countries. Consequently, some elders are not always monitored as closely as apostles would like. On the whole, I think that the system of control over the eldership is considerably tighter in R1 than R2. A small number of sexual scandals have come to light in R1, but without a doubt the majority of the elders are conscientious committed Christians who take their responsibilities very seriously.

Ironically, R2, whose system of control is weaker than R1, have had a number of heavy-handed elders who have not always been picked up by apostles. Abuse of elders' considerable power (remembering Watchman Nee's warnings on this matter) is of considerable concern to all the apostles with whom I talked. Bryn Jones, for example, invited me to investigate and report back any stories of misconduct I could find.[5] Both the formal authority and *de facto* power of elders cannot be understood by the Ephesians ecclesiology alone; the authority of elders derives not only from apostles but also through the acceptance by Restoration members of discipling doctrines. This is crucial, as we shall later see. The Ephesians 4 ecclesiology without the discipling doctrines is unusual but would not promote the radicality that we find in Restorationist churches.

## The Other Ministries of Ephesians 4

Apostles and elders, rather like bishops and priests in the historic churches, have emerged as the primary ministries of the restored churches. Leaders of house groups, and those who take on some leadership function within the local church could be said to perform the function of a deaconate. These people, however, would be seen as those learning in leadership. They have no formal position and there is no developed teaching in Restoration circles concerning a tier of authority below eldership. All members belong to the 'priesthood of all believers', but particularly in R1, some are far more priestly than others.

The teaching concerning prophets, evangelists, and teachers is clear, but in practice these ministries of Ephesians 4 have not emerged in any great number. There are a great many prophecies and interpretations of tongues in Restoration churches, for example, but few formally constituted prophets (or informally recognised prophets for that matter). In Bryn Jones's churches many people prophesy, but prophecies have to be submitted to the elders who then decide whether to release the message to the congregation or not. The early anarchic Pentecostalism is now absent from most Restorationist churches. It is not uncommon in R2, however, for prophetic words and interpretations of tongues to burst forth before asking the permission of the elders and apostles. The same is still true in many areas of R1.

To my knowledge, most local churches would not claim to

have one or more resident prophets. In practice, some people are recognised as having the prophetic word more than others, but they do not emerge with the authority of the prophet which according to Restorationist teaching is second only to the apostle. In R2, as we saw in Part One, Maurice Smith was widely accepted as a prophet to John Noble's apostleship. The leading prophet in R1 has been David Mansell who has combined the role of elder at Turner's hall with an itinerant position as prophet and conference speaker on Bryn Jones's team. Mansell's ministry has been particularly linked with Bryn Jones. (At the time of writing, neither these major prophets of R2 and R1 are exercising their prophetic gifts within the Restoration movement.)

Interchange of role is the key to understanding prophets, teachers, and evangelists in Restoration. Bryn Jones, for example, is widely accepted as having a prophetic gift. He prophesied over the separating (Restorationists do not like the idea of ordination) of George Tarleton as apostle, and David Mansell as prophet back in the days of the early and undivided Restoration movement.[6]

Terry Virgo is seen as possessing the charism of a teacher and so too are Hugh Thompson and David Matthew. Thompson and Matthew are also elders and members of Bryn's team. The latter fact definitely raises their status in the movement, but quite what that status means in terms of Ephesians 4 is not clear. What is clear is Arthur Wallis's role as the undisputed senior statesman and teacher of the Restoration Movement. He is so highly regarded that I believe that most members of R2 also accept him in that role.

Evangelists have not really emerged as a separate category in either R1 or R2. Both Bryn and Keri Jones are excellent platform speakers, and so too is David Tomlinson. R2 has an elder called Rodney Kingston who lives in Worthing. He has undoubted evangelistic gifts, but whether he is seen as an evangelist *per se*, I think is unlikely.

The 'big guns' of evangelism, teaching ministry and prophecy do seem mainly to exist in R1. In R2, David Tomlinson is an all-rounder: he is a pioneering apostle, an evangelist, and teacher. John Noble is a builder and nurturer of churches, and an innovator of ideas. He is not seen as an evangelist. Gerald Coates qualifies as an apostle, but though he teaches and evangelises, his great ministry does not seem to appear in the Ephesians 4 list. Gerald is a sort of spiritual supremo: he conducts and compères conventions and large meetings with consummate skill. He is the best communicator—particularly with the media—that the Restoration Movement has got. (A leader in R1 agreed with me in this observation, but quipped: 'It's what he communicates that bothers me!')

## Apostolic Teams

Unwittingly, I think the establishment of apostolic teams in both R1 and R2 has added another tier to Restorationist organisation. Members of the teams, in becoming associated with the apostles, are endowed with apostolic authority. They become released from their local strongholds to become involved in both regional and international ministries. This also alters the apostle's function: he is now not only the spiritual leader of the churches under his control; he is a leader of a team. The team helps him to evangelise and make local and national decisions, they act as messengers between the eldership and the apostle, and promote both the ideological and commercial aspects of the kingdom. The team is composed of men whose leadership is a leadership that is neither exactly that of the apostleship nor exactly that of the eldership. Or to put it another way: the men take on their new status because they are members of the apostolic team not because they are elders or because they fit into the ministries of Ephesians 4.

I do not intend these remarks to be critical because I hold no special brief for Ephesians 4, but I do think that team development has altered the structure of leadership within the Restoration Movement. I think that both Bryn Jones and Arthur Wallis would want to say that the ministries of Ephesians 4 are essential ministries for the Church, but these should not be interpreted too rigidly. Elders who join apostolic teams remain elders, but assist the apostle in whatever capacity their natural talents and their supernatural gifts allow.

R2's teams are not really so high-powered as R1's. Or, to be more accurate, they are more low-key. Teams in R1, and in particular Bryn Jones's team, were developed as a result of a conviction that an evangelistic thrust was needed to bring the people into the kingdom. Teams are seen as a vital part of Restoration vision: they are a sign that the kingdom is going onto the offensive.

In R2, however, they have not really taken evangelism terribly seriously. Their teams, therefore, have arisen to provide a support network for the apostles in their shepherding of churches and bridge-building with mainline denominations. Gerald Coates, for example, has a team that cannot really be seen in terms of a development of Ephesians 4. His team are an eclectic bunch who help Gerald organise various functions, events, and everyday administrative affairs. I remember meeting Gerald one day with a team member who was introduced to me as an administrative assistant.

The growth of the team in R1 is partly the emergence of a new structure designed to spread the gospel more effectively, and partly to increase the efficiency of kingdom life. Both R1 and R2 would seem to be creating, in effect, a tier of bureaucracy and management to augment the charismatic leadership of apostles.

## The Structure and Practice of Shepherding

In practice, it seems to me, Restorationists have not majored on all the ministries of Ephesians 4: they have created an organisation whose leadership is invested in apostles, apostolic teams, and elders. If the apostles and elders are the foundation stones and bricks of the kingdom, it is shepherding that provides the mortar. In the Catholic Apostolic Church (as we shall see), the adoption of the ministries of Ephesians 4 eventually led to a formal ecclesiastical denomination with the orders of apostles, angels (bishops), priests, prophets, and deacons. If Restorationism had been created around apostles and elders as formal or official ranks within the movement, then what would have emerged would have been a hierarchical church in formal terms only: i.e. an apostolate whose jurisdiction was confined to ecclesiastical matters alone.

The adoption of discipling doctrines, however, alters the formal ordering of the Ephesians 4 ministries, and turns them into a paternalistic network of structured relationships. These relationships extend beyond the church and enter into the homes and communities of believers. To say that this involves a structure again needs some clarification. Restorationists say that discipling is not a structure but a set of personal relationships voluntarily entered into. This is not untrue, but it is misleading. Firstly, not all relationships are voluntary, because children are covered by their parents whether they like it or not. But more importantly, the personal relationships take place within a clearly defined matrix.

Children do not shepherd parents, wives do not discipline husbands, elders do not cover prophets, and prophets, whilst they might admonish, do not rule apostles. God's kingdom is a theocracy, and the spiritual principles which guide it are hierarchical. There is an assumption that shepherds are more mature than sheep, but this is really a very tentative principle in Restoration. There is no guarantee that apostles are spiritually more mature than elderly ladies in the back pew, any more than one can safely assume that husbands are more mature than their wives. The ranks and orders of the kingdom are primarily understood, as we saw in the last chapter, as God's order. Apostles, prophets, elders, husbands, parents, are all the indirect but delegated authority of God Himself. It is for this reason that I think that we have to understand shepherding as a structure and an organisational shape as well as a set of practices.

An outsider who casually dropped into a Restorationist meeting or celebration event, would not pick up this structure. He would notice the freedom of worship, individualistic expression, and the exercise of the spiritual gifts of 1 Corinthians 12. There would be no use of formal titles; apostles and elders being called by their first names.

(George Tarleton, when he was an apostle in R2, did self-mockingly refer to himself as 'St. George'!) But the absence of formal titles only masks the reality of the power and authority of the apostles and elders within the movement.

I think the evidence shows, that in both R1 and R2, shepherding has been more pervasive than the ministries of Ephesians 4. Shepherding adds two dimensions to kingdom life that are missing in the ecclesiology of Ephesians 4. Firstly, it transforms the formal ecclesiastical authority of the apostles and elders into an informal system of paternal relationships. This informalism does not undermine the formal authority; on the contrary, its very humanness reinforces it. Secondly, shepherding extends the influence and control of leaders into every corner of the alternative society. In doing so it blurs the traditional distinction between church and home. When converts join Restoration, they do not become members of a new church: they leave the secular world for a sacred society.

I do not intend to enter into controversies in this chapter concerning possible abuses of discipling. Horror stories certainly abound, but to deal with them now would distort the general picture. (I shall deal with such stories and other controversial issues within Restorationism in the final chapter.)

The extent and level of eldership control is difficult to determine. Shepherding is all-pervasive in the movement, but it is patchy in its application. When new members complete their commitment courses and become a member of their local Restoration church, they enter into a counselling arrangement with the elder. He in turn may assign a mature Christian, such as a cell group leader, to take on a shepherding role. Within the local church, however, the elder is always the senior counsellor. To be counselled means to be taught the principles of kingdom life, and to put yourself in the position of learner. Members are expected to operationalise kingdom principles in their everyday lives, and to be open to correction, admonition, and improvement.

In principle, there are no areas of members' lives which are exempt from investigation. The usual distinction in churches between spiritual matters and personal responsibilities does not exist in Restoration. Personal issues become a matter of concern to elders and counsellors (if they are perceived to hinder personal and spiritual growth). Smoking, for example, is not seen as a personal matter: it is kingdom business.

Teenagers will be counselled not only against premarital sex, but against engaging in any activity which is seen to contradict kingdom principles. Right attitudes of wives to husbands, and husbands' attitudes to work and the world are constantly checked. The elder may often be used to arbitrate between personal rivalries and disputes in the church. A common misunderstanding of shepherding is the idea that elders spend all their time giving orders to their congregations. A much more typical method is open and frank discussion of problems between elders and members. Such discussion is typically in private. Conversation may be heated, and confrontation is often seen to be necessary. Usually, problems are resolved to everybody's satisfaction.

The confessional and counselling aspects of shepherding are not usually ritualistic or formal occasions (though I have heard of a number of cases in R1 which could be described as a formal 'carpeting'). Most discipling takes place within close personal relationships. There are some similarities with the confessional practices of Catholicism and the secular methods of psychiatry, but there are a number of essential differences. For example, one does not typically ask the priest or psychiatrist whether you should marry so and so, or whether you should take job Y instead of X.

In R1, whilst elders do not tell the women which men to marry, it is expected that engaged couples will discuss their forthcoming marriage with elders. Elders certainly would not approve of marrying non-Christians (or self-confessed Christians from Confessions that deny the 'born-again' experience). People, on the whole, are also dissuaded from moving homes or jobs if they take them away from the Restoration ambit. I have heard many (unsubstantiated) rumours that elders have told couples when to have sex, and how many children they can have. It is certainly true that it is not considered inappropriate for elders (and apostles) to seek to influence and direct the financial, social, and moral lives of Restoration members.

Another essential difference between discipling and other counselling methods is that discipleship has a bottom line: and that line is that in the local church, ultimate authority lies with the elder. (A priest can also invoke a bottom line of course: he can refuse absolution.) Similarly, the elder also knows that his authority is accountable to the apostle. It is only when the elder invokes the bottom line, that the whole discipleship system is liable to break down. Either the authority of the elder (or apostle) is accepted, with the possibility of mounting resentment and the likelihood of future rebellion, or members leave. It is usually only when Restorationists leave the kingdom after failing to agree with their leaders, that we hear of how terrible discipling is in practice . . .

Typically the bottom line is not invoked in Restoration churches. The majority of counselling involves the giving of advice, and methods and means for overcoming problems. How to improve your prayer life, for example; or how to improve your temper. Members will be exhorted to tithe more graciously, become more active in the church, learn to cope with the unsaved at work, or an uncaring husband at home. The overall intention of counselling is to make people more responsible, and more spiritually mature. All the leaders insist on this, and claim that the scare stories are the sort of rumours everyone hears, but no one can substantiate. Whether it is true, in practice, that shepherding leads to maturity is a matter of conjecture. It would seem likely that paternalism breeds dependency, and shepherding, instead of producing Christian leaders, merely produces sheep. Perhaps this is merely a long-term worry of mine, or simply a prejudice; the evidence for the effects of shepherding are notoriously difficult to find.

When I visited the Dales Bible Week in 1982, and Festival in 1984, I asked a number of people to describe their experience of discipling to me. None of them gave me any examples of what they considered to be heavy-handedness or inappropriate counselling. One woman told me that the elder had helped save her marriage. A teenage boy claimed that his house group leader, and the group as a whole, had helped him to overcome racist feelings. One boy told how the leader of his 'community church' had helped him stay off heroin and 'pot'. The general image of the elder seems to be one of the elder brother, or one who is more spiritually mature. Perhaps it is natural that committed believers are unlikely to discuss serious tensions and difficulties to an outsider. But the fact remains, that believers often see discipling as a positive benefit.

David Tomlinson gave a good example of discipling problems, and how to deal with them, on Radio 4's documentary, *Front Room Gospel*.[7] A couple joined one of his churches with debt hanging permanently round their neck:

> House group leaders tried to find why their lives were so up and down, and of course found out that they had all these worries all the time, and were constantly going into commitments that they could not keep. Now, as far as we can see, love and faithfulness, and brotherhood, demands that we help each other in those sort of areas. And so in the context of a loving, caring, trusting relationship one person can say to another: 'You've really got to stop this; and before you go and get into any more commitments— before you take on any more hire purchase agreements— you must come and share it with me . . . That's not to say that we are going to lock you up in the church dungeon if you don't, or excommunicate you if you don't. But it is a case for saying that if you want to get out of your problems, you are going to have to open up your life for someone to help you.'

To introduce David Tomlinson here is to introduce a major factor in shepherding which I do not think can be ignored. David Tomlinson can talk with some confidence in the way that he does because he has the sort of personality that seeks to avoid confrontation, invoking bottom lines, and falling out with people. He is a mature, secure person, who does not feel the need to use his apostolic authority to get his own way, ride roughshod over others, or make impossible demands on members. The personality factor will inevitably influence both the content and manner of discipleship. In the fat file that I have collected on discipling abuses, authoritarian and insecure personalities is a dominant theme.

One former member of R2 told me that he had adopted a rule of thumb that helped him judge the maturity and sensibility of leaders. He would score them out of ten. If they said to him: 'Bill' (a pseudonym), 'how are things going? Can I help?' he would give them ten. But if they said to him: 'Bill, God wants you to sort yourself out,' he would give them five. Frequently, according to Bill, they would say to him: 'Listen to what God is saying.' This would merit a score of three. Occasionally, they would insist: 'This is God's word for you, Bill: you must receive it.' (The implication being, felt Bill, or else something nasty would happen to him.) This approach scored zero in Bill's book. According to Bill, the more insecure they were the more they would invoke heavenly backing for their advice.

Whilst I am obviously in no position to endorse Bill's original personality theory, I do think that there is no doubt that shepherding is a system that is open to abuse. Many people would want to condemn the system outright as unbiblical or totalitarian. But even supporters of shepherding recognise the dangers. The very fact that it reaches into every corner of a believer's life, demonstrates that it can be a source of tension and evil as well as a power for good. George Tarleton, former apostle in R2, pointed out to me that discipling is not simply a problem at the eldership level. Who oversees unscrupulous apostles? George believes that the majority of apostles, prophets, and elders, are good conscientious people. Some of these he believes to be deluded and thus potentially dangerous. There are one or two leaders throughout Restorationism as a whole, he believes, who are what he described to me as 'wrong 'uns'.

Looking at the role of women, and particularly wives, in Restoration circles, it is noticeable that R1 and the Basingstoke communities are more committed to the traditional role view than R2. Women are not encouraged to go out to work, and wives are expected to submit to their husbands regardless of whether their husbands are right or not. From a feminist perspective, this information will be all they need to know to condemn kingdom life as yet another bastion of male privilege. Joyce Thurman, who was involved with the House Church Movement when she wrote her book, *New Wineskins*, told me that she found attitudes to women the hardest thing to take. Joyce and her husband are now Roman Catholics (of a charismatic variety) and she finds women far more free and less restricted than those in R1.

In practice, however, the situation is by no means uniform in R1. There is a lot of lip service to submission of wives in the home. In the home, according to the doctrine, the man is God's delegated leader. Wives can and do, however, go over the heads of their husbands to the elders. Elders, whilst respecting God's order in the home, and whilst teaching the submission of wives to husbands, also remind the men that they are supposed to be the head of the wife as Christ is to the Church. In R2, in particular, this is often understood not only to mean that the husband should be caring and respectful, but also that he should encourage mutuality of ministry in the home.

A young wife in Terry Virgo's church in Hove gives her assent to the idea of submitting to her husband, but it is worth noting how she interprets this:

> I don't think it's an authoritarian thing at all. I know that Steve really loves me, and he does not order me to do things. But because I know he loves me just as much as Christ loves the Church, I can relax and be myself fully in that. And yet at the same time, I know that I don't bear the brunt of the total responsibility for the family. He is the head, and I'm happy to be in partnership with him in that.[8]

The submissiveness of wives has as much to do with their social class as their Restorationist ideology. In R1, and more so in R2, there are many middle-class wives who

were already in professional employment when they joined
the kingdom. Becoming Restorationists did not lead to the
wholesale abandoning of professional careers. Many of the
women in Restoration are better educated than their leaders.
Ron Trudinger may write about the submissiveness of
women in *Built To Last*, and he may be quoted with relish
by the men in R1, but some women, whilst accepting the
titular shepherding of their husbands, maintain considerable
autonomy. Having said that, it remains true that there are
many women who claim that they are content with their lot.
I have met wives who see themselves fulfilling a spiritual
function (ministry) in the home, and feel that a woman's
place is in the home.

Within R2, there is a definite mood of emancipation
amongst women. At Festival 84, I heard women publicly
say that they wished to be more involved in healing, water
baptism, teaching, preaching, and forms of leadership other
than 'women's work'. Often in R2, like R1, women's leadership tends to be amongst women. Most women that I have
talked to agree that the man is the head of the home, and
that elders should be men. Nevertheless, many of them
thought that women could and should play a more active
part in Christian leadership.

It might be thought that this issue has nothing to do with
how shepherding works. But it has: Restoration has been
built up on what leaders see as the spiritual order of the
kingdom. Christ is the high priest, and all leaders are men.
The only shepherding role allocated to women is amongst
other women (under the ultimate authority of men) and
children. For women to become more active in leadership,
a change in perception of God's order will need to take
place.

John Noble's wife, Christine, has always been involved
with John's work. John sees Christine as a partner not an
underling. One of the reasons that I take with a pinch of salt
the claim that John is too authoritarian, is his relationship
with his wife. I am sure that Christine would not mind me
saying that she is not the 'model' submissive wife. I remember one incident at Festival 84, when I shared the platform

with Christine Noble on the 'role of women today'. Christine had been waxing lyrically about what women were going to do when finally they got away from male domination. Then calling out to John, who was sitting in the middle of the large audience, she said: 'Is that all right, dear?' The whole crowd, including John, erupted with laughter.

I cannot imagine such an incident happening in R1 (or the Basingstoke communities). Such incidents are not trivial, for they tell us a great deal about the difference between R1 and R2, and the way in which the structure of shepherding is more open to change in R2. Christine's comments and attitude are enough to cause a shiver throughout the whole of R1: women expressing themselves in this way smacks of rebellion in the kingdom. And, of course, in a way they are right . . .

The position of children within the structure of shepherding is interesting. On the one hand they are encouraged to become 'born again' at a very early age, but on the other hand their status in the kingdom up until the conversion experience is not absolutely clear. Once born again, children are encouraged to be baptised with the Holy Spirit. It is not uncommon for seven- and eight-year-olds to speak in tongues and prophesy. The children are also encouraged to dance and sing with considerable freedom of expression. But because for Restorationists, like many Evangelicals, initiation into the Church is conversion, children up until that time are not in the Church but living in the shadow of the kingdom. Shepherding and training for children in kingdom principles must begin, Restorationists feel, before conversion and throughout their formative years.

Ernie Baxter's influence is clearly noticeable in this area. When he was at the Lakes and Dales Bible Weeks, he stressed the importance of physical punishment: 'to break the rebellion of the child'. He taught that the hand should not be used, because the hand should always be the touch of love; and because hitting with the hand can often damage the child. It was recommended to use the strap or a cane, but never whilst the parent was in anger: 'in order that you won't build up resentment.'

Maurice Smith recalls that this advice permeated R2 as well as R1. He remembers a leader living near him buying up a large bundle of canes, which he gave out to members. Ted Rotherham, who until recently was a local leader in the extended branch of R2, regrets the use he made of physical punishment. So too does Maurice Smith. One father in R2 admitted to me that he had thrashed his son in temper; in practice, as he had discovered, it is very difficult to systematically beat someone in cold blood. I recall a letter in an edition of *Restoration* where a woman wrote in, thankful that she had a special wooden spoon which she used for punishment. She hung it on the wall (presumably its visibility had a deterrent effect).

Today, attitudes are changing in this area. Shepherding of children is still a major theme, but methods of correction are not so uniform. Some people, such as David Tomlinson, never did take much notice of this stress on physical punishment. However, leaders in the newly constituted R2 felt it necessary to put on a seminar at Festival 84 to discuss alternatives to physical punishment. John Noble's school reserves the right to corporal punishment, but the Government report notes that the sanction has never been used. I think it not unfair to say that it is normative to use physical punishment within the homes of R1 (and to a lesser extent R2), but it is not compulsory.

On the whole, the structure of shepherding is clear in Restorationism. From the apostle down to the small child, covering arrangements exist for all members: virtually everybody seems to be under some delegated authority. This being so, there is a remarkable fit between the principles and practice of shepherding. More so, I believe, than the fit between the theory and practice of the Ephesians 4 ministries.

Formally, Restorationism is a theocratic apostolate, but in practice Restorationism operates as an interpersonal paternalistic network. The idea of a pyramid structure, or a totalitarian organisation run from the top, is misleading. Restorationism is not yet a formal institution with a clearly delineated bureaucracy: power and authority exist at all levels of the network; they are not invested totally in one man. Discipling gives Restorationism its dynamic and specialness. It is the shepherding structure, above all else, that makes kingdom people radical people. To use a sociological phrase, the level of social control is far greater than the average Christian church. Restorationists say, correctly, that the control exists within the context of a freely entered and voluntary covenant.

Some Evangelicals do not find this reassuring. They point out that the same thing could be said of the cults such as the Moonies and Scientology. Certainly a number of questions are being asked by worried observers. Do apostles accept admonition and criticism from below? (David Matthew says that Bryn Jones does.)[9] Who monitors the apostles? Are abuses merely aberrations from good practice, or are they in the nature of the system itself?

## Meeting Together

If apostolic ministries in conjunction with comprehensive discipling methods provide the basic matrix within which Restoration exists, it must not be forgotten that kingdom life is focused in a number of settings. Ideally many Restorationists in R1 would like to be able to turn their backs totally upon the world, but this is not possible because of work primarily existing in secular society. R2 does not seem so convinced that all modern culture is evil, and even R1 members enjoy some leisure activities outside the 'alternative society'. In both R1 and R2, however, the focus of the kingdom in everyday life is the home, the cell or house group, and the local church. In some cases, as we have seen, this is extended to Restorationist schools.

The Christian home is the nursery of the kingdom. It is in Godly family relationships between the husband, wife, and their children that the reality of kingdom life is practised. Both R1 and R2 are proud of the fact that much of the shepherding input goes into the family. The house groups are in many ways what sociologists call extended families, except that instead of mother and father and children being augmented by grandparents and other kinfolk, they are extended by kingdom people who live in close proximity. The house group is an expression of the family extended into community. Many kingdom people move into the same street. Together they worship, debate, and have fun (and rows) together. Strong friendships are formed and the emphasis is on sharing a common life.

In a way, then, kingdom people form communities by association: i.e. they self-consciously create pockets of the kingdom wherever they go. This is another demonstration of Restorationist radicality. People in the Charismatic Renewal, Baptist or Pentecostal churches, do not typically move in with each other (or next to each other).

Increasingly, however, especially in large sections of R1, the house group is being superseded by the local church. It is difficult to generalise, but in Bryn Jones's churches, for example, the house group is of diminishing concern. More and more time is being spent in church. The building of larger and larger churches in the cities is seen as part of the vision of a light that is both an invitation and a warning to the world. Certainly, R1 is anxious not to hide its light under a bushel: it wants to make a public show of strength. House cells persist and remain as an important daily contact with fellow believers, but it is the church that is the major focus of the local Restoration community.

Local leaders, both elders of churches and house group leaders, regularly meet with apostles or members of apostolic teams. Retreats and regional sessions are regular events. For everybody, however, their liturgical year is punctuated by the celebration occasions. These events perform a similar function to the conventions of earlier Pentecostal movements: they are a special time when God is believed to move and bless in a particularly powerful way. Unlike the day outing of Elim members to the Royal Albert Hall every Easter, or the weekend Easter convention at Bethshan tabernacle in Manchester, Restoration events tend to be residential; the whole family goes along. In the great Dales Bible Week, or Festival week, when you are mixing with literally thousands of kingdom people, there is a feeling of excitement, expectancy, and revival in the air.

The celebrations are regional events which go beyond locality. Hence they are expressions of the larger church and pointers to the eschatological vision of filling the whole earth with the kingdom of God and the final 'restoration of all things'. Celebrations give Restorationists the feeling that they belong to a massive movement. The tiny house cell rooted in the burgeoning local church flowers into the full glory of the restored kingdom. The big events are not simply things that Restorationists happen to attend: they are essential expressions of personal faith and commitment. They are also essential to the overall shape and structure of the kingdom. As one elder put it: 'Can you imagine heaven without the banquet?'

In R2, which for the moment is considerably smaller than R1, the new Festival venue is a means of bringing churches together who normally never meet. It is also an opportunity to express solidarity between the different streams of churches who are linked to the apostolic leadership. R1 tends, increasingly, to stick to regions. Downs Week is really Terry Virgo's patch. The Dales and the Wales Bible Weeks are primarily Bryn and Keri Jones's concern. However, there is an intermingling of churches and leadership at these celebrations. They demonstrate that Terry Virgo, Tony Morton, and Bryn Jones are working together and supporting each other's work.

R1 goes in for far more jamborees than R2. Furthermore, Church House in Bradford acts as a focus once a month for the many fellowships in the outlying districts. R1 does not invite leaders in R2 to their celebrations. R1 leaders do not come to R2 celebrations. Moves are being made to make mutual acceptance of ministries between R1 and R2 a reality and not just a formal agreement. (I think it is going too far to say that even a formal agreement exists.) There are to-ings and fro-ings between some of Terry Virgo's churches and Gerald Coates's, but whether this will come to anything it is too early to say. In many ways R1 and R2 are so clearly moving apart that it will take a miracle for Bryn Jones and Gerald Coates to share a platform together. The separateness of the celebration events highlights clearly that the

Restoration kingdom is a kingdom divided: it has two shapes not one.

Celebration events are special occasions that promote the solidarity of kingdom people, but they are not ghetto events. On the contrary, celebrations are a demonstration of kingdom power to all who wish to come. The Dales Bible Week, for example, has always been an interdenominational occasion. Probably half the people there are not from Restoration churches. (This is one of the reasons that I earlier over-estimated the size of R1.)[10] All of the big residential conventions of Restoration are the showpieces and recruitment offices of the kingdom.

But how does one get into the kingdom? What sort of people will you find there? What sort of life does one lead? How much will it cost you? If you do not like it, can you leave (without hassle)? For those who would like an answer to such questions, perhaps because you would like to join, or simply because you are curious to know what kingdom people do, may I suggest a quick tour in, around, and out of the kingdom.

## Notes

1   In fact teams started earlier in embryonic form. John Noble, for example, had a team in operation as early as 1975.

2   I have never managed to get any accurate figures for the number of churches under the leadership of the R2 apostles. David Tomlinson brought some twenty-seven churches with him. Both John and Gerald have less than that (though with influence inside a number of other churches). The typical R2 church is smaller than R1. The Cobham fellowship is some four hundred, but it consists of smaller units.

3   He means in the sense that Bryn is formally under authority to someone; not whether Bryn ever accepts criticism.

4   Terry Virgo, in R1, is also involved with churches who are not directly under his control (particularly Baptist churches). I also know of at least one elder in his team who is actively involved in inter-denominational work.

5   I did in fact do that, though these were really issues of moral misconduct rather than the direct abuse of power. Bryn made no attempt to hide the issues. In fact no one from R1 has tried to buy my silence, influence what I write, or suggest that I keep names out of it. For my part, I feel that some of my telephone conversations with Bryn Jones were off the record.

6   See Appendix 1.

7   23 March 1984.

8   Ibid.

9   'Shepherds Or Sheep Stealers', *Buzz* magazine.

10   I have written a research note on the methodological difficulties of head counting in the forthcoming *Journal Of Religion*.

## RECOMMENDED READING

There is virtually nothing, though one can glean a little from Eileen Vincent's *Something's Happening* (Marshalls, 1984).

# A KINGDOM TOUR

I am in a position to take you on an exclusive tour to the Restoration alternative society (courtesy of Kingdom Tours). But be warned: this is not the sort of package holiday for the lazy; it is really a trip for intrepid travellers.

In principle anyone can apply for a visa to enter the kingdom, but I am afraid that some of you will be disappointed and refused entry. Years ago, when the kingdom was just starting, it was not so difficult to get in, but now you will have to undergo a commitment course. Commitment courses are not everybody's cup of tea, but at least they do offer you the opportunity to decide whether you really want to go. There is no excuse, when you enter the kingdom, for saying, 'I did not really know what it was all about.'

## How to Get into the Kingdom

Before applying for your visa, you have to know where the official recruitment offices are. There is no problem, for they are all over the place. Firstly, look around your locality and you will probably find a church with the words 'Community' and/or 'Fellowship' in the title. Be careful though: you could easily stumble upon something that looks like Restoration but is not. Ask the right questions: 'Do you believe in delegated authority?'; 'Who is your apostle?'; 'What does Dales Bible Week, or Festival mean to you?' Once you have satisfied yourself that you have got the right place (remembering to check whether you have R1 or R2), stick around, attend the services, and if you decide that you want to go on the tour, they will approach you with the method of applying for your visa (i.e. a commitment course).

Although this is a perfectly legitimate way to get on the tour, I must confess that it is not the way most people get to go. Usually people prefer more organised approaches to the recruitment offices. Most of the people who enter the kingdom are already Christians from denominations or independent house groups, who feel that they wish to live a more radical life. Many of these groups were involved in the Charismatic Movement. Sometimes, whole churches, and often sections of churches apply to be 'covered' by one of the apostles of the kingdom. This often happens after a visit to the Dales Bible Week, or a similar event. It is more likely, therefore, that you will wish to join the tour in the company of your friends and fellow Christians.

Another popular approach to the visa problem is to invite a team of consultants from Restorationist churches to come and teach you about the kingdom. This can happen, and does happen, in churches within the Baptist Union, and traditional Pentecostal churches. A small minority—though an increasing minority—are asking to join the tour as a result of conversion experience either from evangelistic meetings, or from hearing of the kingdom from a permanent resident. This approach is particularly welcomed by Restorationist leaders, as a number of them have told me that those without any previous denominational experience settle down into the kingdom with less trouble. However you choose to come into contact with the kingdom—or however it thrusts itself upon you—ultimately you cannot avoid having to undergo your commitment course in order to obtain your entry visa.

Commitment courses do vary considerably around the country, and all of them, regardless of whether they are in R1 or R2 and are formal or informal, will take several weeks to complete. If you think that you would rather only visit R2 (because you think it is easier to get in) then you may be in for a shock. You will probably have to complete a foundation course on conversion, water baptism, gifts of the

Spirit, tithing, and shepherding. Here is an example from the Romford Fellowship:

In this brief look at spiritual authority we will be touching on submission and shepherding. The spirit of this age is anarchy, independence, rebellion, and anti-authority, and we must always guard that the church is not affected by this. An essential element in the care and concern necessary in church building is spiritual authority by God's delegated authority. Submitting to spiritual authority, in another person whom I can accept as appointed by God, is at the heart of restoration life and growth in church.

Is that too heavy for you? Well if it is, then I'm afraid that you cannot come on the tour. John Noble may want you to fill in a questionnaire to make sure you really want to go (for Restorationists do not want fly-by-nights). But whether you want to enter the kingdom through the recruitment offices of R1 or R2, you will have to be taught the principles of kingdom living in advance. You will be expected to do a fair bit of reading, join in group discussions, and ask questions. After having had some weeks to pray and seriously consider taking the tour, you then have to make a decision. Maybe you will feel pressurised by your local church or fellowship to go, or not to go, but in the end it is you who have to make up your mind. Once you make your commitment to go, and once the leaders of your commitment course accept your commitment, they will give you your visa. Kingdom Tours is now happy to take you into the kingdom. (Rumour has it, that there are still pockets of the kingdom where commitment courses do not yet exist.)

## What Sort of People Will You be Travelling with?

One of the nice things about Kingdom Tours is that you travel with a nice class of people. Mind you, you could feel a bit out of it if you travel to the wrong part of the kingdom. If you go down to Cobham for example, and you are a 'chip butty' person, you will find that they are all middle class down there. But don't worry, the kingdom accepts all types of persons regardless of class, race, or previous experience. As long as you have got your visa, you will be all right. In Bradford and Middlesbrough you will find that communities are much more mixed in their social class.

If you are self-consciously middle class, then you might like to know that the kingdom boasts a very high proportion of professional classes both north and south. These include many small businessmen, estate agents, and civil servants. There are a great many teachers in schools and further education. Nurses are everywhere, and there are no shortage of doctors, solicitors, and accountants. Bryn Jones can boast four Ph.Ds from his church (in various disciplines), and a great many elders have degrees or higher education of some kind. (Most of the apostles do not.) What the psychologists like to call the divergent thinkers—the abstract and conceptual intelligentsia—do seem to be in short supply. There are technicians and engineers, but few philosophers, social scientists, or post-graduate theologians. If you are a skilled worker, with a trade, then be warned. Your tour is likely to be a busman's holiday: the kingdom needs people like you.

Maybe all this class stuff leaves you cold. What difference can social class possibly make in the kingdom? (The same as anywhere else, David Tomlinson would say.) But perhaps age profile worries you? You will be welcome in the kingdom if you are old, but one of the most interesting and surprising features on entering the kingdom is to find how many young people there are. Most churches in Great Britain have an imbalance of old to young (and women to men). The kingdom is replete with children, teenagers, almost as many men as women, and seems to specialise in young couples with young families. Around the Cobham and West Sussex areas, for example, the community dimension of the kingdom is especially attractive to young couples with no extended families to help support them socially and financially.

This sense of community will also appeal to you if you are

unemployed, old, ill, or lonely. If you want to remain socially isolated, or keep numerous and close relationships in the secular world, then frankly I do not think there is much point in taking the trip. Kingdom life, in practice, tends to be a reality shared amongst kingdom people.

If you are black, you will be welcome (though George Tarleton warns that there is covert racism around). Inter-marriage is quite common, and is certainly not frowned upon. There are not many West Indians or Asians in Restor-ation, but numbers are on the increase. If you live in London's inner city, look out for David Tomlinson. He will be especially interested if you are working class as well. Basically, Dave is fed up with white middle-class house church people: the kingdom, he feels, is in danger of becom-ing a cosy club for the better off.

Divorcees get a special welcome in the kingdom (which is not common in many Evangelical circles). You won't get the usual pious patter either about God loves you and accepts you, but you can never marry again. Remarriage in the kingdom is not an automatic certainty, but it is becoming increasingly common.[1] If you are homosexual or lesbian, however, you will not be welcome unless you are prepared to become heterosexual (or, at least, not practise homo-sexuality). Kingdom people believe that you can be super-naturally 'delivered' from sexual perversions. A major leader has declared to his friends that his sexual orientation was changed by God.

## What Sort of Life Will You Lead?

The adage 'When in Rome' is particularly apposite in the kingdom. As I earlier pointed out, you cannot enter on a package tour. Package tour operators cater for 'little Englanders' who go to Spain to eat fish and chips and drink English beer; they do all they can to preserve a semblance of the homeland in the foreign country. This will not do in the kingdom: once you are in, you must leave the old world behind. You will be expected to behave according to the laws and customs of your hosts.

You will spend a great deal of time in worship whilst you

are in the kingdom. The chances are that many of you were first attracted to Restoration by the music.[2] Proof that the kingdom generates its own styles and is not merely derivative, are the number of original songs that have been written. If you are a follower of Billy Graham, and attended Mission England in 1984, you will already be well acquainted with kingdom songs: the Mission England Praise book is full of them.[3] You will soon learn all the words and tunes. I remember in 1982, shortly after I had commenced my own kingdom tour, that I used to wake up in the night with the choruses jangling in my head.

Those of you from the more traditional Pentecostal backgrounds will find the songs in the kingdom not so sentimental and personal as the ones you are used to singing. This is even more noticeable in R1 than R2. 'Jesus, Jesus, Jesus, sweetest name I know (I know, I know)' is far more likely to be replaced by songs centred on God the father and king:

> Father we love you,
> We worship and adore you.
> Glorify your name in all the earth.
> Glorify your name,
> Glorify your name,
> Glorify your name in all the earth.[4]

Many of the songs invoke the glory and majesty of God (and the all-powerful judge, *pantokrator*, is a dominant motif); psalms and scriptural verses are often set to modern music, though the style is more modern anthem and march than rock or jazz. You will hear many groups and soloists; like many of the people who perform at the Christian Greenbelt festival, these songs tend to be 'middle-of-the-road' rock, or American modern country music.

If you go to the Dales Bible Week you may find dancing is more restrained than it used to be, because egoistical dancers were spoiling it for the others. In most corners of the kingdom, however, you will be able to dance and use your body in worship. In every part of the Restored kingdom you will find clapping, hands raised (and shaking), and extempore crying and praying. Worship is primarily understood as a corporate activity: the subjects of the king worship Him together as the people of God. Restorationist style of worship will not appeal to anybody who prefers traditional liturgies. But as these issues are dealt with in the commitment courses, I can assume that traditionalists will not apply for visas. (One elder in the R2 told me that he longed for a formalised liturgy as a contrast to the freer style!)

Worship in church, and the house group, will be Pentecostal worship. 'Signs and wonders' are normal in the kingdom, and you will find expectations are high that God will heal the sick, and deliver people from demons. You may wonder why there seems to be so much demon activity in the kingdom. Unlike you, the Devil does not need a visa to get in. The kingdom is not yet in its spiritual fulness, and sin, whilst it is not expected to abound, certainly exists. You will discover when you first start the tour, that people will naturally expect that you may be smuggling in more than a few secret sins. Elders will determine whether your sin or problem is of demonic origin or some other source.

Demons do not seem to be so prevalent in the kingdom as a few years ago. This is not because the kingdom is now full of holier people, but because many leaders are more careful in seeing demons behind every sickness and trouble. David Mansell, so a number of people have said, has a grasp of psychological principles as well as a fundamentalist doctrine of demons. David Tomlinson makes a distinction between a belief in demons in principle, and actual demonic attacks. He feels that some Restorationists tend to treat demons like the proverbial 'reds under the bed'.

If there is some disagreement on the influence of demons amongst kingdom people, you will find a general acceptance of the importance of the gifts of the Spirit. You will be expected to pray for such gifts; elders will help you to exercise the gift of tongues and prophecy. If you are slightly worried, even though you have completed your commitment course, that the signs and wonders may be a bit over the top (perhaps you have heard non-kingdom people use the word 'extreme'), then you will find them very similar to the practices of the charismatics in the mainstream churches.[5]

You will certainly find that a lot of your time in the kingdom will be spent socially mixing with fellow Christians. To get the most out of the kingdom—indeed, to demonstrate that you are a kingdom person—you become a member of a community church and a house group. That is why a short stay is not really possible. You cannot be a part-time kingdom person, and if you wish to go on tour you have to be prepared for a long stay and take all your money and goods with you. (I did not say the tour was cheap.)

The kingdom encourages parents and children to be involved in church meetings. Crèches are organised both by the local church and the house groups. If you get into financial difficulties, you will find that your close friends in the house group, and others from the church will help you out. David Tomlinson and a few families, for example, wanted to move into London but could not afford the house prices. Festival 84 took an offering of twenty-five thousand pounds for them. A fellowship from the Midlands came down and did all the internal work of plastering and plumbing as a gift to the apostle.

In case you are thinking that such generosity is only for the leaders (and I would be a liar if I did not tell you that they seem to get the biggest financial awards), it works on the local level too. You could be helped with mortgage payments, debts, even school fees. Terry Virgo gives an example of what mutual support means in practice:

> A young man had a chip pan fire in his kitchen, and before nightfall—though the fire had really destroyed most of the kitchen and spoilt a lot of the house—before nightfall, there was a new gas cooker installed and operating by the other members of the cell group who came in and worked hard all evening . . .[6]

Admittedly, some people find the close atmosphere of mutual support groups stultifying. Others find the close scrutiny of the shepherd inhibiting. Even if you have completed your commitment course, and have a general idea of what kingdom life is like, the only way you will ever know how it works out in practice is to practise it.

It is not the case that once you enter kingdom territory, you will never be involved with anybody or anything outside. In R1 and R2 you will find that members go to the cinema, and go out for meals; usually they go with other Restoration members, but not always. In R2, the local church and house groups remain the primary focus of social life, but increasingly other social venues are looked to, such as concerts, pubs, holiday outings. R2 is obviously keen to be more involved in mainstream happenings than R1. John Noble and Gerald Coates, and many of their fellow Restorationists, were to be seen at the Westminster Central Hall in October 1984. There, a 'Third Wave' conference had been organised to introduce John Wimber and a team of over two hundred from California to the Christians of London.

Tony Morton, and a number of Terry Virgo's team were also there. This is probably the greatest intermingling of mainstream charismatics and house church people over the last ten years. However, do not expect much extra kingdom activity if you visit Bryn Jones's branch of R1. David Matthew will tell you that this is a deliberate policy by Bryn's team. Their churches seem to be the most socially exclusivist, and spend virtually no time with Christians from outside their own fellowships. The reason, says David, is that they want their churches to be a cutting edge, an offence and a challenge if you will, to the denominational churches. However, both Bradford churches—along with R1 and the whole of R2—supported Mission England and Mission London.[7]

## How much will the Restoration Kingdom Cost You?

The answer to this question obviously depends on whether we are talking about money, personal freedom, or psychological stability. You will have learned from your commitment courses that there will be a spiritual cost. Becoming members of the kingdom—soldiers of the king—is to turn your back on self-interest, and on being a comfortable member of secular society or mainstream Christianity. People, like Nick Butterworth and Maurice Smith, will tell you that this 'spiritual cost' is just a jargon phrase, meaning that your personal freedom will be invaded, and legalism not freedom will be your lot. Many people, who are still happy in the kingdom, see this as the sour grapes of the disillusioned. To talk of spiritual and psychological costs would take another investigation and merit a further book, but for the purpose of our brief tour I will restrict myself to the practical issue of money.

Here, the commitment courses are quite honest. No one who has opted to go on Kingdom Tours can possibly claim that they did not know how much it will cost them. Tithing is a universal custom in the kingdom.

The practice of tithing, however, varies from church to church. Some people tithe on their gross incomes, and others on their net incomes. To pay the tithe is to demonstrate that you are a serious believer. Not to pay the tithe is evidence of rebellion, dissatisfaction, and a flouting of kingdom authority. The simple fact is, as you will find, that most people pay up without a murmur. People do sometimes get into financial difficulties, but usually they are helped out. As many of the permanent residents are middle class on incomes above the national average, most of them manage quite well. Tithing takes a great act of faith (and heartache for the tight-fisted).

Your tithe will be used primarily to support your local elder and apostolic teams. One rule of thumb that seems to have been adopted in Terry Virgo's churches, is for each local community to pay an average of their earnings to the elder. However, many of the elders get less than that. If you want to know what your local elder and apostles earn, you had better ask them. Bryn Jones, for example, earns thirteen and a half thousand pounds a year plus a car.[8] Such a sum is not unusual in Restoration circles. Whilst such wages would seem a fortune to the pastors in the traditional Pentecostal denominations (and not bad for Anglican vicars either), it may very well be that real wages are higher than that.

Fees and expenses for trips abroad, tax relief (or un-declared income), cars, money for housing, personal gifts, may be extra payments or the fringe benefits of the job. George Tarleton admits that leaders are comfortable and well looked after. Church members may voluntarily do jobs around the house, or be assigned tasks of gardening, painting and decorating. These issues are obviously questions of individual conscience by leaders (and perhaps of interest to exposé journalists). I have no inside information on widespread financial abuse; if it exists on any large scale, it is an extremely well kept secret.[9]

The kingdom is an expanding empire. As it grows it acquires new plant, machinery, and new leaders. All have to be paid for. R1 is fortunate to rely partially on efficient business organisations, but the bulk of the money still comes from members. The primary method of raising money in addition to the tithe, is the special offering.

The amount that you will be expected to put into these offerings will depend on your faith, generosity, and financial means.[10] Special offerings are usually asked for specific purposes or needs. They will not always be for kingdom uses. R1 raised some fifty-eight thousand pounds for the Italian earthquake victims, for example. Usually, however, money will be for supporting Restoration missionary work, helping apostolic teams in evangelistic and international work, developing video and audio systems of communication, and helping with housing for leaders.

You will discover that a great deal of effort has gone into the methodology of fund-raising; this is necessary in our culture as there is a great deal of pain associated with giving away money! The majority of members give without stint in the belief that they are furthering the kingdom and will be supported by God (and each other) if they should personally run short. When special offerings are called for, either locally, or regionally, it is not uncommon for a prophet, or an elder with a word of prophecy, to announce the sum of money that he believes God would have the congregation meet. If say, the target is twenty thousand pounds and only eighteen thousand is raised, it is not unusual for a slip of paper to be handed up to the platform. The leader will announce that a generous giver has raised the extra revenue to meet the target. The announcement is greeted with salutations of 'Amen' and 'Thank you Lord.'

If this strikes you as stage-management or Americanism (which you might also find perfectly right and proper), then I wonder how you will react to the 'heap offering'? This is linked to the idea of the 'hilarious giver': 'the Lord loveth a cheerful giver.' They had a heap offering at the Welsh Bible Week in 1984. People were encouraged to think of giving away money as fun. And so to joyful and playful music, members (and guests) danced and jumped their way to the front and deposited money in a heap. The idea of giving as 'so much fun' obviously worked in this case because the final amount raised was ninety thousand pounds. I was not there, but reports reached me that the Dales raised nearly two hundred thousand pounds.

Perhaps we can see this simply as the razzle-dazzle of American methods. But not all fund-raising is of this type. At the Dales in 1982, the platform speaker asked for financial support for leaders. Quietly, and without fuss, five thousand pounds was raised. Bryn Jones's churches seem to raise more money than the rest of R1 and R2. Nevertheless, all Restorationist churches can gather huge sums of money compared to many mainstream churches. Perhaps we ought to remember, however, that the Church of England is the second largest landowner in England, and many established churches have investments and stock. Restorationist churches have nothing but their members' generosity.

You will find that the majority of Restorationist members support their leaders because they want to extend the kingdom: not because they want to keep a lot of 'fat cats' in luxury. I think it probable that we shall see some of the money being invested in cable and satellite television before very long. If Bryn Jones is not one of the first to establish the 'electronic church' in Great Britain, I shall be surprised.[11]

## Leaving the Kingdom

Some of you who may want to start off visiting R1, may eventually decide to settle in R2. It seems to be a mainly one-way traffic. I certainly know of no major defections from R2 to R1. Many of you who decide to take advantage of Kingdom Tours will no doubt soon apply for permanent residence. But what about those of you who might want to leave? Here, I have to make a confession. The kingdom does not automatically issue exit visas. Perhaps you think this is crazy, and that this extended metaphor of the tour has gone far enough. After all, if you do not like the kingdom you will leave. Who will stop you? It is not quite so easy in practice.

In the first place, people with whom you have been closely associated, who have become your friends, with whom you have spent many hours in prayer, worship and fellowship, are not happy simply to let you go. This is true of all deeply committed religious groups. Try asking the Catholic priest, for example, who decided to give up holy orders, what pressures he was subjected to before he could get out? (And, incidentally, there is nothing intrinsically evil in this; to turn your back on a vocational priesthood is no small matter.) Many Restorationists do not look upon other denominations as alternatives to their own movements. They see them as, at best, marginally involved in the kingdom. To leave the fellowships and return to the world or other churches, they often say, is to risk being sniped at by the Devil. Demons may creep in sometimes to the kingdom, but outside it they are everywhere.

Such a picture may seem strange to someone like Gerald Coates who is worldly-wise (by Restorationist standards) and is continuously seeking *rapprochement* with other religious groups. It certainly is not the case that leaders deliberately (George Tarleton would feel it safer to say 'on the whole') keep believers in constant fear of the outside world. It is the case, however, that many people I have met in R1 and R2 spend so much time together that they are afraid of the outside world.[12]

And so the first problem to face if you want to leave, is that fellowships are unlikely to let you go without a real effort to keep you inside. I know that this is true of many religious groups, including the classical Pentecostals, but in most places the social and moral controls are minuscule compared to the discipleship and close community living of Restoration. Most dissidents in most religious institutions when they lose commitment just get up and leave. But for some Restorationists this involves far more than leaving the local church.

Many people who really give Restoration a try, will probably have moved into the same street as the local cell group. Or, some may have become involved in joint mortgage schemes, or borrowed money. To pull away from such involvement means a radical change to your whole way of life. It may involve legal proceedings, and financial wrangles, if you insist on leaving. If you stay put, but discontinue fellowship, it may lead to ostracism and bitterness.

Of course, you could be lucky. The fellowship may have recognised that you were really only a tourist; a spiritual dilettante, who was at best a fellow traveller, but never really a member of the kingdom. You can be assured that if you persist in flouting kingdom authority, you will be expelled. John Noble is a big man and would not only let you go, but would try and stay friends even if there was a major ideological rift between you. But it is important to realise how both the apostles and the ordinary members of Restoration feel when a genuine member (as opposed to an interloper, or someone passing through) leaves the kingdom. It is as if the father in the story of the prodigal son sees the boy choose to return to the swine.

Leaving the kingdom, then, is as hard as entering it. This is not because Restorationists are narrow, unpleasant, and spiteful people. On the contrary, the difficulty of getting in, and getting out again, is evidence of the seriousness of commitment which the kingdom entails. As I have been trying to demonstrate throughout Part Two, the kingdom is for radicals. I can take you imaginatively on a brief tour, but in reality, Restorationism is the opposite to Canon Ivor Smith-Cameron's house church. There you are welcome to pop in for a quick snack. In the Restorationist kingdom, it is the full banquet or nothing.

## *Notes*

1   Bryn Jones has written a very sensitive piece called 'Is there life after divorce?', *Restoration* (March/April 1984). The Church of England Evangelicals, who seem to find so much difficulty with this issue, could do worse than look into the Restoration approach to remarriage. Basically, Restoration does not take a liberal secular approach. They see repentance as the core biblical doctrine in this matter.

2   Professor Walther Hollenweger and I once discussed the central importance of songs and choruses in the Pentecostal movement. We both agreed that if you were to take away the music, Pentecostalism might not survive.

3   Whereas the new Methodist Hymnal is totally barren. (The Charismatic Movement does not have the same foothold in Methodism that it does in the Anglican and Baptist churches.)

4   Donna Adkins. 1st verse. Copyright Maranatha Music 1981.

5   If one wishes to attack the Restorationist movement on account of the nature of its charismatic activities, then one would need to see this in the context of Pentecostalism as a whole. I have seen things in the Charismatic Renewal *per se* that have been more 'way out' than Restorationism.

6   *Front Room Gospel*, Radio 4, 23 March 1984.

7   Many mainline Evangelicals, however, doubt house church real support and interest in such inter-church evangelism.

8   He told me on the telephone in July 1985.

9   The problem with organisations of the Restorationist sort, is not that they are full of crooks, but that they are often not 'up front' enough about money. A good accountancy system, and an annual declaration of income avoids a lot of unpleasantness and would sink most of the rumours surrounding R1.

10   They are not, however, optional in the kingdom.

11   *Editor's Note:* Under the auspices of the Dales Television Company, Bryn Jones began satellite television, speaking to Europe from Olso, on Sunday 30th June, 1985.

12   Institutionalism can occur in close-knit religious groups as well as formal institutions such as prisons and mental hospitals. See E. Goffman's chapter on 'Total Institutions' in *Asylums* (Anchor, 1961).

# 10

# IS THE RESTORATION MOVEMENT
# A DENOMINATION?

I do not intend in this chapter to make any prescriptive statements about denominationalism. That is to say, I am not concerned with saying whether denominations are good or bad. When Michael Harper, for example, points out[1] that the House Churches (he means R1 and R2) are a new denomination, he is not so much stating a fact as making an accusation. A new denomination for Michael Harper, and most leaders in the Charismatic Renewal, is a disaster and a tragedy. I shall have something to say about this perspective in my final chapter.

The question I do want to discuss, at some length, in this chapter, is a descriptive one: is Restorationism a denomination or not?

## Denomination and Sect as Sociological not Theological Categories

To talk about denominations, sects (or even cults) is really to talk about sorts of religious organisations or movements; it is not to enter into theological controversies. Theology is the knowledge and study of God. Insofar that that knowledge leads to a concern with God's working in the world—His 'economy', to use a theological category—then, of course, His Church is a theological issue. To talk of the Church as the Body of Christ, or the relationship of the Holy Spirit to the Church, soon brings us back to issues of ecclesiology and prescriptivism: how should God's Church be ordered?

I think it is expedient to duck such issues here, simply because we can decide whether Restorationism is a denomination or not without having to enter such controversies. Most people when they think about denominations—how they are formed and what relationship they have to other religious structures—do not immediately start thinking theologically. If they think systematically, they may think in terms of organisational typology. This has been a major interest in the sociology of religion. As a considerable body of knowledge and reasonably clear-cut criteria for identifying religious movements now exist, I intend to approach the denominational question within this framework.

We can start, as sociologists so often do, with some observations from common sense. If you were to ask most people in Britain to name religious denominations they would probably think of the Church of England, Roman Catholicism, the Methodists, and Baptists. Perhaps they might mention the United Reformed Church. The last is the odd one out of this company for two reasons. Firstly, it has only been in existence for a few years (compared to the others). Secondly, the United Reformed Church is probably unique in British religious history as it is a denomination that was not formed as a result of a revival, nor a schism; neither has it emerged from a long identification with our past religious heritage. Instead of being sanctioned by either tradition, schism, or enthusiasm, it was formed out of three existing denominations which desired to come together as a witness to church unity. Thus, the English Presbyterian movement, the Congregationalists, and the churches of Christ became a denomination by fiat: by general consensus the URC was born.[2]

The fact that this is so should alert us to the fact that denominations are not always born out of enthusiastic and sectarian movements that then cool down into denominational respectability. Denominations can emerge in that way, of course, the Quaker movement being a good example. Methodism was certainly born out of schism and religious revival, but the modern Baptist movement (whose roots are only partly in the Anabaptists) was formed more out of doctrinal differences than revivalism. We can note, that with the exception of very rare churches like the United Reformed Church, denominations can only be said to be denominations when they have been around for a while. By the mid-nineteenth century, for example, Methodism had certainly come out of the cold, and was accepted by other denominations as a respectable and responsible church.

On this criteria alone, it is far too premature to call the Restoration movement a new denomination. Denominations do not appear overnight; they slowly emerge until they are seen by existing denominations to be serious contenders (or perhaps, even partners) in Christendom. In my opinion, this is about as far as common sense will take us. Sociologists would want to go further. What is a denomination? they would want to ask, and how do we compare it with other religious structures?

The modern origins of this question go back to the German sociologist, Max Weber. He suggested a dichotomy between church and sect. He saw the church as 'a sort of trust foundation for supernatural ends, an institution, necessarily including both the just and the unjust . . .' The sect, on the other hand, he saw as the 'believer's church . . . solely as a community of personal believers of the reborn, and only these . . .'[3]

Particularly through the influence of Weber's student, Troeltsch, this dichotomy became the basis of much of the subsequent work in religious typologies. The sect was seen as a body of voluntary believers that stood for distinct theological doctrines. It refused to compromise its religious teachings (particularly the belief that it held the unique or most enlightened path to salvation). It refused, also, to compromise with 'the world'. Conversely, many of the earlier sociologists felt, the church as an organisation was universalist in its teaching, but the voluntary principle was unimportant (you are born in the church); and the world was not something to shun but something to be accommodated. The church, then, was broad in its teachings, and sought to dispense supernatural blessings. Its compromise with the secular world (and hence the established political order), resulted in a built-in conservatism. National churches, in particular the historic churches of the Catholic, Orthodox, and Anglican persuasions, are the embodiment of churchness.

Now whilst much of this early work was crude, and inconsistent in some ways as we shall see, it is glaringly obvious from this information that Restorationism does not only fit sect far more closely than church, but Restorationists themselves—on this criteria—would see themselves as sectarian. Their very attack upon denominationalism is that churches contain believers and non-believers, and that these churches are compromising churches.

When I first broached the subject of sectarianism with David Matthew, he was understandably none too pleased with the idea. But, in fact, the real problem with the word 'sect' is not that it cannot be defended as a useful typology, but that it carries with it negative connotations. In short, to repeat an earlier point, it is used prescriptively not descriptively. To use it prescriptively is to talk of sectarian spirits (the spirit of divisiveness, the spirit of separatism). In this sense of the word, there are many sectarian people in traditional denominations. Some Evangelicals—and many broad churchmen—see the Charismatic movement within the denominations as sectarian, even though the charismatics have not hived off to form a new denominational structure. On the same criteria no one could accuse John Noble, for example, of being sectarian: he would walk over broken glass to maintain fellowship with people. Many Restorationists are not the sort of people who want to cut themselves off from the rest of Christendom as 'holier than thou' people.

To be able to use 'sect' as a descriptive category, however, we have to clear up some of the obvious weaknesses of the earlier sociological approaches. Troeltsch, for example, tended to identify sects with the poor and disinherited of society, and 'churches' with the relatively affluent. At least this distinction did give the opportunity for seeing the possibility of a movement from a sectarian organisation to a church (what we would call, these days, 'denomination'). Methodism would seem to exhibit such a movement, for example. Unfortunately, Troeltsch tended to oversimplify.

This becomes clear if we look at America. There we see a pattern of denominationalism but with no established church. Many of the denominations, however, whilst (perhaps) not so universalist in their theology as Weber's understanding of church, are closer to the church type than sect. H. Richard Niebuhr sees the denomination as endemic in American society, because of his belief that 'by its very nature the sectarian type of organisation is valid only for one generation. The children born to the voluntary members of the first generation begin to make the sect a church long before they have arrived at the years of discretion. For with their coming the sect must take on the character of an educational and disciplinary institution, with the purpose of bringing the new generation into conformity with ideals and customs which have become tradition.'[4]

Niebuhr, and a number of American sociologists after him, see all denominations as advanced forms of sects. The sect with its radical uncompromising stance, and with a membership from the lower strata of society, inevitably in time becomes the more affluent middle-class denomination that makes an accommodation with the world. The real problem with this approach is that whilst it fits some sects and denominations, it does not fit all of them. (It also fits America better than Europe.) What we can detect in many sectarian churches is that although they tend to lose the fervour of the first generation, the second and subsequent generations still adhere to specific (and sometimes unique) doctrines; and attempt, quite successfully, to resist the compromising tendencies of denominations.

The first big problem that a sect has to face, is the possibility that it may not survive the first generation. Sometimes, we can detect the beginnings of a sectarian formation (such as the group that surrounded Edward Irving when he was excommunicated from the Church of Scotland) without having any certainty that it will come to anything. Looking at Restorationism at the present time, for example, I believe that there is strong evidence for the emergence of at least one, and probably two, sectarian formations. I can be bolder than that and say that R1 has, even now, all the hallmarks of a new sect. For a sect to become anything, however, it has successfully to make the transition from the first to the second generation. To do this it has to demonstrate stability, continuity with the first generation, a recognised authority structure, and yet maintain its specialness and distinctive doctrines and practices (or adopt new revelations). If it is able to do this, it does not become a denomination; it becomes an established sect.

The established sect becomes a stable—and possibly quite large—sect that never quite becomes mainline: i.e. absorbed into the more integrated church/world compromise of so many denominations. Certainly, it is possible for an established sect to go on to become a denomination; the many American Baptist churches are good examples of this development. Professor David Martin argues, I think correctly, that Methodism was a schismatic offshoot of Anglicanism, but its orientation to the world and its strong universalist appeal has always been closer to Weber's sense of church rather than sect. Methodism is not, then, necessarily a good British example of the transition from sect to denomination (church). What is interesting about so many British sects is how many of them have become established, but have remained faithful to the doctrines of their founding fathers.

Even Quakerism, for example, whilst moving away from an enthusiastic and evangelical beginning to a quietist and eventually reforming sect, has held onto much of the simplicity of its church structure and liturgical practices. The Salvation Army too, despite its almost universal recognition, has maintained its original and unusual military structure. With its uniforms and brass bands (whatever happened to the 'Joystrings'?) and its temperance ideology, it clearly still bears all the trappings of its nineteenth-century origins.

The fact that earlier I could cite the Quakers as still a sect, highlights the possibility, against Troeltsch, that sects need not be organisations of the poor. But if suggesting The Friends as a sect rather than a church-type denomination is pushing it a bit, they are not the only example of middle-class sects. Both the Exclusive and Plymouth Brethren (though more so the Open Brethren these days) have been a middle-class movement. The same is true of the Catholic Apostolics. It remains true, however, that the majority of sects begin in relative poverty. The established sects also typically show an upswing in social mobility and affluence.

The Pentecostal sects in Britain are good examples of this. Indeed, they are excellent examples of sect development from tentative beginnings to established formation. Elim and the Assemblies of God, which were established and secure by the late 1920s, may have lost the fervour of those early days—nobody today would claim that they are living in revival—but they have remained faithful to their early vision. The same is also true of the smaller Apostolic church and the Apostolic Church of Faith sects. They all still stress the specialness and uniqueness of their doctrines.

Elim is probably closer than any established sect in Britain to becoming a denomination. (They call themselves a denomination, but in sociological terms they are a denomination of a sectarian rather than a church organisation.) Whilst it is small, some twenty-five to thirty thousand, it has a firm centralised structure, salaried pastors, and a Bible College with increasingly improved academic standards. It is a partner in the Evangelical alliance, and whilst it still tends to be isolationist and wary of non-Evangelical groups, there is a genuine desire to be more involved in a broader Christian work.

Having tried to introduce some elementary sociological ideas in the area of religious typology, however, I think it is now essential to concentrate on sectarian structures themselves. To say, for example, that sects are groups of Christians committed to the voluntary principle in religion and stand against compromising with the world, is not to tell us much. Clearly there are many different forms of religious sects, many of which are not Christian. Some sects, such as Elim, are essentially 'conversionist' sects in the sense that they wish to bring people to Christ and into the baptism of the Holy Spirit. They do not claim, like the Mormons do, to be the only true church; rather they stress their special emphasis as a Pentecostal church. Quakers, on the other hand, stress the 'reformation' of society rather than personal salvation. Some sects have, if not exclusively, primarily stressed the 'revolutionary' transformation of this world into a glorious millennium. Adventism of various kinds runs through the Millerites of the nineteenth century, the Jehovah's Witnesses, and in Christian organisations such as the Christadelphians.

Other sects have stressed perfect knowledge (*gnosis*) or techniques of divination and healing; Spiritualists and Scientologists come to mind. A few sects have been 'utopian' like the Oneida Community who have attempted to build heaven on earth. Most significantly, many sects have often showed conflicting tendencies towards reformation, revolutionism, conversionism, and utopianism. Just as the enthusiastic Quakers developed into quietists (Dr. Wilson would say 'introversionists'), so did the Catholic Apostolic Church quickly move from a Pentecostal enthusiasm into a sacramental High Church but still with a muted Pentecostalism. Many Pentecostal sects in America have exhibited many different aspects of sectarian ideologies in the earlier stages of development; usually a dominant set of consistent ideas develop. I mention these changes, because it is one thing to identify a sect, but it is quite another thing to identify the way in which a sect will develop.

Who could have predicted, for example, that the Children of God sect, which started out as a fairly typical—though communitarian—version of fundamentalist Evangelicalism, would have moved into left-wing politics, adopted a resident prophet, put 'hookers for Jesus' out on the streets, and ended up promoting paedophilia?

To quote the Children of God here, gives us a clue as to why so many Christians in sectarian formations reject the notion that they are a sect: it is not that they will not (in time) 'come clean' and admit that they are a denomination of some kind, but because they object to being lumped together by sociologists with the cults and non-Christian groups. I think that this is a perfectly understandable reaction. However, there is a misunderstanding here. Sociologists do not call Christian groups sects because they are necessarily weird or heretical. On the contrary, most sociologists are quite aware that many sects are in fact more orthodox and traditional than many so-called mainline denominations. As I shall argue in my Conclusion, sects have resisted rationalism and modernism far better than many of the denominations; notably the Church of England and Methodism.

Sociologists link non-Christian and Christian religious movements together because of their organisational similarities and their general antipathy towards secular society. Sectarian classifications are not theological classifications in any way. The Jehovah's Witnesses, for example, are sociologically similar to the Christadelphians but theological distinct. To call the Jehovah's Witnesses 'heretics' is perfectly in order within the prescriptive bounds of orthodox Christianity; it is out of order for a descriptive sociology.

## Sectarian Characteristics and Restorationism

Dr. Bryan Wilson's approach to sectarian typology is to search for a cluster of typical characteristics. (He is well aware that there are always exceptions to generalisations.) Wilson suggests that the sect is typified by the following:

(a) it is a voluntary association; (b) membership is by proof to the sect authorities of some special merit, such as knowledge of doctrine or conversion experience; (c) exclusiveness is emphasised and expulsion of deviants exercised; (d) the self-conception is of an elect, or gathered remnant with special enlightenment; (e) personal perfection—however defined—is the expected level of aspiration; (f) there is ideally a priesthood of all believers; (g) there is a high level of lay participation; (h) the member is allowed to express his commitment spontaneously; (i) the sect is hostile or indifferent to the secular society and state; (j) the commitment of the sectarian is always more total and more clearly defined than that of the member of other religious organisations; (k) sects have a totalitarian rather than a segmental hold over their members, and their ideology tends to keep the sectarian apart from 'the world'. The ideological orientation to secular society is dictated by the sect, or member behaviour is strictly specified.[5]

Wilson recognises that these are ideal characteristics: in practice there will be both variations on these themes and also some will be stressed far more than others. We would expect, for example, a well-established sect like Elim, which is close to being a denomination without becoming one,[6] to be less totalitarian in its control than the sect in the full flush of its youthful struggle for identity.

Before trying to establish what kind of sect Restoration might be, let us go through Bryan Wilson's sectarian characteristics and see how they apply to Restorationism:

(a) *voluntary association:* both R1 and R2 are committed freely to accept God and be shepherded by His delegated authorities; (b) *membership as special merit:* leaders have to be convinced that members are regenerate—born again— and that doctrine is fully understood as a result of a commitment course (whether formally or informally conducted); (c) *exclusiveness:* this is emphasised far more in R1 than R2, but both stress distinctness; (d) *conception of elect or remnant:* children of the kingdom—special shock troops of the king—with superior teaching to other churches is a strong theme; (e) *personal perfection:* the rooting out of selfishness and rebellion is what discipling is all about; (f) *priesthood of all believers:* a cardinal doctrine, but with an apostolic structure there is a hierarchy of priesthood; (g) *high level of lay participation:* there are no part-timers in the kingdom; (h) *express commitment freely:* this is encouraged and expected, especially in worship; (i) *hostility to secular society:* more true of R1 than R2, but sections of R2 also see the world as Babylon; (j) *commitment more total than other religious groups:* this is a primary characteristic of the radical Christians in Restoration; (k) *totalitarian hold:* far more true of Restoration than not only denominations but other Pentecostal sects.

There are other recognisable signs of sectarian formation in Restoration, but they are more clearly marked in R1 than R2. (1) The move from house fellowships to church and community fellowships. (2) The establishment of a clear hierarchy. (3) The development of teams. (4) Setting up business organisations. (5) The buying up of local churches and buildings. (6) Buying large churches as a foci for apostolic leadership. (7) The gathering together of the local churches in regions, and at large venues, such as the Dales and Festival. (8) The adoption of common liturgical styles and a Restorationist argot. (9) Growing hostility to Restorationism from other sects and denominations.

All these are signs not that a new denomination of a sectarian nature is established, but that it is in the process of becoming established. To say more than that is to go beyond the evidence. R1 does not perceive itself as a sect. R2 perceives R1 as a denomination, but not themselves. Other Pentecostal movements see these branches of the House Church Movement as a denomination (or fast on the way to becoming one). All these perceptions are rarely descriptive. It seems to me that there are a variety of reasons for these groups seeing Restorationism the way they do. For R1 to admit that they have become a sect is to admit that they have failed. R2 if they admit that they are denominationalised, are accepting that they are no better than R1. Pentecostal sects, already established, want no more rivals in an oversubscribed and highly competitive small market. Those in the charismatic Renewal see the new 'denominations' draining the spiritual energy from the mainline churches. For them, a new denominational structure is both a folly and a betrayal.

I think it absolutely essential, however, that we do not dismiss the Restorationist claim not to be a new denomination or sect out of hand. In other words, there are still some factual matters left to be resolved. For example, Restorationists often say that they cannot be a new denomination because they have no constitution or declared articles of faith. This is true in a formal sense only. The Restoration articles of faith are clear enough, and the commitment courses may not ask new members to sign on the dotted line, but the rules are public knowledge. Furthermore, Elim when it started out had neither rules of faith nor a constitution. But Restorationists claim also that thay have no headquarters. This is also true (for now) but sects do not always have a headquarters. The Open Brethren have never had a constitution nor a headquarters, but that does not alter the fact that they are an established sect. The reason that they can be considered so, is not because they are not a significant force in Christianity but because they failed to achieve their original goal.[7] That goal, like Restorationism, was to turn their back upon denominationalism and become no less than The Church.

Restorationists would agree that the Brethren movement failed. They would see this related to the absence of the gifts of the Spirit, and a refusal to accept that apostles and prophets are ordained by God for the Church of today. This time, Restorationists feel, the earlier Brethren vision of going beyond denominations in order to found the universal church, will succeed. The very fact that Restorationists believe this, poses a very interesting problem in our understanding of sects. Does not this idea of theirs— the search for universality and comprehensiveness—sound far more like Weber's church than sect? Most sects arise clinging to one idea, or special doctrine. Often salvation is seen as belonging exclusively to themselves, or they see their own movement as possessing the most perfect expression of it. Sects that turn their back upon the world usually do so with a rising sense of their own self-importance and uniqueness. The restorationist vision does not seem to be sectarian in this sense at all. They want to fill the whole world with the kingdom; and they hope that the whole of divided Christendom will be swallowed up in the restored church.

Dr. Wilson points out that a few special sects do indeed look, on the surface, as if they are churches. Such religious movements, he maintains, are radical reformers or 'restored churches' (his phrase not mine)[8] who seek to bring back a pure unsullied religion which has been lost. In practice, however, they compete with other churches (sometimes aggressively), and become separatist. Their rejection of other religious denominations and structures warrant their inclusion as sects. He cites two historical examples of Restorationist sects: the Catholic Apostolic Church, and Brethrenism.

I believe that modern-day Restoration is the third Restorationist sect to emerge in Britain in the last hundred and fifty years and the first of this century. In many ways Restorationism is a synthesis of the Pentecostalism and apostolic structure of Irving's followers, and the anti-denominationalism, simplicity, and evangelicalism of the Brethren. All three movements reject the old wineskins of the traditional denominations. All three movements, interestingly, are primarily middle class. Modern Restorationism, however, does not have the upper-class flavour of the earlier movements. Neither can we understand it without seeing it in relation to denominational Pentecostalism. It is this Pentecostalism that provides the glue that makes the synthesis stick.

In the next two chapters I want to look at modern Restoration in the light of these three movements: early Brethrenism, Irving and the beginnings of the Catholic Apostolic Church, and the first few years of classical Pentecostalism. The historical perspective lends substance to Dr. Wilson's abstract typologies, and also enables us to understand more fully the nature of restorationist sects.

To end this chapter, however, in order to correct what might seem to be a slur on the intelligence of Restoration leaders, I should point out that many leaders have given these matters a great deal of thought. They all know that movements fail, and they have read church history as much as anyone. John Noble, for example, realised the dangers of denominationalism back in 1974. He takes a line on sectarian development which is quite common in Restoration circles. Like David Matthew, he sees the emergence of new religious movements as a means the Holy Spirit uses to promote aspects of truth that have been lost or neglected. Furthermore, what sociologists might use as a criterion of sectarianism, he might want to see as evidence of bringing truth out of an apostate church. Indeed, I think Arthur Wallis would reject much of my argument on the sociology of sectarianism not only because sociology is still thought of as demonic[9] or subversive of faith in some Evangelical circles, but also because he would see the coming out—the radical separation—as a work of God's Spirit. Denominations have basically had it for Arthur: God is calling His people out, and no amount of sociologising is going to alter that.

My sociologising, however, is not designed to 'rubbish' the work or belittle it.[10] I have deliberately avoided prescriptivism. On the basis of a sociology and history (as we shall see) of religious movements, it simply has to be said—using these criteria alone—that the Restoration movement is the crucible for two emerging sects.

Bryn Jones accepts that the earlier revivalist movements foundered, and that the Pentecostal churches failed to continue their momentum. (I think that Pentecostalism was a Renewalism that went wrong rather than a full-blown Restorationism.) He believes that the Renewal movement can never radically repair the damage done to the Church by denominationalism. Bryn's perspective on revivals shows that he has a sense of history. God, he claims, is calling the Church to Himself. All the great revivals of the past are foretastes of the true deluge of the latter rain. The people involved in these movements (like himself) were certain that they were in the final generation. They were all convinced that their revival would be the final chapter in the gospel story.

Despite these facts, as Bryn sees them, he is convinced that his churches are involved in part of that final chapter. He told me that he would not, he could not, admit that they were going to go the same way as the rest of Church history.[11] I have no doubt that Bryn, David Matthew, and all the leaders of R1 are convinced that God is on course and that they are with Him. But Bryn is no fool. It is not in his nature to court failure. He is a man with a vision, and the idealist in him sees nothing less than God's Church filling the earth in preparation for the King's return. Nevertheless, he knows that revival is not dependent on him. As a last word on the matter, he said to me that whether he was right about his own work, or whether he personally would fail (and even if Restoration became another denomination), God would not give up on His Church. His plans would continue: the kingdom would be restored, and revival would sweep the world.

R2, I feel, might be prepared to settle for less than moving on to build the final kingdom. The pioneers could become settlers. David Tomlinson, for example, who is already convinced that R1 is a denomination, is aware that R2 could also become one. He does not want it to do so, and he is by no means convinced that it will become so. Nevertheless, he would be able to adjust to a lesser victory as long as he felt that he was personally doing God's will.

The biggest problem for Restorationists, it seems to me, is not whether their movement has become denominationalised, but whether they can cope with the fact of it. Denominationalism is a sly process: it sneaks up on you and catches you unawares: when you are an active and committed member of a new religious movement, you are often the last to know that you have been caught.

## Notes

1 *That We May Be One* (Hodder and Stoughton, 1983), chapter 12.

2 Not that everyone played ball: there is still a small Congregational Union.

3 Michael Hill, *A Sociology of Religion* (Heinemann Educational Books, 1973), p. 47.

4 Ibid., p. 58.

5   Ibid., pp. 76–77.

6   Whether Elim can make the leap from its sectarian past to a denominational future is doubtful in my opinion. To become integrated into the mainstream of religious life would be, for them, to risk apostasy.

7   Brethrenism has also over the years standardised many procedures and liturgical practices. These are not uniform, but Brethren can easily recognise each other and feel at home in each other's churches. Some Brethren have no difficulty in seeing themselves as a sect as long as this is understood sociologically. John Boyes, the editor of the *Christian Brethren Review*, for example. See our joint article on the Brethren and the HCM in *CBR*, forthcoming.

8   Bryan Wilson, *Religious Sects* (Weidenfeld and Nicolson, 1970), p. 207.

9   This is slowly changing with the realisation that sociologists are not all Marxists and atheists! The work of Clifford Hill, and Os Guinness has been much appreciated. Christians from an Evangelical background could do worse than start with David Lyon's *Sociology And The Human Image* (IVP, 1984). I think it not unfair to say that Christian sociology is often bad sociology. Os Guinness's work is important here, because he writes good sociology with Christian insight.

10   Some members of Restoration found my comments hurtful in 'The Theology Of The Restoration Churches' because of my use of the word sect. See D. Martin and P. Mullen (eds.), *Strange Gifts, A Guide to Charismatic Renewal* (Blackwell, 1984).

11   What I like about David Matthew is his resistance to pessimism. I am sure that he will read my comments fairly and thoroughly, but I already know what his response will be: 'Scripture makes it plain . . . that sooner or later the pattern of history must be broken . . . One day there will be a generation of the church that makes it to God's ideal . . . Why should not that generation be your generation and mine?', *Restoration* (March/April 1984), p. 22.

## RECOMMENDED READING

Bryan Wilson, *Religious Sects* (Weidenfeld and Nicolson, 1970).

Andrew Walker, 'From Revival To Restoration', *Social Compass* (1985).

P. L. Berger, *The Sacred Canopy: Elements of a Sociological Theory of Religion* (Doubleday, New York, 1967).

D. Martin, *A Sociology of English Religion* (Heinemann, 1967).

# 11

# CATHOLIC APOSTOLICS AND CHRISTIAN BRETHREN AS THE FORERUNNERS OF RESTORATIONISM

Edward Irving, the Catholic Apostolic Church, and Brethrenism are not typically treated together by historians. In my opinion this is a mistake. Both movements were a response to the upheavals of society caused by the French Revolution and what Thomas Carlyle termed Industrialism. Irving and the early Brethren leaders were appalled at the disintegration of the Church into competitive denominations that seemed, to them, devoid of the glory of Christ. Furthermore, there are interesting and important historical and theological overlaps between the two groups. For these reasons, I intend to look at them together.

## Irving(ism)[1] and Early Brethrenism

What eventually became the Catholic Apostolic Church, and a group of Christians who preferred to be called 'Christians' or 'Christian Brethren', were two movements which were born out of an eschatological conviction. This conviction, stated baldly, was the belief that the Second Coming of Christ was imminent.

Prior to the early nineteenth century, the general view of adventism amongst many Protestants was the belief that Christ would return at some date in the future after the world had been rid of Pope and Turk, and subsequent to the Jews being restored to Palestine.[2] The hope of the Christian, therefore, was death; certainly not a hope in an imminent

218

return of Christ to rule in a glorious kingdom. The millennium, in their schema, was usually seen as belonging to history prior to the Parousia.

For those who like their history tinged with irony, the developments in adventist theory, following the French Revolution, and having such major consequences in Protestant Nonconformity, were dominated by the thinking of three Jesuits. Indeed, the beginning of the nineteenth century is the modern origin of a certain brand of prophetic interpretation which has fascinated Evangelical groups ever since. (There were, of course, waves of adventism in the late Middle Ages, and the early seventeenth century.)

W. Cuninghame, in 1813, had published a prophetic work claiming that Christ would return to the earth, personally, before a millennium became established upon earth. This 'futurism' was denied by a growing number of supporters of the writings of Alcazar; he was a Jesuit priest who had died in 1613. He had argued that the prophecies of the book of Revelation had already been fulfilled at the time of ancient Rome. This 'historicism' saw Nero as Antichrist (later versions opted for Caligula), Rome as Babylon, and the millennium as commencing with the defeat of Imperial paganism by an Imperial Christianity in the person of Constantine.[3]

Cuninghame's futurism, however, was supported by two other Jesuit writers. Riberia, who died in 1591, taught that Antichrist would be an actual person who would build a new temple in Jerusalem, forbid Christianity, be acknowledged as leader of the Jews, and eventually become conqueror of the world. This would all be done in a space of a literal three and a half years. Perhaps the single greatest influence on Protestant adventism came from a book that first appeared in English in 1826, to be followed in 1827 by a two-volume edition translated and with a long foreword by Edward Irving. Ostensibly written by a converted Jew, Ben-Ezra, and entitled *The Coming of Messiah in Glory and Majesty*, the book was in fact written by a Chilean Jesuit, Manuel de Lucunza who died in 1801.

In Lucunza's futuristic schema, we get the idea of the Antichrist as a confederacy (of persons), a great deal of emphasis on the destiny of the Jews seen in terms of a separate covenant with God, and Jerusalem as the centre of God's reunion with mankind. When Jesus bodily returns to earth, He will not come initially in power and glory, but secretly for the saints. This 'secret rapture', was to be a 'meeting in the air' where the dead saints and the living faithful servants of Christ would be caught up to meet Him. This advice (interpretation) of Lucunza leaves the judgements and the wrath of God to fall upon the unjust, whilst the so-called Great Tribulation would be missed by the saints. The Tribulation would be survived by some people who would refuse to blame God for their troubles and repent of their sins. These people would constitute the rank and file of the millennial kingdom on earth, which would be ruled by the returned saints and Christ Himself.

Variations on these Jesuit speculations have dominated fundamentalist and some Evangelical groups ever since. In Elim and Assemblies of God, for example, a rather lurid novel, *The Mark Of The Beast*, was all the rage before the Second World War. I read it as a young boy, but had no idea (and probably the author did not either) that the prophetic theories in the book stemmed primarily from the Jesuits! The futurism to which Irving and Darby (the leading Brethren founder) subscribed, was not really a 'latter rain' eschatology. On the contrary, despite a conviction that God would restore His Church in the face of apostasy, this was seen against the background of appalling world disasters and destruction. Irving saw the Church revived again 'terrible and mighty like an army of banners', but he did not expect it to become a mountain that would fill the whole earth. (The vision of destruction which Irving and Darby both envisaged is precisely what modern Restoration opposes.)

What crystallised this vision of the 'last things' into firm convictions which became a major impetus (I believe, *the* major impetus) behind the Brethren movement and the so-called Irvingites, were two conferences held over a number of years. Out of the Albury conferences in Surrey from 1826 to 1830 (and Irving's congregation in London) emerged the group called the Catholic Apostolic Church. The other conferences at Powerscourt in Ireland from 1831 to 1834,[4] gave shape to the movement of Brethrenism. (In embryo, Brethrenism was already in existence as the Plymouth church, for example, was already functioning.)

The people gathered at Powerscourt were mainly—but not exclusively—disaffected Anglican Evangelicals. The Albury circle were broader based, and included not only Anglicans but Presbyterians and Independents. Hugh Drummond who originated the Albury conferences was an Evangelical and so was the Rev. Armstrong (both of whom would become apostles in the new church). However, Edward Irving was neither an Evangelical nor a Low Churchman. His Scottish Presbyterianism was of a High Church variety both in terms of a doctrine of sacraments and holy orders. Interestingly too, John Nelson Darby, the most dynamic and controversial of the early Brethren, held to a High Church theology as far as ecclesiology was concerned.[5]

The members of both conferences were from the middle classes and aristocracy. Many participants were excellent scholars. Albury could boast a world scholar in Hebrew, but many people from both conferences were proficient in Greek and Hebrew and well versed in theology and philosophy. Probably, the Powerscourt group, despite being more uniform than the Albury set, were marginally better educated. Benjamin Newton was, in my opinion, the finest scholar the Brethren movement ever produced, until Darby hounded him out in 1845. The most adventurous and wide-ranging thinker of either group was Edward Irving whose Incarnational and Trinitarian doctrines so excited Samuel Coleridge that he described him as having 'the heart and unction' of Martin Luther.[6]

The two conferences are, in fact, connected personally. Lady Powerscourt attended the Albury conferences. The journal of this young widow reveals her to be closer to the mystical and Pentecostal doctrines of Irving in some respects than the more conventional Evangelicalism of Brethrenism. Irving himself visited Lady Powerscourt in Ireland. Shortly afterwards, a smaller, private version of Powerscourt began before the full conferences commenced in 1831.

A number of Irving's followers attended Powerscourt (though we do not know their names). Brethren historians, on the whole, have not been anxious to show the connections between Irving and Brethrenism. One writer, Timothy Stunt, has made some attempt to show some interesting personal connections.[7] Bulteel at Oxford, for example, was a clergyman who resigned in protest against the apostasy of the Church of England. He was supported by Newton and Darby. Later he joined Irving's circle, and after the great man's death in 1834, he became a member of the Catholic Apostolic Church. Becoming disillusioned with this movement, he again made contact with the Brethren in later years. The Rev. Armstrong, before he became an apostle in the CAC, worked for a time with one of the leading Plymouth Brethren, Dowglass. This gentleman later left the Plymouth church and the Brethren movement, and supported the CAC for the rest of his life.

John Nelson Darby, who was to become the leader of the Exclusive branch of Brethrenism, taught the doctrine of the 'secret rapture'. He denied that he took this from Irving, but on this issue and many other aspects of futurism,[8] it must be said that many of the Powerscourt ideas were very similar to those promulgated through the *Morning Watch*; this was Drummond's own quarterly journal, but also a vehicle for many of Irving's later views.

More broadly, Stunt correctly points out, that both the 'Irvingites' and Brethren were movements in search of purity. For both of them the Church had gone wrong. They both taught separation from the world, and both expected the imminent return of Christ. Neither group held to a narrow individualistic pietism (in the first instance) based on biblical authority alone. They believed in a high doctrine of the Church under the direction of the Holy Spirit. To this, one could add, that both groups had a strong commitment to a universal catholic church:[9] they both believed that they were movements for unity of the Church.

The early Brethren were not aggressively Baptist, and a number of the Anglican members, including Darby, did not see believers' baptism as a cardinal teaching. It is not the case that Albury was Pentecostalist and Powerscourt was not. On the contrary, interest in the restored gifts divided Albury as well as Powerscourt. We can see from the Powerscourt reports, that there was considerable interest in the possibility that divine healing and the charismatic gifts of the Spirit might be a sign of the imminent return of Christ.

One of the Brethren's great leaders, Captain Percy Hall, was particularly keen on the possibility of a new Pentecost. Darby himself (though never Newton) was by no means closed to this possibility.

When news reached Albury in 1830 that there had been an outbreak of tongues at Rosneath and healings at Row in Scotland, there was intense excitement. Irving had already presented a very powerful theological argument in favour of the gifts based on his Trinitarian and Incarnational works.[10] He was desperately anxious to discover whether the Scottish phenomena were really the work of the Holy Spirit or some demonic counterfeit. The Albury group sent an investigative team, which included Cardale who was to become the leading apostle in the CAC. Darby also decided to go to Scotland and see the 'miracles' for himself.

The Albury team came back convinced that the Holy Spirit had been restored to the Church. From that moment, until tongues broke out in Regent Square church in October 1831, Irving and some six hundred people daily prayed for an outpouring of the Spirit in London. Darby, on the other hand, was not convinced of the genuineness of the gifts. He did not like some of the biblical prophecies and doctrines given in 'the power', and as they agreed with Irving's speculative theology rather than his own, he withheld support. A little later Newton attended an Irving Pentecostal service (he does not tell us whether it was Regent Square or Newman Street). The atmosphere there, he felt, was not from God, and he found that he was not able to concentrate on Christ's atonement.

However, what clinched it for the Brethren—and ended any latent Pentecostalism that there might have been—was the discovery that Irving's Christology was heretical. In fact, Irving had already been tried for heresy by the London

Presbytery of the Church of Scotland in 1830. He was found guilty of believing in the sinfulness of Christ's nature. In 1833, after the outbreak of Holy Ghost manifestations at Regent Square, Irving was again tried at Annan in Scotland where he was ordained. The charges were the same and so was the verdict; this time, however, Irving was excommunicated.

Nothing hurt Irving and his circle more than the confessions of a man called Baxter, who in his *Narrative of Facts* revealed that, after supporting Irving, and having been one of the leading prophets in the new group, he discovered to his horror that Edward Irving taught heresy concerning our Lord's human nature. This discovery immediately led to the end of his 'delusion', and he never again found that he could speak in 'the power' (as the Irvingites called being under the influence of the Spirit). For the rest of his life, Baxter remained a respectable Evangelical layman, but a consistent and persistent opponent of Irvingism.

Irving's so called heresy was the peccability (or liability to sin) of Christ's human nature. Darby in revolting against this notion was not only joining the majority of the Evangelical world at that time, but he was also, like Baxter, seeing a direct link between Irving's heresy in Christology and the issue of Pentecostalism *per se*. Newton also condemned Irving on both counts, but in fact his doctrine of the Incarnation was far closer to Irving's than Darby's theology. This was to prove fatal for him when Darby was able to use this as an excuse for railroading him out of Plymouth. There are some very important theological issues which we cannot go into here, but I would like to comment on them briefly.

It does not surprise me that when the Exclusive Brethren in the 1930s made their last attempt as a Christian group to become influenced by an outsider, they chose Watchman Nee. (Yes, the same one!) Nee was involved with the Exclusives for a time, until they ostracised him for consorting with Open Brethren. His spirituality owed much to a Darbyite theology. Both Nee and Darby tended to treat Christ's human nature as unreal. This Docetism, as it is called, with its strong (almost gnostic) sense of the evil of matter, is precisely what Irving had been fighting against. Newton thought that he overstated his case, but he too thought that the ancient teachings of the Church should be preserved: that Christ in becoming human became a real man not a facsimile of a man nor clothed in the unfallen flesh of Adam.

At the very least, the long-standing belief in Brethren circles that Irving was a heretic, and that this *ipso facto* made Pentecostalism suspect, needs challenging. Professor Tom Torrance, and Professor Colin Gunton are just two notable conservative theologians who would defend Irving's orthodoxy. They realise, in a way in which many Protestants do not, that Irving's doctrine is in line with the early Greek fathers and primitive Calvinism as opposed to the teachings of Augustine, Luther, and much later Evangelical thought.[11] (Perhaps it is more curious that classical Pentecostals, neo-Pentecostals, and House Church radicals have, on the whole, tended to ignore Irving; this is mainly due to lack of knowledge of his teachings and theology, but it is also partly due to the fact that Irving was a High Churchman in the strict Calvinist tradition. Modern Pentecostalism has its roots in the Low Churchmanship of the Holiness movements.)

Irving and the early Brethren leaders both wanted to return to a New Testament church. They both believed that God was restoring His kingdom through them. From a modern Restorationist point of view, it must look like a lost opportunity that the Brethren and Irving's followers never joined together. If they had, there is no doubt that what would have emerged would have looked very much like Restorationism. The differences between Irving, his followers, and the Brethren, however, were considerable.

The Brethren movement was initially a Christian reformation of great simplicity. 'Irvingism' is really the nickname of the church that grew up around Irving, but which Irving did not found (as Dr. Wilson incorrectly states).[12] The correct name for Irvingism is not 'Irvingites' but the Catholic Apostolic Church. This movement is complex and only marginally connected to Edward Irving himself, who died in 1834. Nevertheless, Irving's own doctrines shaped much of that church, and so it is worth comparing his understanding of the restored church with the early Brethren.

The Brethren were solid Evangelicals; they were Low Church in practice (though some of them were High Church in theology). Irving disliked what he saw of Evangelicalism. He thought it was tainted with the rationalistic doctrines of the Enlightenment, and too taken up with good works and missionary societies. He thought also that Evangelicalism treated the Bible as an idol as surely as the Catholics treated the church as an idol. Methodism, he saw as subjective, sentimental, and awash in an Arminianism that put faith and self-will before the sovereignty of God. Brethrenism was itself mildly Calvinistic, but in later years it became increasingly attached to the sort of holiness, evangelism, and spirituality that was to be found in the Keswick conventions.

Darby, in particular, but most Brethren too, were iconoclastic on the issue of holy orders. They took the priesthood of all believers literally. There was a genuine commitment to the end of clericalism, and a dislike of any constituted priesthood. Irving, on the other hand, was strongly attached to ordained ministry, and a belief in a purity of holy orders that stems from primitive Presbyterianism in Scotland and earlier Catholic teachings.

Irving, the Catholic Apostolic Church, and the early Brethren were totally convinced that the Holy Spirit should direct the Church. But the Brethren did not see, unlike their rival restorationists, that this would involve either a commitment to the ecclesiology of Ephesians 4, or a return to the supernaturalism of the Acts of the Apostles. Once Irvingism had been rejected by the Brethren, their doctrine of the Holy Spirit develops more along the lines of Quaker pietism than enthusiastic Pentecostalism.

The unity of the Church, Irving thought initially, would take place within the historic denominations. Catholic Apostolics saw themselves as part of the historic Church: a witness and a signpost to the Christianity of the New Testament. The Brethren saw unity being restored not by the establishment of a new sect, but by the re-establishment of the true church. When I heard Terry Virgo say on Radio 4[13] that the Bible only talks of two shapes of the Church—the universal church of the born again, and the local church where believers meet—he was reiterating Brethren teaching.

Irving believed that Roman Catholicism (not Catholics) was beyond redemption because it was founded on a false ecclesiology: that the high priest of the Church was not Christ but His earthly representative, the vicar or pope of Rome. However, Irving warmed towards the episcopacy of the Church of England, which he recognised as a sister church to his own Church of Scotland. He believed, on the whole, that Protestantism would preserve a remnant of the faithful. Brethren were taken with the remnant theology too, but believed that denominations were simply not in the plan of God.

In an interesting way both Irving and early Brethren (like the later Restorationists) saw the Lord's table as a central issue of discipleship. For the Brethren, the breaking of bread was the essence of the Church: it was the bond, or covenant, of members of the Body of Christ. (A hundred and fifty years later, John Noble was to tell me that the essence of the nascent Restoration movement was breaking bread together not doctrines.) Sharing the common table, and following the Apostles' teaching—as the Acts of the Apostles records of the early Christians—was the clear and simple ideal of Brethrenism. Evangelicals as they were, however, the catholicity of their churchmanship was not matched by a Catholic doctrine of sacraments. Irving would have none of this. For him, such doctrines denied both the reality of the mystical body, and the physical means of grace whereby Christians could be united to their Head who is Christ. Irving, in short, believed in the real presence of Christ in the Eucharist (though like the Orthodox, and some Presbyterians before him, he refused to see this in the technical terms of 'essence', 'accident', and 'transubstantiation').

## Developments in Irvingism
Irving's sacramentalism did not include Confession (which the Catholic Apostolics also excluded), but it did include a belief in the sacramental efficacy of infant baptism. All

these, so often neglected, aspects of Irving's teachings explain why after his death the Catholic Apostolic Church should seem to turn their back upon enthusiasm and opt for what looks more like Tractarianism. In fact, Pentecostalism did continue, but in an orderly fashion with set times in the formal liturgy for the utterances of the Holy Spirit.

Towards the end of his life, Irving did seem to believe in a theocratic apostolate. Having said that, we do not know how far he had worked out the full implications of this. Like modern-day Restorationists, the apostles of 'Irvingism' were called by prophecy though in a seemingly arbitrary way. Hugh Drummond, the banker and member of parliament, acting in 'the power' called out a Mr. Cardale to be the first apostle. 'Art thou not an apostle!' were the rhetorical words. By 1832, Cardale and Drummond were both apostles. Irving's circle believed that the correct order of the Church was apostles, prophets, angels,[14] priests, evangelists, deacons, and readers; this full range of holy orders was developed after Irving's death. Before he died, Irving was to discover that the circle was the tail that wagged the dog. He genuinely tried, but found it difficult to submit to the new apostolic authority. After he was excommunicated from the Church of Scotland, Irving was forbidden to officiate as a priest until he was reordained by the apostles. Irving was called to be an angel, and he presided over the church at Newman Street, but under the authority of the emerging apostleship.

Irving's health rapidly failed in 1833, and in 1834, with the blessing of Cardale, he set off for his native Scotland to start a new work there. In October 1834, Irving entered Glasgow clearly dying. On the 7th or 8th of December he died. He was buried in the crypt of Glasgow cathedral under the stain-glass window of John the Baptist.

Like Arthur Wallis, so many years later, Irving was passed over as an apostle. He was the catalyst of the Catholic Apostolic Church, who reverenced him as a John the Baptist, but not a founder of the church. What eventually became the mature church is surely one of the most unique movements in sectarian history.

It was decided that there were to be only twelve apostles

who would have full authority in all matters doctrinal, liturgical, and financial. (Unlike the Brethren, Catholic Apostolics tithe.) Many of the excesses and confusions of the first few years (that is their own perception) were curbed and gradually the new church became established. At first, as they had been so influenced by Irving, the liturgical style resembled the staid order of Regent Square. Soon, however, all vestiges of Presbyterianism disappeared from the church services. They were replaced by a developed liturgy complete with incense, lights, and vestments, and based on Orthodox, Catholic, and Protestant forms.

The church held onto Irving's 'heretical' Christology, his Reformed Catholicism, his biblical prophecies. They developed prophetic interpretations of their own, and eventually melded together a scriptural literalism with a sacramental Catholicism; and a muted Pentecostalism with a number of unique views of their own.

Most significantly, it was decided to choose only twelve apostles as evidence of the restored twelve apostles 'of the Lamb'. They did not accept later interpretations of Ephesians 4, which saw the possibility of more apostles. (Today's Restorationists, for example, see no limit in principle to the number of apostles.) The CAC sought to legitimate their choice of only twelve apostles by the text, 'And round about the throne were four and twenty seats: and upon the seats I saw four and twenty elders sitting, clothed in white raiment; and they had on their heads crowns of gold.' (Revelation 4:4 AV) An Anglican clergyman wrote: 'Yet it is, on the very surface, a large claim, that the Twelve Apostles should be revived in the nineteenth century, in the persons of twelve English Gentlemen.'[15]

The apostles were 'separated by the Holy Spirit' from their secular jobs or priestly charges, and all moved to Albury which became the headquarters of the new church. The CAC did not see—and has never seen—itself as a new sect. Like their contemporaries, the early Brethren, and like their modern Restorationist counterparts, they were reluctant to be called anything. They eventually accepted the title 'Catholic And Apostolic Church' as a result of an accident:

an official from the government engaged in some form of census, asked a leading member of the church what his denomination was called. He was informed that the church member belonged to the 'Catholic And Apostolic Church'.

I cannot go into all the many liturgical and theological innovations of the apostles, their successes, and failures. It would be easy to poke fun at what would seem to be a classical case of Victorian eccentricity. But the curious thing about the CAC is that the more you research it, visit their churches, talk to the last few remaining members, there is a dignity and a genuine spirituality that will not be denied.

The twelve apostles ordained angels and priests, but left no provision for a second generation of believers. They thought that Christ would return before they all died out. Throughout the nineteenth century, the new church continued to grow in Great Britain, Europe, and to a small extent America. In Britain it reached the approximate size of some thirty thousand people. (The same size as the Elim movement today, and Restorationism.)

In 1901 the last apostle died. Henceforth without apostolic authority there could be no more ordinations. Other churches had paid little attention to the Catholic Apostolic Church, and with the death of the last apostle the movement gradually declined. (Though a sectarian offshoot continues to thrive in Europe.) 1902 saw the beginning of the 'Silence': 'And when he had opened the seventh seal, there was silence in heaven about the space of half an hour.' (Revelation 8:1 AV) During this silence, the last moment of human history, the members of the Catholic Apostolic Church have quietly waited for the return of their Lord. They no longer proselytise, and throughout the twentieth century as the last angels and priests died, one by one the parishes closed. In an act of generosity and solidarity with the universal Church, many CAC members were sent back to the historic churches. In 1971, the last officiating priest died, and the liturgy of what had become a worshipping church in the historic tradition ceased. Today, a handful of members still meet at Paddington and Gordon Square. The litany of intercession is still followed on behalf of the universal Church; like Milton, members of the Catholic Apostolic Church insist, 'they also serve who only stand and wait.'

I have met some Catholic Apostolics who see the outbreak of the Welsh Revival in 1904, and the later Pentecostal movements, as a sign of hope that God would fill all His Church (not just their part) with His Spirit. One lady told me that she thought that Colin Urquhart seemed to be a man of God. Other Catholic Apostolics prefer the spirituality of the Orthodox Church to Pentecostal enthusiasm. (A number have joined the Greek Church.) I certainly believe that the CAC has had an internal spiritual history that is quite genuine, but its external role in Christendom has not been to restore the kingdom, but to establish a sect. An old lady of ninety kindly allowed me to interview her. She was married to one of the last priests in the church. When I asked her whether she thought the CAC had become a denomination, she said: 'Well I suppose we did, but we never meant to be.' (I did not have the nerve to ask her about sects!)

## Developments in Brethrenism

And what happened to the fine ideals of the Brethren? At its best those ideals remain today. Donald Tinder's article, 'The Brethren Movement In The World Today', for example, exhibits those ideals. In practice, however, Brethrenism soon after its formation ran into a serious problem. Its seeming simplicity turned out to be a delusion. The breaking of bread with fellow Christians is one thing, but how do we know who are our fellow Christians? Or, put another way: if the common table is not to be defiled, heretical and unworthy Christians must not be allowed to pollute the holy meal. The last supper is marred by the presence of Judas; partakers of the one loaf must be true Christians only. (If this sounds more like a Catholic doctrine than an Evangelical one, it certainly has its counterpart in sacramental liturgies. The Eastern Orthodox, for example, still jealously guard the 'heavenly mysteries' from the heterodox.)

Within the Brethren ranks, the drive for purity became

more dominant than the drive for unity. To some extent Darby's great idealism and vision of one Church resisting the Devil and apostasy, carried with it a quest for purity. Just as today, Restorationists cannot envisage a true church as one that includes the unjust or unregenerate, neither could Darby stand heresy or sin of any kind. This man of extraordinary talents could not resist playing Witchfinder General.

In the early Christian Church, distinction was always made between dogmatic statements, theological opinion, and pious opinion. On the fundamentals of the faith concerning the Incarnation, life, death, and resurrection of Jesus, and the Holy Trinity, there had to be one undivided faith. There was room, however, for disagreement on matters of an important but not essentially dogmatic kind. Darby, to the cost of the Brethren movement, failed to recognise such distinctions.

Darby and Newton had coped with a number of disagreements between them. Darby was irate because Newton was not too taken with his theories of dispensationalism. Whilst the Powerscourt conferences were continuing in Ireland, Newton was holding meetings in Plymouth. Newton would have no truck with a secret rapture, and was convinced that the return of Christ would be a single event. Darby saw the Second Coming in two stages. First, to meet the saints in the air, and second, to return in glory with the saints to judge an apostate church and the Godless world. At first tensions between the two men provoked no more than an agreement to disagree.

In 1845, a follower of Darby discovered some notes taken down by a lady during one of Newton's sermons. These notes seemed to reiterate the doctrines of Irving on our Lord's human nature. Newton was rigorously pursued by Darby over this matter, and was eventually forced to publicly recant. He published a full confession of his errors, but, as Harold Rowdon points out: 'Darby regarded Newton's *Statement* as little more than an effort to throw dust in the eyes of the reader.'[16] Clearly, Newton lost the support of many of his fellow elders at Plymouth. In 1847, he withdrew from the assembly, and played no further part in Brethren history.

The following year brought the split that led to the division of the movement into the Exclusive and the Open or Plymouth Brethren. In Bethesda chapel, Bristol, Müller and Craik, two of the main leaders of the new movement, received a request from two brothers to receive them into fellowship. These men had been in Plymouth. Some Bethesda elders objected. The Woodfalls brothers were examined to test their orthodoxy. They passed the test and were admitted to fellowship and to share in the Lord's table. Darby, who was passing through Bristol on his way to Exeter in April 1848, made it quite clear that he found this judgement unacceptable. He saw it as a means of sneaking Newton's theology through the back door. He insisted that Newton should be publicly condemned.

On the 29th of June 1848, a statement known as 'The Letter of the Ten' was read out at Bethesda. In it, the elders there refused to say any more concerning Newton's doctrines. Soon Müller and Craik were at loggerheads with Darby over this matter. On the 26th of August, Darby published a circular to Brethren assemblies urging them to isolate Bethesda. The majority of assemblies sided with Darby, but a sizable proportion of churches refused to support him.

In a very short time, the churches that gathered around Darby became more and more obsessed with the question of Christian purity. 'Care meetings' or tribunals were set up to vet members' orthodoxy. The Open Brethren were accused of antinomianism, and Plymouth Brethren accused the Darbyites of legalism. (It almost makes the accusations of R1 and R2 against each other seem like an 'action replay'.)

Darbyism, or Exclusivism as it is usually called, has tended towards central control with power residing in one man or an oligarchy—Darby, Kelly, the Taylors *et al*—but it has never really discovered a totally workable and successful system. Splits and schisms have been endemic in the movement. In Dr. Wilson's terminology, the Exclusivists have become an 'introversionist' sect, stressing separation from not only the world but other Christians.

Today, there are only a few thousand Exclusives left. Since the movement came under the influence of the American Taylor dynasty, there has been considerable scandal and confusion amongst the saints. I was impressed, however, by a paper that Bryan Wilson gave at the London School of Economics in 1984. He said that despite media portrayal as heartless bigots, and a strong antipathy towards them from Open Brethren, the Exclusives were in fact a jolly and happy lot in many ways. The families, he pointed out, were characterised by a great sense of fun and togetherness. (This does not apply in a family where a member has rejected the faith.)

We need reminding in our brief review of Brethrenism that no one was more committed than Darby to the restoration of a New Testament church that would replace denominationalism. In the early days of the movement, he was a man of vision as well as bigotry. Despite his inability to accept criticism and tolerate deviations from his own theological system, he was a tireless worker of great intellectual talents. Although he wrote some of the worst English prose that I have ever read, he could write snappy religious pamphlets and coin memorable hymns. From the Greek he translated a new version of the English Bible, and one in German.

Darby was capable of cruelty and unpleasantness towards his enemies. But the man who destroyed Newton, was also the man who was invariably kind to children and people in distress. The story is told of him, that on board ship in order to give a mother rest from a child that would not stop crying, he took the child under his greatcoat and walked with him all night.

It is a pity that Pickering's *Chief Men Among The Brethren*[17] should exclude Newton. Aristocratic and authoritarian he may have been, but he was also an outstanding leader. So many of the first generation of Brethren were men of leadership, culture, intelligence, and principle. Anthony Norris Groves, perhaps the wisest and most catholic of all Brethren, was saintly. One thinks of Lord Congleton who despised luxury and social class; he would not even have carpets in his house. Captain Percy Hall also stands out. He resigned from the Royal Navy because he could not square his commission with his belief that war was against God's will.

The Christian Brethren were primarily a small but significant exodus from the Church of England. Within a few years, they had turned their back upon her ecclesiastical and sacramental traditions. Believers' baptism quickly became the norm, and some of the earlier catholicity narrowed to form a sort of strict and principled Evangelicalism. True to their origins, the Open Brethren have kept the Lord's table open to all who confess Jesus Christ as Lord. Over the years the Brethren have remained a well-heeled religious movement, but have contributed generously to many missionary and Bible societies.

In this century, Brethren have been involved in many inter-denominational activities of an Evangelical kind. Eric Hutchins, for example, was a Brethren evangelist who had considerable success in the early 1960s. Brethren have often been the unsung heroes in interdenominational Evangelical work throughout the world. Unlike many other Evangelical groups, Brethrenism has maintained a high level of conservative scholarship. (The work of Professor F. F. Bruce would be a good example.) For my money the *Christian Brethren Review* is a fine journal of impeccable scholarship.

If I have been seen to digress to say much of positive worth about the Brethren (and the Catholic Apostolics), it is because I am anxious to show that I do not think their work is in vain, or of no consequence. I do think, however, that the movement has not succeeded in its original aims. The sixty-eight thousand or so Open Brethren in Great Britain have maintained their commitment to local autonomy, and have consciously resisted denominationalism. However, a certain uniformity of practice and doctrine has become established which merits the term sect. Many Brethren have remained 'conversionist', but some assemblies are more closed and conservative than others. Pentecostalism has remained a thorn in their sides since the early days of the

Catholic Apostolic Church. Bitterly opposed to classical Pentecostalism, some assemblies have been more open to Charismatic Renewal. Modern Restorationism, more than any other form of Pentecostalism, poses a major threat to the Brethren. As we have seen throughout this book Restoration is replete with Brethren personnel.

Despite the superficial similarities with the Catholic Apostolic ecclesiology, Restoration is really closer to Brethrenism in terms of doctrine and organisation on the local level. Indeed, from them they inherit their evangelicalism, anti-denominationalism, anti-clericalism, and principled views on baptism. Having male-dominated ministries and local elders also owes much to the Brethren, as does the emphasis on the purity of church and separation from the world. Restoration is the direct successor of neither Brethrenism nor 'Irvingism', but it is an amalgam of both. The missing ingredient that binds together the first two restorationist movements into the third and new Restorationism is the classical Pentecostalism and Holiness movements of the twentieth century.

## Notes

1   Irving and the movement which took his name should really be separated, as the latter group included views which were not his own. Catholic Apostles, on the whole, object to the nickname 'Irvingites'.

2   Many mainline Christians were indifferent to the Second Advent. But the rector of Salisbury, Daniel Whitby (1673–1726) made a considerable impact with his views.

3   I am indebted to Harold Rowdon's Prologue in his *The Origins Of The Brethren* (Pickering and Inglis, 1967) for this information.

4   There seems to be some uncertainty as to how long these conferences continued. There seems to have been a conference in 1838, but the earlier ones made the major impact.

5   I recall a lively discussion with Roger Forster, and the family of Mr. Kenneth Frampton on this matter. (It was a fine occasion of Brethren hospitality and open-mindedness.)

6   F. D. Maurice, the great nineteenth-century churchman, also held Irving in high regard. He called the doctrines of the Scottish minister, 'the grounds of all theology'.

7   'Irvingite Pentecostalism and the early Brethren', *CBRF*, No. 10, December 1965. (See also issue No. 12, May 1966.)

8   Darby's dispensationalism, for example, in which he distinguished the Jewish law and covenant from the covenant of grace (for the Church). Dispensationalism was a major contribution of Darby to Brethren thought. (His views look very much like Irving's least satisfactory doctrines.) The notion of dispensations took on extended meanings in both Brethrenism and other forms of Evangelicalism. The New Testament canon, for example, was seen as a dispensation of miracles denied to the later and contemporary Church.

9   See Donald Tinder, 'The Brethren Movement In The World Today', *CBRF*, No. 25.

10   These doctrines and their relationship to Pentecostalism have been admirably treated by Gordon Strachan in his *The Pentecostal Theology Of Edward Irving* (Darton Longman and Todd, 1976). It is to Gordon's credit that we can see the emergence of a new interest in Irving.

11   They expressed their views in my dramatised documentary on Edward Irving, *The Angel Of Regent Square* (Radio 4, 1 December 1984).

12   *Religious Sects* (Weidenfeld and Nicolson, 1970), p. 207.

13   *Front Room Gospel*, op. cit.

14   They believed that the angels of the seven churches in the Apocalypse were not heavenly beings, but bishops or chief pastors.

15  Rev. W. J. E. Bennet, *The Church's Broken Unity* (J. T. Hayes, Lyall, undated but approximately 1867), p. 148.

16  Op. cit., p. 260.

17  Pickering and Inglis (second edition, undated).

## RECOMMENDED READING

Harold H. Rowdon, *The Origins Of The Brethren* (Pickering and Inglis, 1967).

Timothy Stunt, 'Irvingite Pentecostalism and the early Brethren', *Christian Brethren Review*, No. 10, December 1965.

Andrew L. Drummond, *Edward Irving and His Circle* (James Clarke and Co. Ltd., 1936).

Andrew Walker, 'Will no one stand up for Edward Irving?' *The Listener* (6 December 1984).

# 12

# CLASSICAL PENTECOSTALISM AND RESTORATIONISM

## Beginnings

The outbreak of tongues at Row in Scotland, and Regent Square in London, predate the modern Pentecostal movement by some seventy years. It is generally accepted by Pentecostals, that the birth of Pentecostalism began in 1906 at the Azusa Street Mission, Los Angeles.[1] The crucible for American Pentecostalism was the Holiness sects of the nineteenth century. With their Methodistical origins, the two-way path of conversion and sanctification became eventually the 'born again' experience and the 'second blessing'. This second religious experience, or initiation, became the full-blown 'baptism in the Holy Spirit' of Pentecostalism. That Pentecostalism as a mass movement should have its roots firmly in the soil of a Holiness spirituality would not have pleased Irving: he considered such enthusiasm to be sentimental and theologically arid.[2]

In Europe, the picture is a little more complicated. Anglican Evangelicalism and Lutheranism played their part, but so too did numerous Holiness movements. The Salvation Army, for example, with its Pentecostal hymnology—'Let the fire fall, let the fire fall'—combined with the Keswick Conventions (commencing in 1875) to provide a major Holiness momentum. Two Holiness groups, the Pillar of Fire, and the Pentecostal League, contained many churches which were only a breath away from a new tongues movement.

Mrs. Catherine Price of Brixton is credited as the first speaker in tongues of British Pentecostalism. The 1907 date for this event, however, needs to be seen against a much more significant cause of Pentecostalism: the Welsh Revival. This phenomenon, so similar to the American Holiness revivals of C. G. Finney, was nevertheless more than a Holiness revival. Starting in 1904, and continuing in bursts until the Great War, this wave of enthusiasm broke down the traditional barriers between Wesleyans and Calvinists. The revivals had considerable social and political consequences, and had a social communitarian dimension so often lacking in the pietistic Holiness Camp Meetings of North America.

The Welsh Revival coinciding with the great reformist Liberal government of 1905 to 1909, provided part of the fuel for what was to be the last great secular power of British Nonconformity. ('No Rome on the rates!' shouted the Welsh radicals against the 1902 Balfour Education Act.) It also provided power for the nascent Pentecostal movement. Many of its leaders were converted through the preaching of Evan Roberts, the most successful of the many Welsh evangelists, or his associates. George and Stephen Jeffries of Elim, D. P. Williams of the Apostolic church, Donald Gee of the Assemblies of God, are the most prominent examples. The Anglican vicar, Alexander A. Boddy, from All Saints, Monkwearmouth, was also associated with the Welsh Revival.

It was at his church in Sunderland, and under the influence of an English-born Norwegian, T. B. Barrat (who was directly influenced by the Los Angeles revival), that British Pentecostalism got under way in 1907.

The early years of the Pentecostalism movement are marked by a mushrooming of independent groups, rivalries, and opposition from mainline denominations. It is impossible to go into these developments here, but it will be worthwhile to examine the origins of the Apostolic church, and to look at events in the denominationalism of Elim and the Assemblies of God.

# The Apostolic Church

A dispute arose in South Wales concerning the institutional-isation and content of prophecy. Most of the new Pente-costals saw prophecy as an ecstatic utterance to be used for the exhortation and edification of the local church. At Penegroes, however, it was believed that prophecy was to give direction to the church and should be instituted as an ordinance of church government along with the offices of apostle, evangelist, and elder. W. J. Williams became prophet, and his brother (those Welsh brothers again!) apostle. Soon other Welsh churches joined the growing movement founded firmly and self-consciously on Ephesians 4. In 1918, the Burning Bush Assembly in Scotland joined, and later English churches were established.

The Williams brothers had no idea that the new Apostolic church had interpreted Ephesians 4 in a similar way to Edward Irving and the Catholic Apostolic Church. Their discovery of this fact increased their sense of awe and con-viction that this time God would call out a New Testament church in all her glory.

But whilst the Apostolic church developed the most authoritarian and hierarchical organisation within British Pentecostalism (until modern Restorationism), there is little similarity with the earlier Irving experiment. No angels or priesthood emerged. Instead we have in descending order apostle, prophet, shepherd (pastor), teacher, evangelist, elder, deacon, and deaconness. The High Churchmanship of the early Brethren and Irving is missing. So too is the catho-licity and universality of those movements. The Apostolic church is born in sectarianism, and, despite a strong commit-ment to world mission, there has been a built-in separation from the start. This separation has been somewhat foisted upon them: the rest of British Pentecostalism has never really accepted them.[3] Because sectarianism and separatism were built in to the Apostolic church, I do not think, sociolo-gically speaking, that the Apostolic church qualifies as a full-blown restorationist sect.

Nevertheless, they certainly set the scene for modern

Restorationism, and are a vital link with the nineteenth-century movements. Restoration today has partly recaptured the universalist spirit of their restorationist precursors, but their organisation and theology is far closer to the Apostolic church. Apostle Williams did not identify apostleship with either the twelve Apostles of the Lamb (Revelation 21:14) or the twenty-four elders before the throne (Revelation 4:4). He saw a revived apostolate in exactly the same way as modern Restoration.

As Bryn and Keri Jones hail from Aberdare, and as Arthur Wallis and David Lillie were directly influenced by former leaders within the Apostolic church, I think it is not unreasonable to postulate the linkage between the two movements is a substantial one as far as ecclesiological theory is concerned. If this is true, then it reinforces Bryn Jones's insistence, and John Noble's, that their thinking was already partially formed before the Americans arrived. (But did the Apostolic church influence Ortiz and the Fort Lauderdale five?)

Discipling or shepherding doctrines have never existed in the Apostolic church, but the apostolate contains an authority and casuistic power not typical in the majority of classical Pentecostal churches. Unlike modern Restorationism it has remained primarily a working-class movement. Its earlier history and development was marred by prophetic rivalries. Increasingly, over the years, the prophets have been subjected to apostolic and elder control. Apostles were first called by prophecy (this seems to be a universal feature of charismatic apostolates) and emerged as leaders for life.

Clearly, the Apostolic church is closer to modern Restorationism than any other Pentecostal group from the classical era. The Apostolics today, however, are far more denominationally conscious, and far more centralised than the Restorationists. Penegroes in South Wales is now the headquarters of the world Apostolic movement. If I may be allowed a subjective note: the Apostolic church and Restoration look very similar, but in feel and tone they are quite different. Restoration (Two in particular) is theologically similar to classical Pentecostalism, but its spirituality tends to reflect the cosy middle-classness of the Charismatic Renewal.

On Radio 4, in the programme *Front Room Gospel*, I gave the misleading, though unintentional, impression that the Apostolic church was an insignificant sect. This is not so if you look at it in a world context (rather than a European context as I was doing). We have a genuine curiosity here. In Great Britain, the Apostolic church has never really established itself as a major established sect. Today, they have no more than ten thousand adherents; England has some sixty-seven congregations sometimes only numbering a few dozen worshippers. Scotland has twenty-nine congregations (Hollenweger thought more than forty, fifteen years ago), Northern Ireland thirteen, and Wales sixty-one congregations.[4]

At first glance this is surprising. It is certainly not the case that Apostolic meetings are boring. On the contrary, to be impressionistic again, the Apostolic churches that I have attended in Wales were the most emotionally intense that I have ever experienced in Pentecostalism outside Black churches. I recall wonderful *hwyl* preaching and elegant prophecies. Perhaps there is a clue here. The Apostolics in Wales seem to have encapsulated the old Welsh revivalism in an institutional form. There is something essentially Welsh chapel about the Apostolic church that you cannot find in Elim and the Assemblies of God. The main cause for their relative lack of success in Britain, however, is their authoritarian structure, and what many people see as an extreme form of Pentecostalism. Donald Gee's view of the Apostolic church is one I hear from many classical Pentecostals in regard to modern Restorationism: 'To bestow New Testament titles of offices upon men and women and then consider that by doing so we are creating apostolic assemblies parallel to those of the Primitive Church is very much like children playing at churches.'[5]

The Apostolic church has made some modest gains in Europe, but in Africa they have been a phenomenal success. In Nigeria (the home of so many messianic and cross-cultural cults) they have some three thousand congregations, and hundreds more in other countries of the Third World. As a missionary operation, therefore, the Apostolic church is a great success, but operating from a weak home base. There is obviously a cultural factor here. The special emphasis on the prophetic word, and the institutionalism of the charismatic gifts is alien to the individualism and democratic traditions of Western culture. Conversely, the success of ecstatic authoritarianism is to be expected amongst the weakened and dispossessed members of Nigeria's competing tribal structure.

The Apostolic church may very well offer an organisational lesson for Restoration. Can the Restoration structure, which is even more paternalistic and controlled—despite its middle-classness—ever grow beyond a certain level? How can Restorationists persuade the British people, in any substantial numbers, to forsake self-reliance and individualism for a system of paternalism? The Apostolic church faced with a conflict between the prophets and apostles (which the Catholic Apostolic Church faced before them) settled in favour of a dominating apostolate. This led to a certain amount of inbred rigidity, and inward-lookingness: the conversionalist sect abroad is virtually an introversionist sect at home.

The charismatic ecclesiology has not failed as an organisational structure, but it does seem to have built-in deficiencies as far as church growth is concerned. In our culture, at least, charismatic apostolates have so far never succeeded in heading a religious movement of any great size. In this respect, the growth of the more evangelistic apostolic teams of R1 may offer greater flexibility. This partly depends, as it did for the Brethren, on whether the evangelistic thrust is greater than the drive for certainty and purity. In the Apostolic church, apostles are chosen for life. This itself is a recipe for rigidity—for soon turning the new wineskins back into the old. Apostles for life face similar problems to elected trade union presidents (who are elected for life). What happens when personal popularity is no longer recognised, and charisma disappears? The answer is that you are left with the legalistic authority of the office: the charismatic apostolate too easily becomes the priestly magisterium.

Issues of authority, charismatic leadership, and bureaucratic organisation are at the heart of the institutionalisation of Elim. To look at Elim and the Assemblies of God is to look at the most successful of Pentecostal denominations in Britain, and also the last two significant Christian sects to have become established since the First World War. To look at these classical Pentecostalists may very well be Restorationism looking at its future.

## Elim and the Assemblies of God

If the Welsh Revival provided the immediate resources for Pentecostalism, it would not be true to say that the new movement started in a sectarian fashion. On the contrary, the Pentecostal Missionary Union which was founded in 1909 to support the growing band of missionaries and provide them with some training, was an organisation within the churches. Or to be more precise, it was an organisation like the future 'Fountain Trust' that operated within the context of the existing denominations with input from the independents.

Alexander Boddy saw Pentecostalism very much in the same terms as Michael Harper today; and he remained an Anglican vicar all his life. Many other Pentecostalists within the mainline churches saw the movement in ecumenical terms. However, there were so many different groups and organisations, that it was perhaps inevitable that some should crystallise into sectarian formations.

A group of independent churches that eventually became known as the Assemblies of God had many successful evangelists such as Smith-Wigglesworth and Nelson J. Parr. But the two men who really dominate early Pentecostalism, after Boddy, are Stephen and George Jeffries. I have to agree with Walther Hollenweger's assessment that it is unlikely that British Pentecostalism has ever produced a more naturally talented pair.[6]

The brothers were brought up in Maesteg. Stephen was a miner, and George a salesman in the Co-op. Stephen, by all accounts, was a spectacular preacher. He was often carried away by passion, and patches of rhetorical eloquence, amidst a not altogether carefully structured sermon. His reputation as a healer was also considerable. In 1912, he became a full-time evangelist, often supported by his brother George, who was also beginning to strike out on his own.

In 1913 George, and a small group from Wales, attended a conference of Pentecostals at Boddy's church in Sunderland. As a result of this conference, George was invited to Ireland. And it was there, in 1915, that the Elim Evangelistic Band was formed to preach the foursquare gospel of 'Christ the Saviour, Healer, Baptizer, and Coming King'. Elim begins in Ireland and by 1922 there were some twenty-two churches. George, however, made frequent visits to Wales and England, and gradually but not spectacularly the movement began to grow.

On the mainland, many small independent Pentecostal churches also began to be formed (sometimes in houses), and it became increasingly clear that Pentecost was not going to survive in the mainline churches. Strictly speaking, it never became established in the major denominations. Despite the upper-middle-class leadership of Boddy and one of the famous 'Cambridge seven', Cecil Polhill, the majority of established and 'respectable' Christians rejected the new charisma. Both these Independents, and the newly formed Elim churches were almost exclusively working-class. An anti-intellectualism was often seen as a hallmark of the Spirit.

Meanwhile the Elim Evangelistic Band was consolidating. Dominated by the authoritative George Jeffries (who was later to become authoritarian), and aided by the talented E. J. Phillips (who was putting a little organisation into the outfit) the Foursquare Gospellers were making a name for themselves. Stephen Jeffries was soon to fall out with George and end up preaching in the Assemblies of God. But he did not seem to have the temperament for discipline or denominational exactitude. He remained a law unto himself, but made a considerable personal impact wherever he went.

Two dates are crucial in those early days. In 1924, George

Jeffries and his team were out of the country. The Pentecostal Union was abolished and the Assemblies of God came into being as a loose-knit federation of some seventy-seven Assemblies. Jeffries and the Elimites were invited to join, but they decided to go their own way as it seemed to them that 'God's blessing was resting upon the movement'.[7] To be fair to George, he had made moves to create an umbrella organisation in 1922, but the failure to unite the burgeoning Pentecostal movement into one organisation was certainly a failure to create the potential for a mass movement.

Henceforth, the Assemblies of God grew but as a federation of congregational churches. Elim became increasingly centralised in a presbyterian-style church. At first it was dominated by Principal George Jeffries, as he became known, and later by the bureaucratic style of E. J. Phillips and the 'headquarters'. (Headquarters almost had a Salvation Army military sense at first.) Ecclesiological and personality differences were the main causes of division between the Assemblies and Elim. The only doctrinal difference, that remains to this day, was that the Assemblies of God insisted that the 'baptism of the Holy Spirit' was always accompanied by the sign or seal of *glossalalia*; Elim refused to accept phenomena as the external evidence of the inner divine experience. (How different things might have been for Edward Irving, if he had done the same . . .)

The births of Elim and the Assemblies of God are different in kind from the origins of Irvingism, Brethrenism, and the later Restoration. Essentially these other groups were middle-class and 'come outers'; doctrine and conviction rather than evangelistic revival drove them out. Admittedly Irving's congregation experienced supernatural manifestations, and Restorationism arose in a revivalistic milieu (first created by the Renewal). But none of these groups was born out of a revival; most members were existing Christians, not new converts. Elim and the Assemblies had their fair share of converts from existing denominations, but many of the ordinary rank and file members became Christians as a result of evangelistic crusades. Classical Pentecostalism, in short, was far more evangelistic than its neo-Pentecostal counterparts of the 1980s. (And it still is.) But it is 1926 that marks the take-off point for George Jeffries, and confirmed the rightness of his decision, he thought, to go it alone.

In that year, unexpectedly, the famous and controversial woman evangelist, Aimée Semple McPherson, visited Britain from America. George, ever the pragmatist and opportunist, took the bold step of hiring the Royal Albert Hall. It was packed, and although Mrs. McPherson's Hollywood style did not endear her to the British public, she received enormous media attention. The publicity rubbed off on George. In almost no time, he was able to fill the Albert Hall, the Birmingham City Hall, and the great Crystal Palace (before it was burnt down) without any help from Americans.

The American connection was a crucial boost to the Elim movement, just as it proved to be at the Lakes Bible Week fifty years later when Ernie Baxter arrived. Not that George (any more than Bryn) needed American backing to make him shine. He was a phenomenal evangelist. His sermons were short, biblical, orthodox, and beautifully constructed. His voice, as records testify, was rich and musical. His style, on the whole, was reverent, and he had none of the wildness of his brother, and none of the gimmickry of Aimée Semple McPherson.[8]

For a while, the daily press loved this 'mystic of Maesteg'. He was Britain's most successful evangelist of the 1920s and 1930s. The healings associated with his ministry were seemingly authenticated in a way not typically seen in Pentecostal circles today. The *Daily Express* once recorded that over seventy healings took place at one Easter Monday rally at the Royal Albert Hall. Sometimes, on these occasions, the Principal and other pastors would baptise by immersion a hundred or more converts in a specially constructed tank. During a three-week campaign in Birmingham, over ten thousand people were converted to Christ. Many joined Elim, but many more went back to their own denominations or joined a mainstream church for the first time.

Smith-Wigglesworth and Stephen Jeffries also held many successful campaigns, but none of them were quite of the order of the Principal. George Jeffries was a shy man outside the pulpit. He never married. Despite his rather effeminate looks in his early days (at least against his miner brother), and despite occasional whiffs of scandal surrounding his sexuality, there is not the slightest historical evidence that Jeffries was homosexual. (As Restorationist leaders know today, no charismatic leader escapes the rumour machine.) During the height of his power in the late 1920s and 1930s, George Jeffries gained a stature of spiritual authority, so that many Elimites, and others, admit that Jeffries had great personal presence as well as an engaging public persona.

And then, in a way, it all went wrong. Bryan Wilson's excellent account of the Elim Movement[9] sees this as the inevitable clash between charismatic leadership and emerging bureaucratic organisation. Earlier Elimites accused Wilson of taking Jeffries' side against them by talking mainly to his followers that went with him to form a new church, the Bible Pattern Fellowship. Today, however, Wilson's account is given greater credence than it was. Elim leaders seem to be far more objective than they were twenty-five years ago. Not that everyone goes along with Dr. Wilson's account. Some Elim members, who are old enough to remember, prefer seeing Jeffries's fall in terms of spiritual pride, doctrinal deviation, and even personality disorder. It would be true to say, however, that all Elimites, whilst admitting that something went wrong with Jeffries, recognise him as a great man.

This whole story has still to be told, and as Elim have a first-class historian, an open and honest account will eventually emerge. (Pastor Desmond Cartwright, who is writing a book on Stephen and George Jeffries[10] is proud to be an Elim pastor, but he is not afraid of the truth; his work is genuine history, not hagiography.) Elim as a denomination was formed as the Elim Evangelical Alliance in 1926. It was later called simply the Elim Church. More and more churches were bought as a result of evangelistic campaigns. (I remember Pastor Brewster, who was a successful evangelist with Elim after the Second World War, used to buy a church first, and then hold a 'Great Revival And Healing

Campaign' to fill it.) A committee of pastors controlled the daily issues of finance, discipline, and (to a certain extent) doctrine.

Whilst Jeffries went up and down the country with his team, Elim was consolidating as a denomination behind its figurehead. I think it likely that Jeffries did wake up to the fact that the tail was wagging the dog (shades of Irving). He became distressed, by the end of the 1930s, at the centralised control, and urged a move towards congregationalism. But there are some contradictions here. At the very moment that Jeffries was insisting on greater lay participation and local autonomy, his own increasingly authoritarian personality came into play. He was also eager to make the beliefs of British Israelitism a mandatory doctrine of Elim. Whether he was aware of the neo-fascist overtones possible in such a position—especially in leading up to the war with Germany— I cannot say.

The first Secretary of the Assemblies of God, J. Nelson Parr, told me in 1970, not long before he died, that British Israelitism destroyed George Jeffries. 'His theories about the long-lost tribes of Israel,' Parr said, 'became more important to him than the Gospel.' I think it may well be true that British Israelitism unhinged Jeffries a little, in the same way that Dr. Chalmers claimed that biblical prophecy 'unshipped' Irving. But I think this issue has been exaggerated. Jeffries was a diabetic, which was a well-kept secret of the healer for many years. His ill health, unsettled personality,[11] combined with a genuine dislike of the bureaucratic centralisation, were multi-causal factors in his downfall. From an organisational point of view, I think that Bryan Wilson, following the German sociologist Max Weber, was right: sooner or later, charismatic personal authority gives way to more institutional forms.

It was in 1939 that Jeffries resigned from the Elim movement, and after some delay founded the Bible Pattern Church Fellowship (to give it its full title). On the surface this new movement looks to have restoration overtones, because Jeffries wanted a church founded on biblical principles alone. In reality the new sect was a kind of Pentecostal congregationalism with British Israelitism attached. Despite his great popular appeal within Elim—the rank and file members knew little of the conflicts at the top—the new movement never really got off the ground. He made a personal appeal to many pastors in Elim, but many who left to join him soon returned to the parent body. The few churches that made up the new federation returned to Elim in the early 1960s after the death of George Jeffries. (At least the buildings reverted to Elim; not necessarily the small membership of the short-lived Bible Pattern Church Fellowship.)

Whatever the true cause of Jeffries departure from Elim, the split between the Principal and Elim led to the disappearance of the evangelist's charisma. Elim has survived this crisis in its relatively short history, and has matured into an established sect. Its centralised structure seems to have protected it from Restorationist incursions rather better than the local autonomy of the churches in the Assemblies of God.

The Assemblies themselves grew larger than Elim in the number of churches they established. They estimate that they have some sixty thousand members today; I cannot find evidence for such a number and believe that this is a considerable miscalculation. Nevertheless, with its popular Bible College at Mattersly Hall, salaried pastors, and lively evangelistic style, the AOG has developed into a stable sect. Its stability has been considerably rocked by Restorationism in the last five years, but there is no sign that it will imminently recapitulate to the new Pentecostalism.

No mention of the Assemblies of God would be complete without reference to Donald Gee. This man, who so wished that he had had a university education, was in fact endowed with great musical and intellectual gifts. He never pretended that the Pentecostal movement had succeeded, and he wanted the AOG to join the World Council of Churches. Gee was an excellent example of a person who belonged to a sect, but who was totally devoid of the sectarian spirit.

History is cruel. I think it a shame that George Jeffries,

who was probably Britain's most successful evangelist and healer of the twentieth century,[12] should have been completely forgotten. Like Irving before him, the final events of his life obscured his successes. Unlike Irving, however, who at least died infamously, George Jeffries died a nonentity.

## The Historical Lessons for Restoration

Elim and the Assemblies of God were able to grow to their present stability and size (I think twenty-five to thirty thousand, and thirty-five to forty thousand respectively) as a result of emerging beyond the revivalism of the first generation into the relative security of established sects. The initial impetus of classical Pentecostalism, which was a revival with a strong evangelistic emphasis, failed to consolidate the new charismatic organisations into one movement. We have briefly looked at the three main sects that grew out of the early revivals (there were other smaller and short-lived groups), and have noted that Elim itself split. The Assemblies of God have consistently shed churches in various directions (most recently to R1). Such evidence poses the question: is Pentecostalism schismatic by its very nature? Whilst, I feel, that Restorationists would want to answer with an emphatic 'No!', many of them recognise that the historical omens, at least, are not favourable.

Restorationism did not begin like classical Pentecostalism. The fuel for the movement both in terms of rank and file members, and the spiritual energy originated in the Renewal;[13] whereas the ideology, organisation, and leadership lies outside the Renewal. This, at least, has some similarities with the nascent Renewalism of Boddy and the early Pentecostalists.

The failure, however, to move over to a large-scale and successful evangelistic movement, may lead Restoration to become no more than a small introversionist sect of the size and significance of the Apostolic church in Britain. The emergence of teams, especially in R1, at least point to an evangelistic development. There would seem to be a tension here. On the one hand Bradford, the most centralised, organised and separatist group, is also the most evangelistic.

R1 as a whole, as it is presently constituted, is more evangelistic than the more liberal and ecumenical R2. It is too early to tell whether conversionist or introversionist tendencies will win out. Despite its Pentecostalism, Restorationism resembles not only the ideological restorationism of Brethrenism more than it resembles Elim and the Assemblies of God, but also its development is closer to nineteenth-century restorationism.

Modern Restorationism, however, starts from a far narrower religious base then the nineteenth-century movements. In short, the new groups have been predicated upon a classical Pentecostalism, Independents, and a neo-Pentecostalism from within the mainline churches. But neither the Anglican, Methodist, or Catholic churches have provided major input. Most personnel have come from the Baptist Union, the Open Brethren, classical Pentecostalism, and earlier house churches such as Wally North's fellowships and Chard.

The neo-Pentecostalism (which is itself a mutation from the classical style) is essentially overshadowed, therefore, by sectarian inputs. Table 2 shows how we can relate Restoration to present sectarian groups and nineteenth-century movements. The historical perspective demonstrates that the third bite of the Restoration cherry is from a more sectarian point than earlier movements. Indeed, the third bite has to be seen in the light of classical Pentecostalism. Restoration is not a direct descendant of Brethrenism or Irvingism: it would not have come to life without the theology and experience of twentieth-century Pentecostalism. It is this Pentecostalism that mediates, or binds together the two earlier restoration movements into its modern form.

The history of Elim and the Assemblies of God is crucial to an understanding of Restoration not because origins are similar, but because, it seems to me, the evidence is fairly conclusive that Restoration will end up in the classical Pentecostal camp. If R2 makes too many overtures to the mainstream churches, it will simply be sucked back into the Renewal. R1 will either grow through evangelistic endeavour, or shrink to become an introversionist sect. Even if Terry Virgo and Tony Morton cease to relate to Bryn Jones, their organisations are too large to disband. Their future is either to disappear within the first generation or survive in some other sectarian form; perhaps with people from R2. The Bradford group already have a built-in head-quarters at Church House, a strong organisation, firm and charismatic leadership, and money. They look dangerously like a sect within a sect: if R1 disintegrates in its present form, the Bradford core will survive on its own.

The point I am trying to make, sociologically speaking, is that there is no middle ground between the sects and the denominations. Whichever way Restoration goes, whether it be to adopt a more modest conversionism such as Elim, or the introversionism of the Exclusives, whilst it stays outside the mainstream it will remain a sect.

Colin Urquhart, one of Britain's best-known charismatic leaders, has recognised, correctly in my own opinion, that there are two parallel structures of Pentecostalism: the classical sects and house churches outside the mainstream, and the Renewal inside. I think, however, that he is mistaken in thinking that he holds the middle ground between the two. His Bethany Community, and the new Bible College in Sussex, are far more likely, whether he likes it or not, to take him into sectarian territory. Indeed Colin's books and sermons are not so much reflective of Anglican Renewalism as reminiscent of 1950s American revivalism.

If Restorationism still wishes to become 'the mountain' to fill the whole earth, then it will have to go onto an aggressive evangelistic offensive. So far neither R1 nor R2 have conducted campaigns anywhere near the scale of George Jeffries and the Elim evangelistic team. Ironically, to date, restorationist sects, have not grown at the rate of the less universalistic conversionist sects of Elim and the Assemblies of God. The desire to establish the New Testament church order, for committed Christians only, has led to an inward-lookingness that tends to inhibit church growth. Modern Restorationism, like its restorationist precursors, resembles a movement fallen between two stools.

In many ways, Restoration has already succeeded

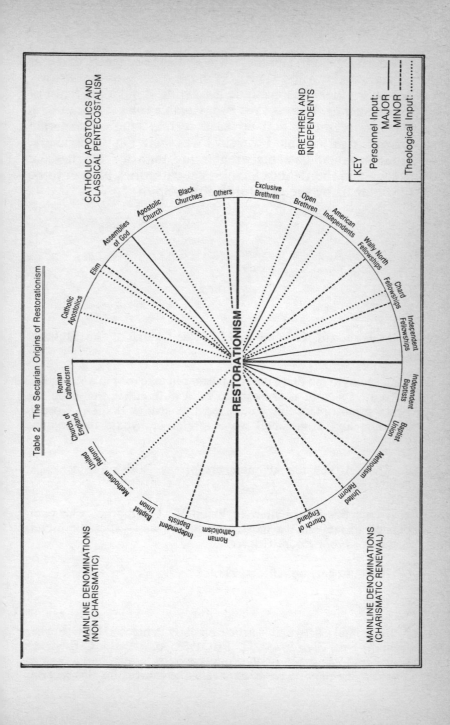

Table 2  The Sectarian Origins of Restorationism

**RESTORATIONISM**

CATHOLIC APOSTOLICS AND
CLASSICAL PENTECOSTALISM

BRETHREN AND
INDEPENDENTS

MAINLINE DENOMINATIONS
(NON CHARISMATIC)

MAINLINE DENOMINATIONS
(CHARISMATIC RENEWAL)

KEY

Personnel Input:
MAJOR
MINOR -------
Theological Input: ..........

Catholic Apostolics
Elim
Assemblies of God
Apostolic Church
Black Churches
Others
Exclusive Brethren
Open Brethren
American Independents
Wally North Fellowships
Chard Fellowships
Independent Fellowships
Independent Baptists
Baptist Union
Methodism
United Reform
Church of England
Roman Catholicism
Independent Baptists
Baptist Union
United Reform
Methodism
Church of England
Roman Catholicism

wonderfully well. The historical evidence suggests that it is unlikely that it will do better than the other groups. History, however, offers lessons to be learned: it is not a predictor of events; neither does it exist by inviolable rules. I do not wish Restorationism to end up as a certain kind of sectarian formation just so that I can say I was right. On the contrary, nothing would give me greater joy than for the laws of history and the fallible sociological categories of men to be blown apart by the gale force of the Spirit.[14]

## Notes

1  I have heard 1885/6 quoted by some Church of God Holiness groups.

2  It seems to me that Pentecostalism can take root in a Reformed Calvinist soil, but it is likely to be a different flower from the Pentecostalist plant that we are used to. I think that Dr. Gordon Strachan and Tom Smail would prefer to bypass the holiness route.

3  Though they are all members of the British Pentecostalist Fellowship.

4  I owe this information to Philip W. Cawthorne, who complained to me—in the most gentlemanly way—after the broadcasting of *Front Room Gospel*.

5  Hollenweger, op. cit., p. 193.

6  Ibid., p. 199.

7  Desmond Cartwright's article on early Pentecostalism, 'Echoes from the past, *Elim Evangel* (5 Feb. 1983), p. 6. Pastor Cartwright's series in the *Evangel*, phone conversations, letters, and a copy of an academic paper have been invaluable sources for this section.

8   After Aimée's infamous disappearance, George Jeffries was asked to go to Los Angeles and take over her Metropolitan Temple. It is difficult to imagine a more opposite pair in the whole history of Pentecostalism. (George's refusal was Elim's gain.)

9   'The Elim Foursquare Gospel Church' in *Sects and Society*, Greenwood Press, 1978. Hollenweger's criticisms of Wilson are themselves now out of date.

10   *The Evangelists: The Lives of Stephen and George Jeffries* (Marshalls, forthcoming).

11   By the 1940s, Pastor Cartwright reports, nobody knew where they were with George: he was uncertain, and constantly changing his mind.

12   Evan Roberts may be able to claim a great success as an evangelist *per se*; but he was no healer.

13   It seemed too complicated to outline this in Table 2, but the Restorationist membership from the Renewal has tended to come from its periphery (and, of course, other Independent churches).

14   See my article, 'Pentecostal Power', in *Of Gods And Men*, ed. E. Barker.

## RECOMMENDED READING

Desmond Cartwright, *The Evangelists: The Lives of Stephen and George Jeffries* (Marshalls, forthcoming).
Donald Gee, *Wind And Flame* (AOG Publishing House, 1967).
Walther J. Hollenweger, *The Pentecostals* (SCM, 1972).
Bryan Wilson, *Sects and Society* (Greenwood Press, 1978).

# 13

# THE KINGDOM UNDER ATTACK

One of the most significant ways that Restoration can demonstrate that it has really arrived on the religious scene with a vengeance, is the fact that it is increasingly being opposed and resisted. This is not simply because it is new: it is because it is radical. Opposition has not come, on the whole, from secular opponents. Non-Christian parents have expressed concern for their children,[1] and as I mentioned at the beginning of the book, the national press has been sniffing around hoping for a sensational exposé. Restoration-ism cannot really expect to avoid the full glare of publicity because it is a high-risk religion. By that I mean that it avoids cosy, safe Evangelicalism, and opts for a radical alternative to mainstream religion. Its high charismatic profile, Americanised business methods, and above all, its commitment to paternalistic yet intense relationships inevitably means that it is always walking in the shadow of sensationalism and scandal. Some Restorationists, I know, see the press (including the religious trade press) as vultures just waiting for something to go wrong, so that they can swoop in and make a killing.

To date, however, the major opposition to Restoration-ism has come from fellow Pentecostalists and Evangelical groups. Much of this criticism has been muted. A number of Evangelical leaders, for example, expressed 'grave concern' to me, but were not prepared to be quoted, or see their names in print. Classical Pentecostals have been particularly reticent in this respect.

A far bigger problem for me, as a researcher, is that many of the criticisms levelled at Restorationism have been based either on hearsay evidence, or, if based on direct experience, have lacked corroborating evidence (such as documentation, further witnesses, etc.). For example, David Tomlinson related the story of the elder who supposedly possessed the front door keys to everybody's home in his fellowship.[2] I have heard this story in four different places, but nobody has been able to find me the bunch of keys or the keeper of the keys. And again, I was told the story of a young woman who was apparently told by the elder that she was not to use contraception; the informant was unable to provide me with the name of the woman, or the fellowship to which she belonged!

Furthermore, when people have been prepared to talk to me, I have to take into consideration, if they have recently left R1 or R2, that their disillusionment can lead to a bitterness that distorts what really happened to them in the kingdom. Taking all these factors into account, there are four criticisms, it seems to me, that present a serious challenge to Restorationism. None of these challenges are invented by me. I have selected them as the four most coherent and persistent attacks, I have heard, against the Restoration kingdom.

## 1 Restorationism is Destroying the Charismatic Renewal

The problem here is that Charismatic leaders are rarely specific when they accuse house churches of being sectarian. Do they mean R1, or R2 in its strict or extended form, or do they mean churches outside this rubric? Consider Tom Walker, one of the leading Anglican Renewalists in Birmingham:

'I'm concerned with the House Church Movement because it seems to me that a movement that pulls believing Christians out of established churches, is going against what The Spirit is saying to churches all over the world. And that is, that there should be new life and a real unity within the established churches . . .'[3]

When I talked with the Rev. Tom Walker, whilst he could not necessarily give me a definition of the House Church Movement, he could give me examples. In particular, he was concerned with the Dales Bible Week phenomenon. Having talked with Douglas McBain and Michael Harper,[4] they are obviously worried about those house churches that stress distinctiveness of doctrine, and in particular shepherding principles. However, even this is misleading, because both these leaders of the Renewal are seeking a *rapprochement* with the John Noble, Gerald Coates, David Tomlinson fellowships. It is really the Bradford churches of R1 that they are bothered about, and groups like the Basingstoke communities in my extended usage of R2.

Since I commenced this book, new evidence has come to light that the Renewal is consolidating and growing at the grass roots level (at least in the Church of England).[5] Therefore, the accusation against Restorationism is not that it has completely sunk the Renewal, but that it is always launching torpedoes against it. From the Renewalist standpoint, the *raison d'être* of their movement is that it promotes an organic (as opposed to bureaucratic) ecumenism: the renewal of the local churches is a call to the unity of the Church. God the Holy Spirit, they feel, wishes to revive existing structures, and prevent the creation of new sectarian enclaves.

This 'reformism' is precisely what radical Restorationism rejects. Renewalists see new structures as competing with the existing churches. This competition they see as dividing the Body of Christ, and weakening the power of the Holy Spirit. Renewalists reluctantly accept the classical Pentecostalists (despite a middle-class bias), because they were there first. But the establishment of house churches they see as a betrayal of all that the Renewal has stood for.

It is a matter of fact, that a great many of the rank and file members of the Restoration movement were involved in the Renewal. However, few were members of the historic churches (though I have met former Anglicans and Catholics). Or to be more accurate, few congregations or large groups moved over from the historic churches, or indeed Methodism and the United Reformed Church. Those former

Renewalists who came over to Restorationism wholesale, often did so as a result of a visit to the Dales Bible Week, or Downs Week. Leaders of the Renewal perceive R1 as more enticing to the neo-Pentecostals of the mainstream churches than R2. Bryn Jones denies that his churches have advocated that Christians should leave denominations. Consider his reply to such an accusation:

'Such a thing has never been preached to my knowledge. I have made it very clear on a number of occasions that where a denominational church is against the authority of Scripture or things of the Holy Spirit, there is no obligation on any Christian to stay in that church.'[6]

But there is a certain lack of ingenuousness here. There can be no doubt on reading Arthur Wallis's book, *The Radical Christian*, or the 'Church Adrift' series in *Restoration* magazine (as we have seen) that R1 believes that all denominations fail to live up to this criteria. Denominations are not in God's plans; the Church cannot be renewed from within the existing organisational structures; apostolic and discipling structures are the essential not the secondary features of church structure.

If Restorationists do begin to say that the Church can be renewed from within, after all, what reasons do they have to continue their separate existence? In America, the Fort Lauderdale five succeeded, for a time, in integrating their shepherding system inside some mainline churches. This is precisely why the discipling issue was so much more divisive in the United States than it has been in Britain: it split the Renewal from within. British Restorationism has peeled off layers of the Renewal from without. As I was at some pains to point out in Part 1, Restorationism is not a mutation from the Renewal; despite overlapping with Renewalism, its existence was separate from the start.

In fact, Bryn Jones makes a point of not having apostolic control over congregations or groups within the mainline churches. It would appear, however, that Terry Virgo has a more flexible arrangement with groups still inside Independent and Baptist Union churches.

Since I started writing this book, I have seen some

convergence between R2 and mainstream Renewalism. A mutual recognition of ministry, an acceptance of the *de facto* reality, and an acceptance of each other's territory, may yet lead to some reintegration of house churches with the Renewal of the mainline denominations. I cannot see this happening in R1, or some sections of my extended use of R2. Reintegration may be too strong a word for R1, but greater co-operation is certainly hoped for amongst some of Terry Virgo's elders.

I think it true to say that most Restorationists do not see themselves as deliberately setting out to destroy the Renewal. It is more the case, they feel, that God is showing them something about the nature of His Church, that Renewalists are not yet seeing. Arthur Wallis is unequivocal on this issue of divisiveness. For him it is a question of truth; Christ came not to bring peace but a sword:

'I think that one always has to bear in mind that truth is always divisive. When the truth of the Gospel comes it divides between those who receive that truth and become Christians, and those who reject that truth. When the charismatic movement came, the truth concerning the Holy Spirit became a divisive point. And we feel that we are simply proclaiming—with no intention to divide—what God has shown to us about the church. Some receive it, and some do not.'[7]

Radical Restorationists do not deny that Renewalists are 'born again' and Spirit-filled Christians. But they do feel that they are out of step with God's purpose 'for this generation'.

I agree with Michael Harper that Restorationism took some of the heat away from the Renewal movement especially after the closure of the Fountain Trust in 1980. Between 1980 and 1982, the Dales Bible Week became a major focus for many nomadic Pentecostalists, and some disaffected Renewalists. By the end of 1984, however, after the visit of John Wimber from California to Great Britain, and after evidence began to show that the Renewal was still consolidating, Restorationism seemed to be slightly less of a threat.

But in fairness to Restorationists, it must be said that

it is oversimplistic to suggest that they are dividers, and Renewalists are unifiers. Caustic critics of the Renewal, such as the Rev. Peter Mullen, would claim that the Renewal does not form new churches, but it does divide congregations.[8] The parish church can consist of the 'in group', and be divided into those with the 'Baptism' and those without it. I attended a Catholic church a few years ago, where there was a church within the church. Natural reconcilers like Tom Walker and Michael Harper within the Church of England know that the tensions within any form of Pentecostalism are liable suddenly to cease being creative, and become destructive. It has yet to be proved, in my opinion, whether Pentecostalism in its 'posher' charismatic form can be successfully grafted—on a long-term basis—into traditional churches without discerption. In this respect history is more on the side of the Restorationists than those in the Renewal.

## 2 Restorationists Deliberately 'Poach' Church Members, and Divide Congregations Against Themselves

This is a very serious claim, and is really an extension of the first challenge. There are two things that can be said with certainty. First, it is the case that a majority of Restorationists are 'come outers' from the denominations, independent assemblies, and established sects. Second, it is not the case that there is a conspiracy, an elaborate plan, or a concerted effort to break up other churches.

It is true to say, however, that churches and fellowships are sometimes broken up; often before the new breakaway group call in an apostle to oversee them. I have met a number of cases where apostolic direction has been subsequent to a split or local schism. More straightforwardly what happens is this: the new teaching arrives in the local church, and gradually it takes root. Either the whole congregation are wooed over, or a sizable minority leave. That power battles arise, and unpleasantness and unhappiness can occur is without doubt. The churches who have felt themselves to be the most vulnerable to incursions or takeovers (as they see it) are congregational-style assemblies that are relatively autonomous, and democratic in leadership.

Even centralised churches have been vulnerable. Six Elim churches, for example, have seceded from the parent body, and a sizable number of individuals. But it is the Assemblies of God, Evangelical Free Baptists, Brethren Assemblies, and churches of the Baptist Union that have been the most effected. The heartland of the Renewal (Anglicanism and Catholicism) have been barely touched. A number of leaders in the locally-structured churches have been bitter because their democratic processes have been abused, they feel, by a religious group that practises no democracy within its own ranks. When Dr. David Russell was General Secretary of the Baptist Union, he received a number of complaints from long-standing Baptist members who complained of being, in effect, ousted from their own churches. As the present General Secretary, the Rev. Bernard Green put it:

'We have even got a situation where half a church has left and set up in rivalry in the building next door. Now, even allowing for our respect of their integrity that seems to us to create a picture of the Church which does not always reflect love as the first gift of the Holy Spirit . . . I think of one particular church (which I must not name) where all membership was cancelled and people were told that they could only be members in the future if they signed a covenant which was newly written; one clause of which was "I promise to give total obedience to the leaders of the church." These people refused to sign, and they were excommunicated immediately.'[9]

Pastor George Canty of Elim (now retired, but still an itinerant evangelist) highlighted the problem of walking out of a church and leaving the rest of the congregation saddled with the mortgage debts on the church building.[10] The issue of trust deeds and debts is a major factor in these disputes. But these cases are rather vague. I would like to offer two case studies which are more specific.

The first case study involves Goos Vedder, who is now a member of Bryn Jones's team.[11] In 1974, this Dutch evangelist and fellow worker with 'God's Smuggler', brother Andrew, was invited to pastor Hoole Baptist church. He was already known and liked there. Within a year, however, many of the Baptists complained at the charismatic emphasis, and the influx of new people who supported this new style of ministry. Unlike the Rev. Bernard Green's story, the new people had not become church members and had no right to vote. A church meeting was eventually held, and there was a vote of no confidence in the pastor. Half the meeting supported the motion, but as a two-thirds majority is needed to remove a pastor, a situation of stalemate prevailed. Goos Vedder sought advice from the local Baptist superintendent, but he could offer no solution to the problem.

Goos Vedder then went to see Bryn Jones, whom he had known for some years. Eventually he decided to leave the church, explaining to the congregation that there was no point in him staying if there was not total confidence in his leadership. He did not, however, give the statutory three months' notice, but left almost at once. He announced from the pulpit that if there were any of the congregation who felt towards him as a sheep towards a shepherd, they were welcome to join him.

A week later a fellowship commenced in the Arts Centre. At first a large group of one hundred or more turned up to support him. From the start Goos Vedder made it clear that the church would be run on shepherding lines (remembering that Ern Baxter had not yet been to the Lakes). Many left at this news. In January of 1975, Bryn Jones, Keri Jones, and Peter Paris came to commission Goos as pastor of the new church.

The fellowship sank to about thirty in number, but then began to consolidate and grow. This story of Goos Vedder is interesting because it allows us to see the problems from both perspectives. One charismatic pastor still in the Baptist Union complained to me bitterly: 'If they must go, they must, but why do they always have to take a group of followers to support them?' This is a fairly typical reaction to such stories, and it is certainly true that once a faction has been established it usually is resolvable only by schism. In Goos Vedder's case, however, he was in a particularly difficult position. He was the formally constituted pastor, and the democratic meeting had not secured enough votes to remove him. And it is at this juncture that we see the radical cutting edge of Restorationism: if the church will not obey the voice of the Holy Spirit, then it will be left to its own devices.

We can recall Edward Irving when he was excommunicated from the Church of Scotland at the Annan presbytery: 'As many as will obey the voice of the Holy Ghost, let them depart.'[12] Or again, when the trustees of Regent Square locked him out of the church in London: 'Surely disappointment and defeat will rest upon it for ever. God will not bless it . . .'[13] Vedder's appeal, therefore, is to obey the voice of the Holy Spirit. We are back to Arthur Wallis: 'truth is always divisive.' To stand for truth, purity of gospel and ministry, often cuts across personal relationships and friendships. The Puritan radicals of the seventeenth century believed in love, but they dared not risk being polluted by an apostate church that refused to heed God's message. Darby believed in one world church, but he could not accept a luke-warm or heretical believer at the common table.

One could argue that Vedder was forced out, or that he did the decent thing and left. As to whether you think it was a decent thing to set up a rival church, depends on whether you think people were obeying the voice of the Spirit, or 'the rebellious murmurings of the heart'.

My second case study involves a fellowship that had already broken away from the local Baptist church. John and Liz Race, who gave me this story, have done so because they feel that it is essential that people know the way in which recruitment and commitment programmes operate in practice. Giving me their names, as they have done, is to risk further ostracism, they feel, from people who are still their friends, but who no longer share religious worship with them. Unlike most other stories of this nature that I have received, this one was well documented, thought out, and reflective. It obviously took great courage for them to give their version of events. They felt that names should not be fictionalised, but they accept that other people in the story may very well interpret events differently. Essentially, John and Liz Race are charismatic Evangelicals; they see Restorationism as something potentially dangerous and sinister.[14]

After a group of people left Romford Baptist church to join John Noble's fellowships (John Race does not say when), a small group who stayed in formed a charismatic core within the existing church. (My idea of the church within the church.) In time the charismatic group gained supporters including an elder, a few deacons, and the church secretary. This secretary, Mr. Brian Smith, opened up his house to the group and became one of the leaders. Some thirty or so people would meet for praise and exercise of the spiritual gifts. Some members of Romford Baptist church knew nothing of this activity. Tension arose between the pastor, The Rev. Norman Wright, and the group. (Rev. Norman Wright was President of the Baptist Union, 1984–5.) Apparently he was deeply upset about remarks accusing him of 'grieving the Holy Spirit'.

It was suggested by him that the group should be disbanded, or curtail its activities. After much prayer, soul-searching, and fasting, John tells us, the group began to reform outside the Baptist church. John and Liz removed their son from the Sunday school, but they did not formally resign from the church. In the summer of 1983, after a visit to the Shepton Mallet Bible Week (R1), Mr. Brian Smith formed a caretaker leadership of himself and five other men. This was supposed to help them through the transition from a disbanded group to a new fellowship. Mr. Peter Birchinall, a much-respected elder at Romford Baptist church, resigned and joined the leadership of the new group.

In September 1983, the new group started meeting for worship in the YMCA. They called themselves Emmanuel Community Church. John and Liz Race insist that neither they nor many of the group had any idea at the time that choosing the title 'Community Church' was in any way associated with the Restoration movement. In October 1983, it was agreed to establish links with John Singleton and the North London Community Church (one of London's fastest-growing churches, incidentally). There seems to have been some confusion as to whether links should be made with R1 and R2. Originally, they had talked of bringing in Tony Morton and Arthur Wallis. That they decided to choose John Singleton is interesting. He was at one time associated with Bryn Jones and David Mansell, but had now branched out on his own. I think it safe to say that he is now firmly in R2, as I saw him and his wife at Festival 84. (David Tomlinson confirmed that he is no longer in R1.)

It was suggested that John and his team should be brought in as consultants (at least that is how John Race saw them). The Emmanuel Community Church were told that these men 'were humble men of God who were farther along the road that they were now travelling'. The group were told that they would be taught 'restoration principles' and how to 'build relationally'.

At first, says John Race, it was by no means clear what this new radical teaching was all about. By the end of October 1983, Peter Birchinall left the fellowship and returned to Romford Baptist church; he was not happy with these new teachings. John Race believes that Brian Smith already knew what Restorationism stood for because he read *Restoration* magazine, and had attended the Dales Bible Week. He had also organised the visit to the Shepton Mallet Bible Week. Before the rest of the group knew of it, he had read Trudinger's *Built To Last* under its original title. (I am not aware of another title for this book, and wonder whether John Race means Trudinger's earlier book, *Cells For Life*.) At this time, says John Race, the full implications of Restorationism were not spelled out to the group.

Indeed, for the next month, John recalls, Singleton and his colleagues talked much about love, sharing, and being radical, but nothing specifically Restorationist was discussed. During this time, however, John and Liz read Trudinger's book, and began to understand not only what Restorationism was about, but began to be deeply concerned. Here are some of John's notes:

(1) The concept of delegated authority and submission to leadership. Trudinger writes (p. 126) 'Every man needs another man with delegated authority as a shepherd over his personal life. Every leader then, himself needs a leader—a voice from God, we may say.' This passage concerned me very much. The phrase 'over his personal life' is unscriptural and open to abuse in practice . . . It places men as mediators between God and men. Extremely dangerous.

(2) The concentration of power in the leadership. The removal of decision-making from the church members. Trudinger writes (p. 117): 'In a restoration church, the elders or the leaders in plurality, are the door of the fold.'

John and Liz were particularly worried about the insistence on tithing. John wrote in his notes: 'A new legalism was being imposed. Christians should obey the dictates of their conscience and should be free to distribute their money as they felt led. There is no NT support for tithing.'

John disliked a section in Trudinger's book (p. 155) where he says: 'So in a community of God's pattern each one is committed. There are no peripherals . . .' John felt that it was unhealthy to build a fellowship without a fringe membership. He thought that the ideology of 'no peripherals' would alienate the faint-hearted.

These points, and many more, were raised at a special meeting held in Brian Smith's house. John Singleton and David Halls were there from the North London Community Church. According to John Race, the book was more or less dismissed by the North London team; the Emmanuel fellowship were told that its teachings were not going to be implemented. (A number of leaders in R2 do, in fact, consider Trudinger's book to be extreme.) After the meeting Liz told John: 'We may have won a battle, but we have not won the war.'

'How right she was,' said John. Soon afterwards, the group returned to those very same principles of commitment and shepherding, that had earlier been dismissed. No cell groups or home groups were established during this time, but the group were told that they would be established after commitment had been made to the new principles.

John thought that there was a lot of double talk around.

Commitment had two sides to it. On the one hand, it was said to be a commitment to one another, a commitment to God and the Bible. The bottom line or the undertow was that commitment really meant being committed to the leadership and being willing to do what you were told. There was much talk about being free in worship and community. On the other side this meant you would be free provided you had the blessing of the leadership. On the one hand we were told that we were not going to have any authoritarianism or heavy disciplining. On the other side we were taught submission, delegated authority and the pitfalls of ecclesiastical democracy. Democracy became something of a dirty word. Theocracy was the way ahead.

John and Liz Race sent me their comprehensive commitment course. After completing it, they felt unable to make a further commitment, and withdrew from the emerging new Restorationist church. John took a rather personal line. He thought that Mr. Peter Birchinall was a stable and sensible person. After his voluntary withdrawal, he felt the remaining leadership was too autocratic. John felt that the dividing line between theocracy and autocracy was too thin. He felt that despite the grand theological structure, the whole thing was a golden opportunity for the power-seeking, and for authoritarian personalities.

John and Liz Race would like to remain friends with members of the Emmanuel Community Church, but they are convinced that Restoration principles are wrong and/or dangerous. They object to the way the teaching was introduced; they felt that they were hoodwinked to a certain extent. Finally, they felt it was wrong and divisive to make the congregation, who had worked to closely together, agree to the new thing, or get out.

There are, of course, many ways to interpret John and Liz's story. I can see no evidence, for example, that John Singleton and his team did anything improper; they responded to an invitation by the Emmanuel Community Church to come and run a commitment course on Restorationism. However covert this might have been at first—or, if you prefer, after the 'softly softly' approach—it was clear by the end of the course what Restorationism entailed. I put it to John Race, that the real damage was not done by John Singleton, but the group themselves when they decided to set themselves up as the charismatic group within the Romford Baptist church. That is where the division started, not at Emmanuel Community Church.

You could argue that Restorationists typically exploit such divisions. But in this particular case, although John's story exemplifies how Restorationism can move in and take over a fellowship, it also demonstrates that the work of division and separation had begun before Brian Smith took over. I am not sure whether John really favours this interpretation, but he does feel that things got a lot worse when Brian Smith became leader. Restorationism was not a ground swell movement within the community, says John, it was pushed from the top.[15]

If Restorationism is built upon a spiritual rebellion and not upon truth and holiness, as Edwards claims,[16] then we can note that the problems that Bernard Green and John Race discuss are rampant within the Restoration kingdoms themselves. David Tomlinson told me that he abhorred the sectarian spirit that sought to divide and break up churches. He pointed out that he had written to Bryn Jones and begged him not to set up an R1 church in Birmingham where there was a thriving fellowship under his care. Cardiff would seem to have churches from the extended R2 and R1. Gerald Coates admitted that he had a small group that were probably seen as a thorn in Tony Morton's side in Shirley, Southampton. There has certainly been tensions between Terry Virgo and some of Gerald and John Noble's churches. Some leaders from R2, I know, see Maurice Smith as a pied piper as he calls people out from under their noses.

Every time R1 or R2 fragments, the issues of division and 'poaching' come home to roost. R2 leaders do not see themselves as poaching members from R1. Neither do R1 leaders see themselves as competing with R2. Nevertheless there is covert rivalry. All this is strangely reminiscent of the development of the Exclusives and Open Brethren a hundred and twenty years ago.

Two things need to be said in concluding this section. First, the blame for divisiveness that has taken place in the formation of Restorationism cannot be placed entirely on the shoulders of the new groups. Hardened attitudes have existed on both sides. Very often Restorationism only moved in when divisions had already occurred. It is far more typical of Restorationist leaders that they were invited into new fellowships, than that they moved in.

Second, as Rosemary Hartill reminded Bernard Green, 'People in glass houses should not throw stones.'[17] Only a short while back, in the history of the Church, the Pentecostals seceded from the mainline churches. They claim that they were driven out (or the Spirit 'bade them go'). Only a few years before them, the Brethren separated from the Church of England (primarily) because of principles. Restorationists claim that they are doing the same. The Baptist movement itself has its modern origins in the seventeenth century, when, like the Methodists one hundred years later, they could no longer relate to the historic tradition.

Restorationists believe that they are building the Church. They believe that this cannot be done from within the existing religious frameworks; so they have moved outside them to try something new. If Restorationists in peering back at these groups may dimly perceive their own future, these newer denominations in looking at Restorationism are seeing their own past. An argument many Baptists and Methodists have put to me, is that today things are different: we do not need to divide any more; ecumenism is the thing. This is not only sociologically naive, but logically untenable. The same argument could have been, and probably was, put at every subsequent divide of the Protestant Reformation. If Restorationists are to be blamed for stealing sheep, dividing congregations, and causing discerption, then it is difficult to see how this differs from the schismatic behaviour of established and respectable churches in the early days of their development.

## 3  Restorationists are Doctrinally Deviant and Self-Deluded

Curiously, these two criticisms are often presented in juxtaposition. This is so, I think, because there is the suspicion by some that the shepherding system breeds dependency by followers and delusions of grandeur in leaders. I do not feel sufficiently trained in psychology to comment on this in any elaborate way. I can say, however, that I have seen no evidence to suggest that Restorationism breeds a certain kind of personality. I share with Eileen Barker both the conviction and experience that people labelled as 'brainwashed' or 'weird' turn out on investigation to be just like anybody else.[18] If it is the case that Restorationism attracts a particular type of person, then it will involve a large-scale psychological study to determine this.

I have heard recently, that people have been leaving the American Shepherding movement in droves. It is alleged that there are many psychologically damaged people.[19] The Rev. Peter Mullen is collecting a file of case studies both inside the Renewal and the house churches. I do not wish to appear too sanguine concerning this issue, but I prefer to reserve my judgement until the evidence is a lot clearer than it is now.

This idea of 'damage' is usually aimed at the discipleship doctrines. And some critics of Restoration see a connection between psychological effects and doctrinal deviation. Classical Pentecostals, in particular, insist that the movement that prides itself on abandoning extra-biblical teaching, is itself built upon non-biblical teaching. This view is shared by many Renewalists. They claim that Scripture simply does not support the discipleship as taught and practised by Restorationists. Unfortunately, this argument tends to be a non-sequitor for both Restorationists and their opponents: one group insists it is biblical, and the other group insists that it is not. It is sufficient to note, however, that Restorationists are out on a limb on this one. Evangelicals, classical and neo-Pentecostals are not persuaded that shepherding structures can be deduced from biblical principles. Without being way out on a limb, of course, Restorationism would have little reason for claiming distinctness and special revelation. Without a commitment to covenanted relationships, Restorationists would not be radicals.

This is particularly true when linked to the charismatic apostolate. The general view of apostolic structures within Elim and the Assemblies of God, as we have seen in Chapter 12, is that they are fictional creations having no relationship to the power or the legitimacy of the New Testament offices. Anglicans, such as Tom Smail and Michael Harper, believe that there is a uniqueness about the original twelve and a special place for Paul.[20] The so-called apostles of the 'risen Christ', such as Timothy and Barnabas, they understand in an episcopal sense of bishops not in a charismatic sense of anointed ones. (Though, of course, these particular examples may very well have been men with charismata.) Such a view, which is similar to that held by most Catholic and Orthodox groups, could never be acceptable to Restorationists; such a view tacitly accepts some kind of apostolic succession. If such a view gained ground in Restoration circles, the whole legitimacy of their position would be denied. The Brethren coped with these issues by a radical anti-clericalism that denied the priesthood altogether.

A number of Brethren have told me that the Restorationists are clericalists albeit in a charismatic form. Apostles, prophets, and elders are in effect, they claim, holy orders. Whilst I think there is a great deal to commend this argument, I do not think that it is the case that Restorationists really think in these terms. The reason, I believe, lies in the absence of a High Church theology which underlay the earlier Restoration movements. Modern Restoration, in theory, holds to universality and catholicity, but their immediate roots are in classical Pentecostalism and modern Brethrenism (as far as their churchmanship is concerned). The full ecclesiastical implications of a restored apostolate have not really fired their imagination in the way it did the Catholic Apostolic Church.

A criticism that I have heard from such disparate groups as the Ichthus house churches, classical Pentecostals, and Baptists, is one I first heard from Maurice Smith: Restorationism is an extreme form of legalism. This legalism, he believes, characterises both R1 and R2 and any other shepherding system. Maurice Smith thinks that legalism is repressive and builds up resentments and rebellions; specifically, he believes Restorationism breeds guilt by always stressing the shortcomings of believers. Striving for perfection, under delegated authority, he believes leads to a sense of inadequacy and perhaps despair.

It is certainly true that the anarchic freedom of the early days gave way to a strong authority imposed from the top downwards. I think it also true to say that Restorationism's strong sense of community and solidarity does not leave much room for personal deviancy in the kingdom. But I think that it is untrue to say that life is bound by rules and regulations at every turn. I am not sure, for example, whether Maurice Smith is aware of the changes taking place in R2 since he left. Nor do I think that it is possible to generalise about the kingdom: the application of Restoration principles is patchy and reflects personality factors of leaders and social class to a certain extent.

Perhaps one of the most serious criticisms of doctrinal deviation and its relationship to self-delusion comes from George Tarleton. A former apostle in R2, his apostleship was recognised by Bryn Jones and John Noble. In 1974, George Tarleton and David Mansell were both prophesied over by Bryn Jones and called to their charismatic commissions.

George believes that doctrinal and psychological factors have combined to ruin what he believes was a genuine movement of the Holy Spirit. I spent some hours talking on the phone to George Tarleton, and it has obviously been a painful experience for him first to recognise, and then accept that he was deluded. He kindly sent me a written statement or testament on 'The One That Got Away':

One of the main reasons I quit was the growing awareness that the freedom—which had given this movement its dynamic—was being eroded away. The 'freedom' it now boasts of is only when it is compared with something formal. Britain's poverty trap can look like heaven if you're starving in Africa.

Tithing was the warning bell that law was back with us again. Under the euphemism of a 'kingdom principle', this unbiblical practice was imposed by Bible lovers. The letter was replacing the Spirit. Institutionalism was setting in. A new denomination was being born.

That was really sad—realising that we had given birth to another sect. Especially when one of the main aspects of our vision was that there was one church. The reality was that there were thousands of sects and we were adding to that number. Nothing is more painful than the death of an illusion.

The greatest damage was done by the submission trip which the leaders went on. Due to a lack of spiritual authority, submission to men was imposed on the church. These men merely passed on their insecurities, their modified middle-class values, and a christianised form of right-wing politics. (How anyone with an ounce of discernment can see Mrs. Thatcher as a prophet is beyond me!)

Then there was my 'liberal' views about the authority of the Bible, the place of women and the humanity of Christ. They were beginning to be a source of embarrassment. Slowly it dawned on me that the doctrines people cling to are those which suit their personality.

When creative praise degenerated into a series of action replays, when individuality was being strangled to death by submission, when impressing became more important than expressing I knew it was time to leave. Discarding my siege mentality, I had to get out of the ghetto. Away from the doctrinal dualism which saw everything as either of God or the devil.

The last message I was allowed to deliver at a large gathering was a plea to stop evangelising the world and start loving it. Well I have now taken refuge in that world, setting up my stall in the market place. From here my view of the world has changed. I see God deeply involved with it. Far from writing it off, he's changing it because of the love affair he has with this world of ours.

When George Tarleton left R2, he took no followers with him. He has moved down to the New Forest, and taken a secular job. His telephone is ex-directory, and his address unavailable. He is convinced that the splits and factions of the Restoration kingdom are ultimately God's will: they will prevent a really large denomination being formed.

## 4   Restoration is Not Brotherly Love: It is Big Brotherly[21]

When we were preparing for the programme *Front Room Gospel* at the BBC, inevitably—as it was 1984—the question of 'Big Brother' cropped up. By far the most serious criticism against Restorationism is that it operates a system of sinister control over members' minds and lives. I can state unequivocally, that most of the stories circulating about Restoration are either lies, expressed but not yet realised fears, or exaggerated accounts. Shepherding, in the majority of cases, takes place within admittedly paternalistic yet caring relationships.

In preparing for the Radio 4 programme, however, I did come across a definite syndrome: there were people who were frightened to talk, or who felt that talking would only damage the good they felt still existed in the movement. I received a number of complaints and letters concerning the Basingstoke churches, for example, but absolutely nobody would talk on radio. And then Rosemary Hartill received a letter from a man in Basingstoke that contained some hard-hitting observations and some shocking stories. Before we went on the air in March 1984, he too had withdrawn, saying he had changed his mind.

A number of friends, and people I trust, have handed me stories that led me to believe that in the kingdom not all was sweetness and light. These stories, however, were virtually impossible to check out. Following Bryn Jones's invitation, for example, to report on discipling abuses in R1, I have not been able to find one story that stands up. Because of the number of complaints I received, and the people who delivered them to me, it is my personal opinion that the discipling controversy is going to stay around for a long while yet. Pockets of abuse do exist, I am convinced.

The Basingstoke *Gazette* carried out its own investigations in 1982.[22] Like myself, they found that the majority of people refused either to talk, or to give names. Only Mrs. Dominique Lawson would allow her name to be used. She joined the Community Church in the mid-1970s. At first she was grateful for the way her husband was helped financially; he was unemployed at the time. Gradually, she claimed, the church took over their lives. 'We had to look happy and smiling even if we were not feeling like it. We had to seem united and happy, when underneath it was just awful.' She claimed (though this is not what I would call hard evidence) that members had to consult leaders if they wanted to change their jobs, their cars, or their homes. Eventually the Lawsons wanted to move, and they were told that the time was not right. They moved anyway, and left the church. A deputation arrived and tried to persuade them to rejoin. 'They said that outside the church we would not survive,' said Mrs. Lawson.

I have met people, whose experience seems similar to Mrs. Lawson's. But such stories are not typical. Clearly some of the members I have discussed this with in R1 and R2, were as outraged as I was at such stories. A number of leaders knew of such stories in other groups, but preferred to turn a blind eye because the persons concerned were not under their authority. This has a slightly humorous side to it for anybody from a Catholic or Orthodox tradition: it would seem the problem of jurisdictions has been inherited by Protestant sectarianiam after all; apostles can no more tell other apostles what to do than diocesan bishops!

After the first broadcast of *Front Room Gospel* in March 1984, some letters reached me containing stories, allegations, and in some cases stronger evidence of discipling abuse. A few people agreed to be named. One man came to see me, whose story was quite different from the others. It involved not only him, but most of his church. The story was different for another reason. He not only came to see me for a day, but he brought with him a written statement carefully thought out, copious correspondence between himself, his apostle/prophet, and other letters between himself and Gerald Coates. In addition he brought some tapes of the man to whom he had submitted his life. These tapes included informal conversations (as well as formal addresses) on how to successfully discipline wayward members.

The apostle concerned is from my extended use of R2, and we have met him before as one of the 'fabulous fourteen'. His name is John MacLauchlan. In view of the serious nature of the allegations made against him, I contacted John MacLauchlan, who has kindly replied to the substance of the complainant's allegations—made in some detail in his written statement. The complainant is called Ted Rotherham. He is well known in R2 circles as he was around from the early days of the Leprosy mission. Although never a national leader, he was a respected elder of a small church in Surrey.

It is not my intention in this case study to say that every word of Ted Rotherham's story is true. He is prepared to defend every word of his story even though he realises that it makes him out to be a dupe. I believe that he is a man of integrity, and is concerned that others do not make the same mistakes as he did. It is not my intention either to suggest that John MacLauchlan is a wicked gentleman. He denies absolutely Ted's version of events. I do not believe that John MacLauchlan is a liar; both he and Ted perceive each other and the world in a totally different way. As they no longer share the same *Weltanschauung*, it is perhaps not surprising that they cannot agree on the nature and facts of the dispute between them. What Ted's story illustrates—and it is essentially Ted's story that we shall be looking at, not my version of it—is the potential dangers and problems of a discipling system.

After the split of Restorationism into R1 and R2 in 1976,

John MacLauchlan and Graham Perrins continued to see themselves in an apostolic role, but tended to conflate, in practice, the offices of apostle and prophet. From about this time, Ted Rotherham's church came under John MacLauchlan's influence, and they were proud to be associated with a man whose reputation as a scholar and level-headed person was high in Restoration circles. Ted's Camberley church in Surrey continued to have fellowship with Gerald Coates, who was very popular with the people there. Ted takes up the story:

It was in the autumn of 1979 that I was summoned to see John Mac at his home near Yeovil. He asked me a question: 'Who is your father, Gerald Coates or me?' I did not feel the need to make such a choice but was told: 'It's either Gerald or me.' At that time I was not aware of the division between them and with some reservations had to choose John for his long-standing input into my life.

Ted began to realise that some leaders were competing for leadership. His church was told to withdraw their small financial support for Gerald, and stop 'relating' to him. In February 1981, a conference was held at John Mac's home. There, Ted says, he was asked to relinquish all authority to John. Ted again:

He then laid out his objectives to have concentrated input with monthly visits to bring us in line with the same ministry as his own fellowships at Yeovil. This consisted of personal foundations, corporate foundations, tithing, giving oneself, and attitudes in daily living. We were told that if these aspects of teaching were not changing our lives that we would have to move to Yeovil within twelve months. I was very uncomfortable with this statement and said so and began challenging John on many areas of his direction, and was subsequently told that the word of God to us was that we would have to move and that we would never have another word . . .

My wife and I were in complete turmoil and desperate to know what we should do. We had decided not to go; a few others said that they would submit to John and could not agree with us to stay. The majority stood with us but were very confused as the fellowship had now been dissolved and I had stood down after twelve years' leadership in what was a very loving and friendly fellowship.

Ted went to see Gerald Coates, and although he sympathised with Ted, felt that Ted had to sort it out for himself. I discussed this with Gerald, and I do not think he was saying to Ted: 'You've made your bed, now lie in it,' but I do think he was saying to Ted: 'You've submitted to another man's authority; sort it out with him.' In the event, Ted and his wife decided to capitulate and confess their wrongdoing to John Mac. Ted continues:

I was told to apologise to everyone in the church for my actions and put my house on the market right away. The move was on and by now we were all moving with the exception of two young men. There were the problems of jobs, children at 'A' and 'O' levels. We encouraged my wife's elderly parents to sell their home and move away with us to the West country.

Ted felt that now everything would be all right. John had assured him that the move would not effect his shepherding relationship with the fellowship. A move was effected to Martock in Somerset. In a few weeks a local house church leader called on Ted, and informed him that he was no longer to have responsibility for the Camberley church. Those who had not yet made the move would now, like Ted, submit to him as John's delegate. John could only be contacted, Ted was told, through the mediation of this new leader, Keith Impey. Ted insists that John MacLauchlan had promised him close personal contact after the move that would include regular lunches and consultations. In the event, says Ted, it was nine months before he saw John. Ted felt humiliated.

Some were now moving into Martock whilst others were told to move to Yeovil and we began to meet at Keith's house. I was a sheep amongst my own sheep having to get permission what I should and should not do, being directed to help with the decor and garden of other leaders.

Ted and some others were encouraged to give money from the sale of their houses to help others move down from Camberley. Keith, according to Ted, told them that they were not getting jobs because they were not giving money when directed. False prophecies were often given, says Ted, and when they failed they were told that God had changed his mind. He remembers an incident of a girl who was told that she would not get a job because she had not mastered a smoking habit. The prophecy was given as a 'word' (*rhema*) direct from God. (The girl did get a job.)

After some twelve months, when Ted felt cut off, isolated, and humiliated, he and his wife decided that enough was enough. Through one man, they realised, they had come to believe that they were the unique expression of the Prophetic Church on Earth. Yeovil was to be the centre of the true Church radiating out to the whole world. Ted recalls: 'I had lost my leadership, function, sheep, job, friends, financial help, and was very disillusioned.' On the 25th of March 1983, Ted decided to finish with submission to men and cast himself on Christ alone. Several days later, John MacLauchlan rang to say that he could no longer cover Ted and his wife, but they were welcome to choose somebody else from Yeovil. Ted made it clear that he would submit to nobody. John then replied: 'In that case I will not allow anyone access to you because of your actions.'

The ill-feeling continued, claims Ted, and he was asked to move out of the area so that he would not attract others to himself. He asked John MacLauchlan what was the Scriptural basis for not allowing others to see him. 'Ted,' he replied, 'you should know that we don't work from Scriptural principles.'

Ted and his wife are still in Martock. They claim that

others are now coming out, and that the prophet's kingdom is breaking up. Ted insists that the basic problem in his life has been looking to external authority to lead him into truth. All his attention, he says, was given to making the effort to live up to other people's expectations. Ted is now part of Maurice Smith's support group for, as they see it, the casualties of shepherding. Whether Maurice's 'new thing' will turn out to be yet another twist in the sectarian spiral remains to be seen.

Ted's story (and this is a very shortened version), he hopes, will help stop people being deluded like himself (and help prevent others being duped). He sees submission and discipling practices as a trap:

> Having the desire to know and please God, enjoy fellowship with others, you commit yourself to 'The Fellowship' and subsequently the 'Authority' of those 'Over' you. No longer do you act independently but through the leader by direct intervention or seeking advice and guidance from him. Should this conflict with your own feelings the choice you are facing is do what you feel is right and face the consequences, or deny 'your spirit' and give way to the one over you. The latter denies direct communication with God and embraces a structure held together by Law leading to fear and condemnation.

John MacLauchlan wrote to me on the 1st of December 1984, and Keith Impey on the 3rd of December. Both categorically deny Ted Rotherham's account: John MacLauchlan (first paragraph):

Dear Andrew,
Thanks for your letter and copy of Ted's material.
There are really so many inaccuracies and outright lies in Ted's account that I can see no profit in commenting on them in detail. The Lord has not taught us to defend ourselves in such circumstances. Ted will account for his statements to a higher authority than ourselves! . . .

Keith Impey (paragraphs five and six):

> For a man who was so confused and attacking anything
> and anybody in sight at that time, it is ironical that he can
> remember with so much clarity exactly what was said and
> done.
> In truth and reality, he cannot and he only has his impres-
> sions upon which he is basing his comments. Those
> impressions are born out of bitterness and resentment.
> They do not represent the real issues and the facts . . .

John MacLauchlan did make some personal accusations
off the record, but then Ted Rotherham also made some
personal accusations off the record about John.

Ted Rotherham felt it right that John MacLauchlan
should have the right to reply, but warned me that John
was extremely plausible, intelligent, and believable. John
MacLauchlan wrote in paragraph four:

> I must say that I think it unwise to publish an account
> such as Ted has written for you. He is a plausible man who
> has done much harm to the work here. My main mistake
> with him was to leave him in leadership as long as I did in
> the hope that he would mature and stabilize . . .

Neither John MacLauchlan nor Keith Impey actually
rebut any of the specific facts (except one; see below) or
incidents of Ted's account. John explains why in the final
part of his letter: '. . . I trust that your readers will accept
that I consider it inappropriate to enter into controversy in
the forum of your book, over the specific allegations made
by Ted . . .' What John does do is offer us, in contrast to
Ted, his view of the Yeovil fellowships:

> . . . We remain 'unaligned' with any group. I have
> always (publicly, including during the days of the so-called
> 'fourteen') opposed any moves towards national leader-
> ship or organisation. We would not call ourselves a
> 'House Church' (we meet in all sorts of buildings!) but

simply Christians meeting together in the Yeovil area. We acknowledge without reserve God's moving with groups of all kinds, and have no exalted opinion of ourselves. There are many approaches that would not be appropriate or God's will for us, but we respect the right of each group to build as God directs, and would not dream of criticising them. The body of Christ in a universal sense has many varied members.

We resist all attempts at producing or imposing *uniformity* among the churches. Our unity must be based on mutual respect and recognition, not on anyone's attempt to modify all others to harmonize with his views. There is no 'New Testament church pattern', as the church is an evolving entity, called onward by the word of God towards a consummation in Christ that we can only at present glimpse. (It is this refusal to accept that a New Testament pattern is currently binding on us that is misrepresented by Ted . . .)[23]

What readers will, I am sure, realise is that they are being presented with two different versions of reality. Even such a strong case as Ted Rotherham's story is by no means clear cut. Without a great deal more material witnesses, collaborating evidence, etc., it is very difficult for us, in any objective sense, to decide which version we choose to believe. Personally, I am convinced that both Ted and John presented me with the truth as they see it. This book is not a court of law, and it is not for us to decide who is right and who is wrong.

It is the purpose of this book, however, to attempt to investigate every aspect of kingdom life. Whilst I do not feel that it is my place to arbitrate, I do feel that it is proper that I should air the sort of complaints that exist against Restorationism. John MacLauchlan put himself in my hands as far as editing his letter is concerned (last paragraph), and Ted Rotherham gave me full permission to edit as I saw fit. Ted's complaint was the best documented of any I received, but it is not unique; there are six other stories on my files which differ in detail and the personnel involved, but are similar in complaint.

The Restoration kingdom, both R1 and R2, is a radical kingdom, and radicals attract opposition in a way in which conventional Christians do not. Some Restorationists see criticisms as attacks of the Devil. But it is my experience that many Christians outside the kingdom are not so much censorious as curious. This curiosity is sometimes married to anxiety. Most people simply want to know what the Restorationist kingdom is really all about. The kingdom is not really under attack from without (though it has many rebellions from within), but it is being seriously probed.[24]

## Notes

1   A number of parents contacted me after the first broadcasting of *Front Room Gospel*. Two of them were desperately worried about their teenage children, and felt that house churches were manipulative, and dangerous. (I was visited by three parents, and spent an afternoon with two sixth-formers from the west country.)

2   *Front Room Gospel*.

3   Report on Dales Bible Week, for *Sunday*, Radio 4, 8 August 1982.

4   Both involved conversations for BBC programmes that were, in the event, not used. Subsequently, I talked to Michael on the telephone and came across Douglas McBain's article in the August/September 1984 edition of *Renewal* magazine, 'Emptiness at the Centre'.

5   This information from the Church of England Board of Mission and Unity, is the first strong evidence that Michael Harper's assertion that the Renewal is quietly but surely expanding, may be correct after all. It looks as if I will have to revise my view that the Renewal has entered decline; eating 'humble pie' is part of the social scientist's stock in trade!

6   *Buzz* magazine, August 1984.

7   Dales Bible Week, see note 3.

8   For his most stringent criticism see 'The Curse Of The Hallelujah Chorus', *The Guardian*, Saturday 28 July 1984.

9   *Front Room Gospel*.

10   Ibid.

11   This case study is from Joyce Thurman's book, op cit.
    However, Bryn Jones pointed out to me on the telephone in July 1985 that he and Goos were already in a covenanted relationship before Goos became the pastor at Hoole Baptist church.
    The experience at Hoole, says Bryn, led him to build up his own churches and not work inside existing denominations. (This whole story is really, then, a major factor in the direction of the Bradford-based R1 churches.)

12   From my dramatised documentary on the fall and restoration of Edward Irving, *The Angel Of Regent Square*, Radio 4, Saturday 1 December 1984.

13   From John Miller's article 'Tongues drove him from Regent Square's pulpit', *Reform*, December 1984.

14   I was very impressed with John Race's intelligence and thoughtfulness. We had many long conversations on the phone, and he sent me a fourteen-side statement, and a number of further letters. (All quotes are from John's statement.)

15   I think it fair to say, that whilst John and Liz did not like the implications of Restorationism, their beef is really with the leadership of Emmanuel Community Church.

16   Gene Edwards, *A Tale Of Three Kings* (Christian Books, California, 1980).

17   *Front Room Gospel*.

18   E. Barker, *Moonies* (Blackwell, 1984).

19   Certainly Maurice Smith says so.

20   Tom Smail, for example, thinks that Paul can legitimately claim to have been a witness of the risen Christ. There is certainly no doubt that tradition has accorded St. Paul a unique status (after the twelve).

21   A statement used by Pastor George Canty of Elim on *Front Room Gospel*.

22   *The Gazette*, Friday 8 October 1982.

23   John MacLauchlan's groups are from my extended use of R2 and I thought it only fair to give John the chance to present his work and commitments his way.

24   I have not really probed into the many allegations of financial or personal misconduct. This book has attempted to be a work of understanding; not an exercise in exposé journalism.

## RECOMMENDED READING

'Shepherds Or Sheep Stealers', *Buzz* magazine (August 1984).

Gene Edwards, *A Tale Of Three Kings* (Christian Books, California, 1980).

Michael Harper, *That We May Be One* (Hodder and Stoughton, 1981).

Alan Munden, 'Encountering the House Church Movement: A Different Kind of Christianity', *Anvil*, Vol. 1, No. 3, 1984.

Joyce Thurman, *New Wineskins: A Study of the House Church Movement* (Verlag Peter Lang, 1982).

## EPILOGUE:

# DOES THE KINGDOM HAVE A FUTURE?

It is possible that the whole Restorationist movement will be dead and buried within five years. But I doubt it. Too much effort, commitment, loyalty, leadership, money, plant, and idealism exist for them to be simply blown away. I do not think that the kingdom is yet built in its final form; neither do I think that we have yet seen the final permutations between R1 and R2. Bryn Jones and his churches, for example, may well emerge from R1 as the 'Harvestime Church'. I think it likely, also, that Gerald Coates and his colleagues will eventually come up with an eye-catching name for their groups which will facilitate a clearer identity. My crude algebraic rubric will not survive. The terms R1 and R2 have been created by me only to help us identify religious formations in the making. There is no church in existence called Restoration (One or Two).

There is no doubt, however, that R1 and R2 do refer to a specific reality within that general designation, the House Church Movement. I believe that reality to be the first emerging indigenous sectarian formation of any significance, since the establishment of Elim and the Assemblies of God in the 1920s. Restorationists are not yet an established sect. A revival amongst either the classical or neo-Pentecostals is going to leave the house churches vulnerable to erosion from either side. Conversely, the Restoration movement if it continues to grow—and I think it will do so—may draw out more disaffected Renewalists and traditional Pentecostals.

As I mentioned in Chapter 12, I think it is likely that

the Restorationists will end up in what is already an over-subscribed classical Pentecostalism. But if, and before, they end up there many questions have to be answered. What future role will the Renewal play in fanning the fires of sectarianism? If the Renewal has another significant round of revivals, will there be another sectarian spin-off? Can Restoration become other than another Apostolic church? Will we see the emergence of conversionist (and expansive) groups, or introversionist (and contracting) sects? Will Bryn Jones's segment of R1 be able to resist the prosperity doctrines of the American Bible belt as they enter Television evangelism? (If they do not they will find the mainline churches—and the whole of the British evangelical world—against them.)[1]

If the Restoration movement succeeds in its original aims, and Bryn Jones's and David Matthew's optimism and faith are rewarded, nobody will be happier than me. Nothing could be more exciting for a Christian than to see the vision of a united Church fulfilled. (As to whether such a Church would look like Restorationism is another issue.) On principle, however, I do not particularly want to belong to a perfect church; though I did once. Metropolitan Anthony of Sourozh once told me, when I was searching for the allusive 'true fellowship'; 'If you find the perfect church, don't join it: you'll spoil it.'

The quest for the purity of a lost religion, or the power of forgotten charismas is like the quest for the holy grail: only the pure in heart find it, and they discover that it is not 'of this world'.

But if Restorationists have to settle for less than the Church filling the whole world, has their work been totally wasted? Is being a sectarian such a terrible thing? Are Salvationists less committed Christians than Catholics? Have the Quakers done nothing for our society? Can a 'born again' Baptist be as significant as a broad churchman? Maybe Renewalists still have much to learn from the classical Pentecostalists, whom they have somewhat disparaged.[2] Black Pentecostals, with their oral culture, may yet teach us Westerners how to do theology in our fellowships rather than leave it to the academics in the senior common rooms. Restorationists have not persuaded me that their song is one I want to sing, but I have been deeply impressed by many of the singers. They won my respect by the quality of their lives.

All too often, it seems to me, traditional church people only see emerging sects as failures, mistakes, or proof of the declining power of religion as an integrating force in our society. We have talked about the lessons of sectarian history for new sectarians, but there are also lessons to be learned for the historic churches. As secularisation[3] inexorably continues its way, religious decline is unlikely to be halted. In Western capitalist societies and the centrally planned socialist economies, the material and technological world dominates reality. Neither socialist nor capitalist economics are informed by religion. (I have met Christian businessmen, but where are the Christian economics?) Science and industry perform adequately without religious principles being evoked. As Edward Irving stood on the brink of the modern system of Industrialism, his prophetic denouncement of that system was not that it was informed by science and rational economic principles, but that it was Godless. He saw capitalism as Mammon: 'the basest spirit that ever fell from Heaven'.

Today, the mass media and the state invade our homes and privacy, dictating our fashions, wants (labelled 'needs'), without a second glance at Christian values. Despite the rise of the so-called moral majority in North America, and the growth of Jerry Fulwell's 'religious Right', no dent seems to be made in the consumer materialism of the American dream. On the contrary so often the American dream and Christianity are presented as synonymous. No less an authority than Billy Graham has been warning not to let the token 'born again' be taken for the reality.[4]

Everywhere we look in our culture, religion has been pushed to the periphery. It has become one of the consumer options in a pluralistic society. Christianity is now part of our leisure time (usually on Sundays only). Weber's concept of the broad church, universalistic and embracing the world, is in fact the world embracing the church. British people can see some Anglican bishops talking with fire and vigour about politics, and yet unable passionately to defend the faith. In the British Council of Churches, debates in the General Assembly are notable for their conjoining of secular politics and Christian concern. If George Tarleton can talk of a 'christianised form of right-wing politics' as characterising Restorationism, then the BCC, in my experience, often presents itself as a 'christianised form of left-wing politics'.[5] The Church as 'The Church' is often seen by its members as failing to speak with authority. (Unfortunately, some Christians mistake notions of authority for certainty; and the drive for certainty can lead to accepting authoritarianism as a substitute for spiritual authority. No Christian can know all the answers; even the Lord Jesus admitted that He did not know when the end-time would come.)

Professor Alisdair MacIntyre sees the failure of religious authority as part of the overall crisis of Western morality.[6] The problem, he believes, is that there is a failure to recognise that the doctrines of progress and the principles of the Enlightenment have also brought with them a moral relativity; an end to the shared moral universe that dominated Europe from antiquity to the eighteenth century. Not only formal religious institutions are in decline, but also the moral 'symbolic universe' which may rarely have been followed, but at least it was accepted as being there.[7]

Modernist principles, from the Enlightenment of the eighteenth century onwards, have invaded the Church. Rationalism, moral relativism, and secular criticism have in the words of the French sociologist Durkheim moved from the 'profane' to the 'sacred'. The Catholic anthropologist, Mary Douglas, has a fascinating thesis that is based on the ritual fear of pollution: things have their natural place and should not be displaced. It is perhaps obvious that you do not keep coal in the bath, but so often Christian churches do not seem to realise that they have internalised methods and theories that are not appropriate to their nature. The Scriptures are no longer a sacred text: they are objects of scientific investigation. Divine liturgies are no longer acts of sacred worship; they are do-it-yourself pop concerts. We have replaced holiness with wholeness, confession with therapy, prayer meetings with workshops, and even on BBC Radio *Lift Up Your Hearts* has given way to *Thought for the Day*.

C. S. Lewis, in an argument not dissimilar to Alisdair MacIntyre's, warned that the Church was being swamped by modernism and the forces of modernity.[8] Forty years on, the question has to be asked: 'Can churches, in the traditional denominational sense, resist secularisation and preserve the purity of the gospel?'

To attempt to answer this question, I will take an historical example. In the early days of the Byzantine empire, one of the besetting sins of all historic churches began. (The Eastern Orthodox churches have been particularly affected.) This sin is 'erastianism' or bowing to the state and over-identifying with the political establishment. In many ways this erastianism had many positive features. There was a genuine attempt to Christianise every aspect of culture; there was a spiritual power behind every emperor. Gradually, however, the imperial might of the state and the sovereignty of God the judge (*pantokrator*) became confusingly intertwined.

Charles Williams refers to this experiment of building the Church on earth, through the social structures of society, as a 'flawed icon'.[9] Today, the Orthodox church recognises that as far as its own Tradition is concerned, the purity of the gospel and the radical dimensions of Christianity were preserved not through the splendour of the Byzantine courts, but through the monasteries. The 'God-possessed' men and women ran out into the desert not to run away from God, but to tackle the Devil head-on. The great spiritual and ascetic prayers of the Church were established by the monks, not in the courts of the emperor.

We are a long way from Byzantium, and monasteries are few and far between; and not typically part of the Protestant tradition anyhow. But perhaps the despised sects have a lesson to teach us all? It depends on how serious we think the situation really is. Professor MacIntyre sees the whole of our modern culture poised between agreeing with Nietzsche that there is no objective basis for morality, or turning back to the Classicism of our Judaic Christian heritage. Bishop Lesslie Newbigin, in *The Other Side Of 84*,[10] urges the churches to think again about their tacit acceptance of modern critical rationalism and turn back to the fundamental 'canonical faith'.

But it will not be easy for churches to do this in our essentially secularised world. The great historic churches were built up in pre-industrial societies that were dominated by organically functioning communities. In the early years of industrialisation, the parishes—with their extended families and kinship networks—preserved a semblance of the old order. Now the communities, living parishes, and the extended families are almost gone. (No wonder that Restorationism appeals to the lonely middle-class families in their nuclear isolation!) Not only has secularisation taken over the educational, welfare, and industrial sectors of society, it is destroying the very fabric and structure of religious life itself. Perhaps the sect, with its close-knit voluntary association, and committed camaraderie is a better sociological bet for survival than the old church. The broad church as the leavening and integrating force of secular societies has had its problems since Constantine. But in the context of modern pluralistic societies—plural in the sense of mixed social classes and mixed religions, or no religion—I wonder if it has a future at all?

I am by no means convinced that Restorationism provides a content that will bring the Church into unity. Many other sects are heretical, and could not possibly do so. But I am not talking here about content, I am talking about context. It seems to me that the shape and organisations of sects preserve them from the incursions of secularism better than churches. A sect, in some respects, resembles a diaspora church. Diasporas are emigré churches that are 'scattered abroad'; wrenched out of their natural settings, they are tossed like seeds into alien soil. These seeds are then 'gathered together' to become little enclaves of tradition in the foreign environment.

Professor MacIntyre sees the diaspora (he mentions the Greek church in America) as messages of hope: living and sacred texts amidst a world that does not even recognise a spiritual tradition. Perhaps we can say the same things about sects? They are cast out—or pull out—of denominations. If they are sometimes guilty of a 'siege mentality' this is because they have seen what a policy of open arms has done to the churches.

To talk about world revival is a fantasy in the face of the merciless pressures of modernity. Before the great march forward takes place, there has to be a retreat: a preservation and conservation of our sacred heritage. Before we take on the world, we have to call for a halt to it in our churches and denominations. The battle is not out there in some supposedly wicked world: it is at home where the enemy lurks. The Church in the face of modern Western culture, cannot artificially recreate parishes, rural districts, or a bygone age: but she can form sects.

I am not suggesting that Christendom can survive on sects alone. It was, after all, the patronage of the bishops that preserved the autonomy of the monastries. I do think, however, that the Church of Christ desperately needs sects. It is curious that orthodoxy, even though it is divided up into separate little parcels and intermingled with heresies, can be found to exist more in Christian sects than many Christian churches. If we look at Restoration as just one more sect in a long line of Protestant disasters, then we are failing to rise to the challenge and critique it offers to conventional and denominational Christianity. It is by no means clear whether Restorationism will survive, but will the churches?

Sitting in Bryn Jones's office one day, I remember warming to his vision of the kingdom. For a moment we forgot that we were interviewer and interviewee—potentially even enemies—because we were overcome by the magnitude of the thought that the kingdom of God would overcome the corruption of a fallen world.

Coming home from Bradford, however, I reflected on how I saw the kingdom in a less literalist and monolithic way than Bryn. I could not see how the gospels point towards an earthly millennium, or a massive corporation, or a giant assembly of the saints. Subjectively after months of 'heap offerings', video messages of 'God's men of the hour', the excitement and praising, I wondered what all this had to do with the kingdom. Was Restorationism a sect standing against the forces of modernism, or empire-building by a small group of men? The answer I realised was that it was probably both. I did know that the sheer tension of Restorationism had left me with an overwhelming need just to stand in my church during the divine liturgy and hear the opening words: 'Blessed is the kingdom', and know that it was there in the stillness and the quiet.

But Bryn was to have the last word. On the train, I took an old *Restoration* magazine out of my briefcase. In it he sets out the yardstick to measure all new movements of the Spirit of God. I am content that the Restoration kingdom should be measured by this. Let it determine its own future:

> The charismatic awakening that does not deal with the root of independence, individualism, sectarianism and denominationalism will be deficient as far as the heart of God and the need of our generation is concerned. It will inevitably follow the well-trodden path of decline back into the slough of spiritual paralysis and sectarian strife.[11]

## Notes

1 A former member of R1 has told me that I have underplayed the Americanisation of Bryn's team. Since 1979, he claims, Bradford has become less of a community and more of an American-style mid-Western teaching centre.

He also claims that despite the fact that American prosperity doctrines have recently split R1's Bath Fellowship, such doctrines are increasingly finding their way into Restorationist teaching.

I am not sure whether such doctrines have, in fact, arrived. For a clear understanding of what these doctrines entail see 'Monopolising Faith' in *Buzz*, December 1984.

2   Some of the most impressive and balanced Pentecostals are to be found in the classical sects, and newer black churches. Men like Pastors John Lancaster and Julian Ward of Elim; Pastors Quay and Don Allan of the Assemblies of God; Pastor Brian Long of the Apostolic Church of Faith; Pastor Alvin Blake of the Calvary Church of God in Christ; Pastor Ridley Usherwood of Overstone College. And last, but not least, a woman pastor of considerable gifts, Pastor Io Smith of the New Testament Assembly.

3   This is a rather slippery and unsatisfactory word. By it I mean here, the disengagement of religion from the governmental, bureaucratic, industrial and scientific spheres of life; in short, the pushing of Christianity out of public life into its own private world.

This private world is itself increasingly being invaded by the ideologies of the modern world; more aptly termed modernism or secularism.

4   Talking to him at Lambeth Palace, to launch Mission England in 1984, I was impressed with his thoughtful and reflective approach to religion in America.

5   Or so it seems to me after four years on the board of the Ecumenical Division, and one year as the Russian Orthodox representative on the General Assembly.

6   *After Virtue* (Duckworth, 1980).

7   Usually called 'Classicism'. C. S. Lewis called it the Tao.

8   For his best critique of the modern mind see *The Abolition of Man* (Fount paperback, 1978).

9   Charles Williams, *Descent of the Dove* (Longman, London, 1939).

10   BCC publication, 1983.

11   *Restoration* (July/August 1978) p. 12.
Bryn Jones shall have the last word in the notes too, for his article ends: 'So it is that thousands of us are committed to pray and work for nothing less than the great restoration of the Church of God to its spiritual foundation—God's spiritual government and Heaven's divine power. Revival must become a Restoration!'

## *Author's Postscript*

It is in the nature of a book of this kind that it will be out of date as soon as it's in print. Since this book was completed and submitted for publication two significant events have occurred: (i) Tony Morton of R1 and Gerald Coates of R2 have shared a public platform together. (ii) Bryn Jones has 'released' his fellow apostle Tony Morton, and Terry Virgo to a wider and a more independent ministry.

*Appendix*

# THE SEALING OF GEORGE TARLETON

The choosing of apostles, in the early days of the Restoration movement, was a recognition of ministry that was then confirmed by fellow leaders, and sealed by prophecy and prayer as the confirmation of the Holy Spirit. The recognition of George Tarleton's ministry as apostle, and David Mansell's as prophet took place at the Chingford Fellowship on the 7th of April 1974.

With permission from George Tarleton, I have assembled from tapes Bryn Jones's vision and prophecy concerning George's ministry.

(1) A long prayer from John Noble.

(2) A prophecy (person unknown to me).

(3) *Song:* Father we adore you,

Lay our lives before you . . .

(4) Bryn's vision: 'As we are praying for George, I am seeing the mountain of the Lord encircled around by many ministries holding hands. They are all ministering to the body, all ministering to the mountain of the Lord. But there are gaps, and through these gaps the enemy has come and the grass that should be green has been burned. It has been burned black.

'And these have been the intrusions of the enemy that have come in where ministries have failed to adequately minister to the mountain of the Lord; failed adequately to take care of the saints. And the enemy has come in and burned and burned, and burned the green grass.

'And then George comes up the mountain and he begins

to speak right where the gap is. And he comes to speak not to the mountain, but he speaks to the ministries. And they pull closer together, and close the gap.'

(Amen)

'And then I see him take off in an aeroplane and he goes to other places across the land—across the globe—and he does this: he goes where the ministries are, and he speaks to them to close the ranks, to close the gaps, to pull in line and adequately cover the saints of God.

'And God witnesses that this will be his apostolic calling; that it will have prime focus, prime attention not to all the saints at local level . . . but that God's going to make him a voice where there are gaps in the ranks of the ministry. And he is going to be used of God to strengthen the ministry of the Church.'

(Hallelujah!)

'He is going to have some word from God that will be just what they need; that will pull them together—to protect the mount of God.'

(Amen)

(5) Prayer (from person unknown to me).

(6) Bryn's prophecy: 'Say not that this is too high a calling. Think not that it is too large a sending. But I say to you that I who have purposed before you came forth of your mother's womb, will achieve in you that thing for which I have destined you. For you have heard this night from my servant, of the calling of destiny. You have heard already of that hand heavy upon one. And you have known this in your own life.

'But you have been conscious too of the weakness within yourself, conscious of your haste, conscious of your impatience, conscious of the times you've spoken when I did not speak. But this does not disqualify you. For I being mindful of this will choose you and still send you. And I will make up all the cracks, and I will fill up all the gaps within you that you may fill the gaps in others.

'And I will draw your scattered thoughts together, that you might draw together their scattered thinking. And I will speak to you that you might speak to them. And they will know that God has spoken.

'You shall not stay in any one place beyond my time of appointment. But you shall go in, close the rank, and come back swiftly, says God.'

(Hallelujah! Amen!)

There are further prayers, praying over, and praise of George. He is commended to the Lord, and the congregation. George emerges a full recognised apostle, and remains so until he leaves the Restorationist movement in 1984.